S E E I N G
F I L M S
P O L I T I C A L L Y

SUNY Series in Radical Social and Political Theory
Roger S. Gottlieb, editor

MAS'UD
ZAVARZADEH

SEEING
FILMS
POLITICALLY

STATE UNIVERSITY OF NEW YORK PRESS

Published by
State University of New York Press, Albany

© 1991   State University of New York

For information, address State University of New York
Press, State University Plaza, Albany, N.Y. 12246

Production by Marilyn P. Semerad
Marketing by Fran Keneston

Library of Congress Cataloging-in-Publication Data

Zavarzadeh, Mas'ud, 1938–
    Seeing films politically / by Mas'ud Zavarzadeh.
        p.   cm. — (SUNY series in radical social and political
    theory)
    Includes bibliographical references.
    ISBN 0–7914-0526–5. — ISBN 0–7914-0527–3 (pbk.)
    1. Motion pictures—Political aspects. 2. Motion pictures-
-Philosophy.   I. Title. II. Series.
PN1995.9.P6Z38   1991
791.43'01—dc20

                                                                90–9688
                                                                CIP

10 9 8 7 6 5 4 3 2

برای
محسن ، ماهرخ، منیژه

مسعود

This book is for
Mohsen, Mahrokh, Manizheh

CONTENTS

PREFACE

Although the focus of my discussion here is on film, this is a book on the politics of cultural intelligibility and its inscription in the dominant ideology. I will explain why it is important in critical readings of texts of culture to emphasize "domination" and the way it is obscured, and I will show how the structures and logic of domination can be displayed by an ideology critique that produces oppositional intelligibilities. As part of constructing such intelligibilities, I have engaged postmodern film theory in the opening part of my discourse. Although I have not elaborated on "theory" as such here—because I have dealt with the subject elsewhere (Zavarzadeh, 1989)— I hope it is clear from my discussion that I approach theory as a practice that foregrounds the politics of intelligibility as a means of enabling readers to intervene in the production of social meaning and to transform social relations.

Theory, in other words, is not a metalanguage but a critique of intelligibility: a display and displacement of the politics of the dominant "truth." However, the hegemonic uses of theory marginalize such critique; it is therefore all the more necessary to engage in theory as critique—especially at a time when "theory" is under attack both by deconstructionists, who regard theory to be the discourse of mastery in which the local, the cellular, and the particular are erased, and also by such "politically" interested groups as centrist feminists and other liberal social movement activists, who, like deconstructionists, fear that theory destroys the local and the particular. I believe the increasingly populist "resistance to theory" is part of the contemporary conservative attack on conceptuality (as historical grids of intelligibility). And, along with the inscription of the particular and the

experiential, it is a mode of the postmodern return to the empirical. The empirical, I argue, is not "the real" but the product of
the discourses of the dominant ideology. Most of my discussion is
therefore directed at the politics of the ideological production of
the "real" ("experience") in contemporary film.

My use of a language which, at times, is not the language of
the common sense and thus not always easily accessible is problematic, even contradictory, in a book that claims to approach
theory as a critique of dominant intelligibilities and seeks to be
an ally of the reader in the production of oppositional intelligibilities. Indeed, some readers may find my language filled with
"jargon" and at times quite opaque. I have engaged in a double
move here: on the one hand, making use of common sense and
commonsensical discourses; on the other hand, interrupting
them. Through such disruptions, I have attempted to demonstrate, by using other registers of language, that the common
sense is a historical product and not a natural "given." Once it is
placed in the space of other languages, it loses its "natural" hegemony and becomes only one of the many possible ways of talking about the "real" and not "the Only One." It is thus necessary, on the one hand, to talk with and to the common sense and,
on the other, to interrupt it (no matter how rudely or "jargony"),
because the common sense is the language of domination. In
fact, it is much more pernicious than other languages of domination because, unlike them, it is represented as the "natural" way
of talking and thinking. Jargon, by its very articulation, is self-
foregrounding; it is, to use Roland Barthes's words, a mask that
points to itself and thus does not hide itself or represent itself as
"natural." However, those readers who find the language of the
first three chapters too opaque may wish to begin reading the
book with Chapter 4 and then come back to the opening chapters after they have reviewed the discussions of the films. I
should add here a note about the last chapter which is written in
a form that might strike some readers as "odd" and even
"confusing." The chapter is written as an "alphapedia"—a renarrating of Bergman's *Fanny and Alexander* around "alphabets."
Such a move further loosens what is commonly regarded to be
the unique aesthetic logic of the film and performs its arbitrariness which is the arbitrariness of ideology that represents itself

as necessary. The "alphapedia" also prevents naturalization of my own renarrating as a mode of reading.

The films I have chosen to discuss belong to the category that I call "trivial," and I have indicated the reason for my choice. The trivial is the space in which the daily is negotiated; it is the space that is represented in the common sense as "real," "natural," and as such, it must be denaturalized by ideology critique for social transformation.

Teresa Ebert read this book as it was (re)written and critiqued it extensively: not only did she discuss these films with me, but more important, she resituated many of my original articulations in a more politically and theoretically productive problematics. I am grateful for the sustained intellectual support Roger Gottlieb, Ernest Callenbach, Robin Wood, Brian Henderson, Donald Morton, and Peggy Gifford have given the project. I would also like to thank Bryan Bates, Dana Foote, and Marilyn Semerad for their editorial help.

Parts of this book have appeared in earlier forms in *Film Quarterly, Telos, Enclitic, Syracuse Scholar, North Dakota Quarterly,* and *Cineaction.* I would like to thank the editors of these journals for their interest in these texts.

In the "Introduction" to the revised edition of her book, *Women's Oppression Today,* Michele Barrett exemplifies the political situation in which *Seeing Films Politically* is being published. It is a situation marked by the retreat from radical politics. Indeed it is a time when "politics" itself has become a species of ludic "etiquette": concepts deployed in the analysis of the social are no longer judged by their transformative and explanatory power but by such considerations as whether they intellectually offend (are crude) or give pleasure (are non-offensive—a quality that is given social acceptance by being represented as "subtlety"). The political and social conservatism that is legitimated through the guise of analytical subtlety can perhaps be best seen in Barrett's own "new" reading of contemporary feminism. She opens her "subtle" analysis by putting in question the very concept that enables a feminist social analytic to have any radical and transformative purchase on the reality of contemporary patriarchy. "Oppression," she now believes, is not an adequate analytical concept for feminism because it "looks rather crude" (1988, v). Rejecting "oppression" in the name of analytical "crudeness" is, of course, an ideological alibi: the trope of her entire new approach in which the radical global analysis of capitalist patriarchy is marginalized in the interest of a harmless, reformist, "local" and "molecular" "reading."

In these ludic terms, *Seeing Films Politically* is indeed a "crude" book. Not only does it affirm the need to deploy such concepts as "oppression" but it also stands for a radical global analysis that displays the dominant logic of oppression and exploitation underlying all seemingly separate ("local") social practices. Keeping in mind this new conservative climate, some of those who have read the manuscript of the book have pointed to its "prosecutorial style" and have also suggested that I tone down my analyses and make them more indirect and "subtle" since my relentlessness "exasperates" the (subtle) reader. I have written on the political need, at the present time, for "crudity" (in the sense avoided by Barrett and others) as an intervention in bourgeois subtleties, and I believe "exasperation" is the "other" of "pleasure": the "other" the reader must come to terms with in order to move beyond the complacent bourgeois discourses of "tone," "style," and "readability."

This book is for three persons who have suffered so much from the ruthless subtleties of capitalism...

Mas'ud Zavarzadeh

Berkeley, California

CHAPTER 1

TALES OF INTELLIGIBILITY

1

This is a contesting, some would say contentious, book. It inquires into the ways ideology circulates in some of the films of the 1980s and helps to establish an "imaginary" relation between the spectator (the subject) and the world. Through such imaginary relationships, the discourses of ideology turn the opacity of the world into a luminous intelligibility that not only makes sense of the reality "out there" but also, and more important, creates meaning for the film's viewer, who becomes in this process a knowing subject.

My aim in this book has been to show how seemingly innocent films—what are usually taken to be neutral aesthetic acts of entertainment—are sites of such ideological investment. I have engaged in a series of ideology critiques because I think it is politically urgent to inquire into the operation of ideology: the unchecked domination of ideology limits historical possibilities and produces a world in response to the needs of the dominant class, the privileged gender and the hegemonic race in a society; consequently it subjugates all other needs.

Film is one of the most powerful of what Foucault calls "technologies of the self," through which the social order fashions the kinds of subjectivities required for its perpetuation (Martin, Gutman, and Hutton, 1987, 16–49, 145–62). In engaging these technologies of the self and the subjectivities they produce, I have contested not only the films themselves and their ideological construction of the real, but also the spectator who responds to that ideology, by producing intelligible "tales" from these films. I have also questioned the practices of the dominant forms of film theory and criticism, which are more interested in the formalist study of the immanent properties of filmic texts than in

the effectivity of film as a mode of cultural and political subordi-
nation. The dominant (poststructuralist) film theory, which succeeded the "mise-en-scene" based ("auteur") film theory over
two decades ago, has institutionalized a mode of textualism that
has effectively suppressed all but formalist readings of film.
Obviously, film theory, in the last few years, has widened its
hermeneutic horizons—as a result of a crisis that has beset bourgeois philosophy in general and poststructuralism in particular—and moved beyond the standard issues dictated by its tutor
disciplines of psychoanalysis, semiotics and an ahistorical almost
"generic" notion of "ideology." Still, a formalist analytics is the
only institutionally legitimate mode of critical and theoretical
intelligibility in film studies. The widening of the scope of
inquiry, to a large extent, has to do with the routinization and
collapse of "narratology" as a theoretical project. Most of the
"new" studies, led by such conservative film archivists–historians
as David Bordwell (1985, 1989) are simply relegitimating empiricism. They deal with a rather local history of the forms, industry,
and technology of film (Gomery, 1986; Izod, 1988), or they are
simply a reification of "experience" (James, 1989). In either case,
they are not directly involved in ideological struggles over the
"meanings" of the signs of culture produced in films

I will explore some of the implications of the ruling formalism and its dogmatic regime of close textual readings in the following pages. The institutional power and cultural prestige of
postmodern formalism (both the mise-en-scene school and poststructuralism) and the more recent revival of the Russian formalist theories of close reading in the works of such neoformal-
ists as Bordwell, Thompson, and Staiger has produced a climate
of understanding in which some may find my book too "ideological" and in "bad taste," simply because its insistence on certain
political and economic imperatives overdetermining the film's
aesthetic integrity offends commonsense empiricism and the
belief in "experience." At a time when even some of the most
institutionally influential histories of the cinema are being written in terms of the categories of formalist aesthetics (Bordwell,
Thompson, and Staiger, 1985), formalist and mainstream film
critics and theorists may find my book disrespectful of the textual difference and aesthetic specificity of the filmic experience.

Thus they may marginalize its "argument" about film as the discourse of ideology as mere "assertions" that violate the "uniqueness" of each film in its "totalization." What is *assertion* and what constitutes *argument,* of course, is itself the site of political contestation (Zavarzadeh, forthcoming). The "argument" that does not support the dominant intelligibilities and, therefore, is denied the cultural validation of the institutional "center" has always been read as "assertion" for reasons that I shall discuss throughout this book.

In a sense, however, both the general public and the formalist critic would be correct. I question the validity of empiricism, common sense, and experience as guides to understanding the cultural "real." Common sense and its discourses of experience and empiricism, in my view, are modes of ideological subjugation that produce the obviousnesses of culture and fashion the appropriate forms of subjectivity necessary for the existing social order to maintain itself. It is equally true that I do not respect the uniqueness of the film text, either on the individual textual level (which renders each individual film a unique aesthetic act) or on a collective level (which constructs films as a particular class of cultural artifacts distinct from any other artifact).

The dominant mode of reading films, which is devoted to the protection of the aesthetic "uniqueness" of each film, is in the last instance itself an ideological alibi. The defense of the aesthetic uniqueness of a film is articulated in its textual difference; to be more precise, it reproduces, in the domain of the arts, the privilege and sanctity of the unique, free individual as sovereign subject: it reproduces, in other words, the ideological discourses needed for the naturalization of the existing social arrangements. Capitalism depends on the idea of the "different" individual, who, in his absolute irreplaceability and freedom, engages in free enterprise in a free market. The privileging of the difference and singularity of film text, in short, is a legitimation of this ideological demand for the free, unique, and entrepreneurial individual. Ideology critique violates the principle of uniqueness by demonstrating that the logic of patriarchal Eurocentric capitalism underlies seemingly different, heterogeneous, and nomadic texts. Consequently it is attacked by mainstream film criticism and theory ostensibly on the grounds that it is a "reductionist" reading: it reduces the rich reversible plurality of the film and imposes a closure on it. The actual reason for these attacks, however, is that ideology critique displaces the individual by pointing out the global structures that in fact construct his seemingly "natural" uniqueness and freedom; it thus puts in question the very fundamental ideological grounds of contemporary capitalism.

Protection of the uniqueness of the film ("individuality") is thus the main purpose of all modes of bourgeois film reading— both by humanist (conservative) critics and by postmodern (radical) theorists. Supporting the cult of uniqueness, in his *Concepts in Film Theory*, Dudley J. Andrew, from a humanist perspective, writes: "In asserting a total view of the cinematic complex (from the dark caverns of spectator psychology to a global network of socio-economics) modern theory has forsaken the enterprise of criticism. How can the study of individual film be important to anyone who senses the single voice of ideology emanating from every film? Criticism in this context could only be redundant" (115).

The (poststructuralist) "theorists" whom Andrew attacks, however, far from opposing the unique, reproduce it in their own new languages and analytical procedures. Writing from within poststructuralist problematics, Andrew Higson (1983) attacks radical critics who place their analytical emphasis on economics and its consequent ideological effects, because in their reading, "All films will seem to be smothered by a blanketing 'dominant ideology'" (86).

By turning away from the political economy of signification and focusing instead on the "immanent" formal strategies of signification, poststructuralist critics effectively cut off any relation between global political, ideological and economic structures and the "local" politics of signification. Poststructuralist theory, in other words, is as much invested in the defense of the "local," the "cellular," and the "nomadic" in film as is traditional criticism. Other theorists, who do not share the philosophical assumptions of the poststructuralists, also focus on the unique qualities of the film text. In his *Narration in Fiction Film*, David Bordwell, for instance, writes: "If ideological analysis is to avoid vacuous overgeneralization, it must reckon in the concrete ways that narrational process functions in filmic representation" (1985, 335–36). The commodification of the "specific" is not by any means limited to film critics and theorists. Film makers are equally emphatic about preserving the singularity of the film. Malcolm Le Grice, the avant-garde film maker–theoretician is highly conscious of the relation between the formal properties of film texts and their politics, but nevertheless insists in his *Abstract Film and Beyond* that film should be "essentially 'cinematic'—not dominated by literature or theatre, nor for that matter by painting or music" (1977, 32). The fetishization of the concrete and the uniquely specific is part of the bourgeois empiricism whose politics and epistemology I will discuss later in this chapter.

Traditional criticism and ludic postmodern theory—which I will discuss in the next chapter—then, do not differ in their support of the specific but only in the way they articulate the unique and different. Whereas, humanist critics privilege the unique by appealing to the unitary consciousness and experience of the singular subject, postmodern theorists locate it in "language"—the style of the narrational process, "textuality," "excess," and the "surprising" movement of unrepresentable "difference" (Derrida, 1982, 1–27; Clifton, 1983; Barthes, 1977, 52–68; Heath and Mellencamp 1983; Bordwell, Thompson, and Staiger, 1985; Lyotard, 1984, 82). The valorization of the uniqueness and specificity of the filmic experience is among the discursive apparatuses ideology employs to "aestheticize" itself and place its products under the interrogative immunity usually offered to the arts in bourgeois circles. In doing so, ideology prevents detection of the operation and materiality of its discourses.

This book is an overtly polemical intervention in the way contemporary film criticism and theory make sense of film. Films in this book are read not as aesthetic acts but as modes of cultural exchange that form (desired) social subjectivities. Implicit in my approach, of course, is the assumption that culture (that is, the "real"), at any given historical moment, consists of an ensemble of contesting subjectivities. Films are not merely aesthetic spaces but political ones that contest or naturalize the primacy of those subjectivities necessary to the status quo and suppress or privilege oppositional ones.

Formalist mainstream criticism is too busy investigating the immanent logic of signification in the film to be able to inquire into such questions. Its main interest is in the rhetoric of enunciation: *how* meaning is constructed in the chain of signification *in* the film *itself.* My interest, on the other hand, is not so much in *how* (rhetoric) but in *why* (politics): *why* these films mean what they are taken to mean in the common sense of culture. Formalist (poststructuralist) theory, of course, rejects the distinction of "rhetoric" from "politics" and insists on their sameness and identity: politics is a mode of rhetoric and the rhetorical is inherently political. This new orthodoxy has allowed contemporary film theory to focus exclusively on the immanent negotiations of the sign in the film and to bracket the political economy of signification and subjectivity that relate the local immanent politics to global social struggles. In reading the rhetoric of the film as its politics and seeking its politics in its rhetorical procedures, the dominant tendency inquires into the ways that ideology is inscribed in the film's own formal work. Although this mode of reading represents itself as a critique of ideology and in opposition to the ruling social order, it is in fact complicitous with that order. In the pioneering and highly influential text, "Economical-Ideological-Formal," which opened a new phase in the criticism of ideology in postmodern film theory, Marcelin Pleynet, for example, states that the revolutionary effectivity of resistance films is primarily a matter of "formal research" into the material specificity of cinematic texts and has very little to do with economics (1978, 153–54).

The political, Pleynet believes, is situated in the cinematic apparatus itself, which offers a view of reality that is in essence ideological: the cinematic apparatus records the world (the real) according to the rules and laws of Renaissance perspective. Because quattrocento optics is based on a metaphysical fiction about the "real" and the particular position of the "subject" in that logocentric "reality," the modern cinematic apparatus is, according to Pleynet, inherently "ideological." The role of ideology critique, consequently, is to tease out from the specific cinematic text and its unique formal arrangements the singular manner in which the ideological apparatus inscribes itself. Not only does Pleynet reproduce the "unique" in his theory but, more important, he manages to "formalize" ideology. By "essentializing" the cinematic apparatus, he attributes to it an "inherent," and thus ahistorical, ideology and in doing so effectively erases the role of class struggle in the organization of the social: the political is the effect of the formal maneuvers of the cinematic apparatus itself and not the outcome of historical social contradictions. This is basically the same position shared by such other theorists as Jean-Louis Baudy (Hak Kyung Cha, 1980; De Lauretis and Heath, 1980). Even critics such as Jean-Louis Comolli, Jean Narboni, and their followers—all of whom go beyond the formalist limits set by Pleynet in their understanding of the political—never transgress the boundaries of immanent politics. According to them, the most effective critique of ideology is an "immanent" one offered from within the film text by means of its own formal procedures (digetic verisimilitude, continuity editing, and the like) and thus is respectful of the film's individuality and uniqueness (*Screen Reader 1,* 1977, 2–11, 36–46). This view is shared by more recent (and politically far more conservative) theorists such as Peter Brunette, David Wills, David Bordwell, and other formalists. In *Narration in the Fiction Film,* Bordwell concludes that the political in the film is an effect of the immanent properties of the film and the conventions of form: "By focusing on the individual psyche and maintaining a shifting narrational game with the spectator, *La guerre est finie* transmutes political material into a unique treatment of the conventions of a particular narrational mode" (1985, 228, 335). The *other* possibility—that the political transgresses and transforms the formal—is thus ruled out. For Brunette and Wills the political is the local effects of the operation of the signifier in its distancing of the signified (1989, 11–32).

The most useful critique of ideology, according to dominant film theory, is one performed in the film's "own terms" and not from an external position (economics, for instance) that violates the artistic integrity of the film. Dominant film theory, in other words, essentializes the film's "own terms" and protects them from a global political and economic interrogation. However, there are no such things as the text's "own terms." What are often regarded to be the film's "own terms" are in fact the dominant ideology's "own terms," which are protected in the guise of an aesthetic philosophy. We also need to keep in mind how what one historical era considers to be a unique work's singularly "own terms" are rejected by another historical period as "extraneous" to the immanent organization of the signifiers in a text.

To inquire into the cultural and ideological *why* of films, I have written what might be called transgressive critiques that aim at overthrowing the overt "tale" (meaning) of each unique film and indicate the "other" tale that is suppressed by the dominant one. The displacing of the dominant tale (and the subjectivities it produces) has been done more or less by pointing up and foregrounding what is always in full view but, because of the limits set by ideology, rarely suspected of being anything other than the natural order of things.

To be more precise, instead of focusing on the formal aspects of the film, I have concentrated on the ideological conditions of possibility of the formal and have chosen one specific site of the film to inquire into the way that film produces the kind of reality supportive of the existing socioeconomic arrangements. This filmic space I have called the *tale:* the way that a film offers a narrative—and proposes that narrative to be a paradigm of intelligibility—not simply through its immanent formal devices but also by relying on historically dominant and contradictory assumptions about reality. The film exerts its greatest cultural impact through its tale. By means of its tale the film naturalizes the limits of ideology, and then, by appealing to the commonsensical "obviousnesses" it has produced, the film instructs the audience on how to make sense of the global reality of the culture—how to fit together the details of reality to compose a coherent model of relations and coherence through which an all-encompassing picture of the real emerges. Within the frame of that picture, the viewer situates herself in the world her culture allows her to inhabit. In my treatment of the tales of these films, I have bracketed formalist questions and have not asked *how* a particular tale means but rather *WHY it means what it is taken to mean.* I have, in other words, found the political (why) to be a more effective mode of inquiry than the rhetorical (how).

2

The study of narrative elements in films in postmodern theory has more or less followed the formalist narratology based on a distinction between the *events* of a film and the manner in which these events are represented in its *text*. Different schools of theory and criticism have given varying names to these narrative components, which are called *diegesis* and *discourse* in dominant formalist film theory. Russian formalists who first proposed this binary model for the analysis of narrative designated events as the *story* and called the text *plot*. In their formulation, as Tomashevsky has put it, the story represents the causal-temporal relationships that constitute a narrative: how various incidents are chronologically ordered and related to one another in terms of cause and effect. The actual narrative text may or may not follow this (underlying) pattern, but when one paraphrases a narrative and abstracts the story from the text, one usually (re)arranges the narrative in terms of its story line: chronologically and causally. This is one reason why the story has been regarded by some critics to be closer to the logic of reality as we live it and thus the primary element of narrative as distinguished from the plot. Plot is the way in which events are "arranged and connected according to the orderly sequence in which they were presented in the work" (Lemon and Reis, 1965, 67). Tomashevsky summarizes the Russian formalist view of these two fundamental components of narrative: "the story is 'the action itself,' the plot 'how the reader learns of the action'" (67).

This bipartite division of narrative components informs the works of such contemporary narratologists as Todorov and Chatman, who categorize them as *story* and *discourse,* and has become one of the established features of postmodern narrative theory. Bordwell, of course, directly reinscribes the categories used by the Russian formalists: "I argue" he writes, "that filmic narration involves two principal formal systems, syuzhet [plot] and style" (1985, xiii). Some theorists like Genette have maintained the essential division between story (*histoire*) and plot (*recit*) but have added a third dimension which they call *narration*. Christian Metz, in his *The Imaginary Signifier: Psychoanalysis and the Cinema* (1982), gives a psychoanalytical twist to these two categories. He regards story to be a disguised discourse and as such the enabling condition of a mode of "voyeurism" in cinema. In more sustained deconstructive readings of narrative, this separation of the elements of narrative into story and discourse, like all other binaries of culture, has been seen as a manifestation of a logocentrism that attempts to capture the (illusory) presence and plenitude of a world beyond signification by setting up hierarchies. In structuralist narratology, story is implicitly given priority over plot because its logic and behavior is considered to be closer to the logic of actual life. Story, in other words, has been treated as the privileged term in relation to which plot is a mere secondary entity because it is a treatment of the story. Plot is assumed to be entirely dependent on the story, whose incidents it merely reorganizes for a more effective presentation and impact. However, poststructuralist rhetoric holds that what passes as a story (the primary term) is actually solicited and produced by the rhetorical demands of the secondary and supplementary term (the plot).

Contemporary criticism of film, like the criticism of other modes of cultural narrative, is very much under the influence of the theories of Russian formalists and French poststructuralists. Formalist poststructuralist theory has been particularly productive in providing insights into the workings of filmic discourse. In its most recent configurations, this form of critical theory has brought together psychoanalytical and semiotic investigations with more established forms of narratological inquiry, and the result has been brilliant analyses of the processes of signification in the filmic text. This line of inquiry, even when it deals with (immanent) politics, however, is unable in the end to address the question of the effectivity of film as a cultural act of exchange and communication that provides the viewer with a grid of understanding on which the real of social practices is located. It is ultimately descriptive (rhetorical) and not explanatory (political). Films are not enclosed constructs, as neonarratological models assume, but are instances of cultural acts in terms of which the viewer negotiates his way through the realities of daily practices—all of which are organized, in the last analysis, to confirm the dominant social relations. The final outcome of these cultural acts performed through films is to situate the viewer in a subject position in terms of which his daily practices are seen as significant and he is perceived (by himself and others) as their author and origin. If film criticism and theory is to be more than a mere formal analysis of the organization of the internal space of narrative, then it should investigate the ways in which film performs its cultural role as the producer of class subjectivities. In such an investigation, the narratological project—with its immanentism of story and discourse—will not take us very far. We need to go beyond narratology.

I have located my inquiries not in the "told" (I am thinking of the "past tense" as a narrative marker), that is to say, not in the "story" nor in the "telling" (discourse), but in the "tale": the global *effect* of the film text. Unlike traditional narratological inquiries, then, I have foregrounded the "tale" and focused not on the panhistorical immanent structures of narrative but on the consequences of narrative. My notion of "tale" also allows me to move away from the more recent neonarratological film studies that concentrate on the narrative's immanent textual "materiality" (which actually means "language") and instead to deal with its posttextual outcomes. By the *tale,* then, I do not mean the events or the happenings or any other exclusively immanent aspects of the film. Rather the tale tracks the activities through which the spectator chains together the film's signifiers on a cultural grid of intelligibility—an ensemble of assumptions and presuppositions about the "real"—into an account that makes the film socially intelligible. By making sense of the film, the spectator does not merely engage in an aesthetic act but a political practice: a practice that also enables her to make herself intelligible as a cultural entity—she achieves social "reality" as a "subject." The "tale" of the film, in other words, constitutes the individual ostensibly as a "free person" (whose freedom is manifested in his "interpretation" of the film) but in actuality situates him as belonging to a particular social class. The tale articulates the viewer through the process of sense making, locating her in the social relations of production. Constructing the tale, then, is a necessary cultural skill by which the spectator learns how to sort out the diverse codes of culture, such as gender, sexuality, class, parenting, and to establish a relation among them. In other words, in producing the tale, the spectator learns the ideological syntax of his culture (its class relations) and demonstrates his ability to provide coherent tales—as maps for dealing with the real—and thus proves that he is a symbolically competent and ideologically reliable person. He can be trusted with positions of authority (employment). Cinema is an ideologically useful institution because it helps to produce tale-making subjects out of individuals—especially in a largely postprint, electronic culture.

In producing the tale of the film, which is not a "positive" entity but a hermeneutic construct, the spectator is situated by the framing ideology (not the film itself) in the specific viewing position—subjectivity—that renders its discourses inevitable and invisible at the same time. The film naturalizes this viewing position as the given, the obvious, and the only proper position for the spectator. All modes of films, in different ways, resecure the subject positions needed for reproducing the existing social relations: the realist text (classical Hollywood cinema) reproduces the position of knowing that constructs the subject as coherent, unitary, and stable. However, dominant ideology is not monolithic, and in fact the invisibility (obviousness) of its "domination" is established by the fact that through its diverse discourses it articulates all the historically available domains of social life. To do so at this historical juncture, it needs not only coherent subject positions that respond to a more or less traditional mode of intelligibility (low-tech economy) but also postmodern subject positions that function with agility and without the cumbersome discourses of coherence in more advanced forms of economic activities (high-tech practices). The avant-garde film text articulates the inner economic tensions and contradictions of late capitalist ideology and contests the unitary subject of the realist cinema, thus constructing the subject as inherently unstable, changeable, and even contradictory. These two modes of subjectivity are far from being incompatible, as postmodern film theory maintains: realism is viewed by ludic postmodernism as producing "reactionary" subjects whereas the avant-garde is seen as constructing "radical" subjects. They are in fact complementary. Late capitalism requires not only coherent subjects but also undecidable ones that respond to the economic needs of the social regime that Baudrillard calls *simulation*. In the ideological seams and folds of the ruling practices and aesthetic and social contradictions, of course, other cinematic articulations take shape, such as what I shall call *critical cinema*—a Brechtian kind of cinema of political self-reflexivity that provides the spectator with the space to critique the everyday "from a social point of view" (Brecht, 1979, 86) and thus approach the social as something that is not natural but always demands an "explanation" (125). I shall discuss the (non)relations between form and the emancipatory potential of a film later.

From the positions of knowledge produced by the film text (realist or avant-garde), the existing reality (coherent—"original"—or simulatory) seems to be the only possible one: all other constructions of the real are seen as void of legitimacy. In producing tales, it must be emphasized, the spectator is produced as a female or a male, a white or a black, an upper-class or a working-class subject. In a sense constructing the tale of the film is an indication of ideological skills: a mark that the subject has learned the "proper" codes and practices through which the socially needed "reality" can be made intelligible. Film, as an ideological apparatus, then serves as a means for making sure that the subject is equipped with the elements of the cultural logic of the (dominant) real.

My statement should not be conveniently read to mean that all viewers of a film produce exactly the same tale. Quite the contrary, the dominant frames of intelligibility provide a great deal of interpretive "freedom" and latitude for differences among the tales produced by viewers. In fact it is through this interpretive freedom of texts of culture (film as well as other cultural products) that the ruling ideology establishes its democratic legitimacy and consequently, without overt violence, secures its hold on the limits of understanding.

In the dominant ideology of the democratic state, the subject is represented as a rational (namely, overwritten by the logic of ideology) person who in the privacy of her consciousness can discover the "truth" of cultural texts such as films. Because it is the allegiance of the "free" subject that the state demands, differences in the interpretive construction of the tale (which in fact affirm the ideological "truth" about the "free" individual consciousness) are not only tolerated but in fact actively encouraged.

The dominant ideology however firmly asserts that, in spite of all the differences in reading the tale of the film, there is a core of truth (immanently) in the text itself, and the ultimate goal of viewing a film is to have access to this truth given in the text by another consciousness (the director). In postmodern film theory, as part of its renovation of the discourses of dominant ideology, the "apparatus" and not the "director" is seen as the organizer of the film's signifiers. I shall call this new device a *consciousness effect* as it simply transfers the location of the subject so that it can more effectively produce the new subject for postmodern capitalism, in which there is very little use for the subject as "auteur." The Subject (I shall refer to director–auteur apparatus as the Subject—with capital *S*), needless to say, not only inscribes the idea of the subject in the project of interpretation but also stands for the authority of the social order that is itself organized by the prevailing class-gender-race relations. In constructing the tale, the spectator is free to "interpret" it in anyway that his individual consciousness instructs him as long as his different interpretation accepts the authority of the immanent properties of text itself and thus respects its empirical existence. Although the tale is not a "positive" entity that can be pointed to, the dominant frames of intelligibility make sure that tales follow the reigning (ideo)logic and are not constructed arbitrarily by labeling counterhegemonic tales as eccentric, off-beat, and wayward, thereby rendering them unintelligible. Thus, one of the practices that the viewer learns in constructing the tale of the film is, of course, the proper mode of situating himself in regard to authority. The only limits on the viewer's freedom in producing the tale of the film come in the recognition of the higher authority of the text itself—which is an ideological alibi for the authority that is (immediately) often termed *God* (the origin of all meanings) or *State* (the regulator of meanings) but is, in fact, the mediated authority of the free market forces that mark the produced meanings of texts of culture as purchasable-intelligible or worthless-nonsense depending on their relevance to the dominant economic regime. In regarding individuals as free and allowing for differences in their interpretation of the tale—yet at the same time subjecting them to the authority of a higher power (the immanent properties of the text itself)—the dominant ideology preserves the notion of the free person who can enter into transactions with other free persons in the free market but who is at the same time obedient to the laws of the free market that legitimate the dominant social order.

Contemporary mainstream film criticism accounts for the process of spectatorship and subjectivity in terms of the immanent formal operations of the film through the concept of "suture." Theories of suture are, on the whole, more interested in the poetics of the "desire" the film arouses in the viewer and in the immanent "pleasure" and "displeasure" (lack) he experiences in the process of viewing than in the political economy of spectatorship: the production, exchange, and consumption of cinematic discourses and the pleasures and securities offered by them at historically specific moments in relations of production. History in theories of suture is reduced to a matter of psychoanalytic development—the history of the subject in the move from the imaginary to the symbolic—thereby effectively erasing the role of viewing as a process producing class subjects. Thus the spectator, in mainstream theories of suture, is seen as the subject of *jouissance*—in a state of half-forgetting, voyeuristic-exhibitionistic delight in a darkened theatre, the spectator engages in a pleasurable regression to the pre-Oedipal, fusional moment of identity with an ideal image (mother).

By positing a necessary "absence," mainstream suture theory, especially in the writings of Oudart, Dayan, and Heath, offers a theory of the subject (formation) that erases the socioeconomic and political conditions of subject(ivity). Absence, in Lacanian psychoanalysis, is the trope of the unconscious that is believed to produce the speaking subject. Suture theory in its articulation by Oudart, sees the continuity and coherence of filmic narrative to be an effect of an absence that is sutured through the cinematic process of shot–reverse shot editing. The spectator, Oudart assumes, always experiences plenitude, fullness, and *jouissance* in his or her encounter with the first shot, which is unencumbered by limits ("the fourth side, a field of pure absence" [Oudart, 1977–78, 43]). However, he or she soon becomes aware of the "absence," which is condition of the presence. In the words of one of Oudart's followers: "When the viewer discovers the frame ... the triumph of his former *possession* of the image fades out.... The spectator discovers that his possession was only partial, illusory. He feels dispossessed of what he is prevented from seeing. He discovers that he is only authorized to see what happens to be in the axis of the gaze of another spectator who is

ghostly or absent" (Dayan, 1974, 56). It is this "another spectator" who is called "the Absent One" and whose absence the
reverse shot attempts to efface and thereby create an impression
of auto-intelligibility and transparency for the film—effects that
are then assimilated by the spectator. Suturing then, makes film's
ideological effects unobtrusive by, in Dayan's words, substitution
of the "message" for the "code"—a fictional character for the
"absent one" on the level of cinematic enunciation (56).

In poststructuralist film theory, *Ideology* is a synonym for
representation and has very little to do with the radical notion of
ideology as the diverse practices serving class interests.

However, whether suture is deployed on the level of
"shot–reverse shot" editing (Oudart), "point-of-view" editing
(Dayan), or in a much more generalized sense as the condition
of cinematic enunciation and communication (Heath, 1981, 97),
it is grounded on the notion of "absence" and thus accounts for
the formation of the subject in terms of the unconscious and
immanent laws of the symbolic order (language). The subject, in
short, is "explained" in terms of the mechanics of discourses of
subjectivity and their inner dynamics. To be more precise,
through suturing the gaps and absences in the film, the spectator
is sutured into the film, which provides the subject with "pleasure" through a replay of its history and a recapturing of *jouissance* of the imaginary. Film viewing then is the effect of the
experience of pleasure of oneness, and this oneness is severed
from the collectivity of the social and the political economy that
articulates the subject into relations of production. My point is
that seeing films is a political act, and as such it is more than the
experience of pleasure; it is a "knowledge" lesson through which
the subject is "taught" how to be what Pecheux calls a "good
subject" and is placed in its position in social relation (class).

Stephen Heath, for example, regards suture to be "the relation of the individual-as-subject to the chain of its discourse
where it figures missing in the guise of a stand-in" (1981, 52). By
positing "meaning" as the effect of the immanent and transhistorical laws of signification (Derrida, 1982, 1–27; Lacan, 1977,
30–113) the chain of the discourse occludes class relations. In theorizing suture immanently, postmodern film theory proposes that
the production of subjectivity is a formal, and thus an ahistorical,

process and consequently severs it from the global political, economic, and ideological practices of the social formation. Even such theorists of suture as Daniel Dayan, who have attempted to connect suture to the working of ideology and to relate the spectator's "resistance" (engendered by "pleasure") to the subjectivities offered by the film, have in fact reproduced a formalism in that they have substituted an inquiry into the *rhetoric* of subjectivity—*how* ideology legitimates certain subjectivities—for an interrogation of the political economy of interpellation—*why* certain subjectivities (class relations) are legitimated at specific historical moments to begin with (Dayan, 1974).

In the poststructuralist film theory of suture, the form of the film provides the space of subjectivity in which the subject's history is reenacted from imaginary plenitude to symbolic lack as he is "sewn in" to the discourse of the film. The form of classical cinema (realist film) is thought to be oppressive, regardless of its content. The avant-garde film, on the other hand, is deemed to have a liberatory effect. The content of such films may be quite repressive—sexism, classism, racism—but as long as the form transgresses the codes of classical Hollywood cinema, it will (automatically) be productive of nonrepressive subjectivities. In all its forms, through the idea of suture, ludic postmodern film theory posits the spectator as essentially a passive person. My theory of the tale, on the other hand, proposes the viewer an active tale maker situated in social contradictions of her culture. Some of these active tale makers are also "oppositional" tale makers.

3

The viewer, in his role as a maker of the tale, does not function as a unique individual consciousness who "authors" the tale but rather operates as the ensemble of structures of difference (class relations) in which various frames and codes of intelligibility intersect and enable him to recognize meaning in the film's signs. The tale, I propose, is the narrative (filmic) space in which the viewer by his practice of tale making is made intelligible to himself as the subject of class and constituted as a structure of signification (that is to say, of "difference").

Unlike story and discourse, which are enclosed diegetic

spaces, the tale operates on the boundaries of the narrative-spec-
tator-culture series. The cultural impact, for instance, of *The Big
Chill* is the effect of the tale that the viewer produces about intimacy in contemporary America. The tale offers a model for
making culturally approved forms of friendship intelligible. It
instructs the viewer on how to recognize "genuine" forms of
friendship (that is to say, those forms that correspond with the
subjectivities required by the existing relations of production)
and to distinguish them from "false" modes of intimacy (namely,
those that threaten the existing models of human relationship
made "obvious" by ideology). Through the theory of intimacy
produced in the tale (by the spectator according to ideological
markers of the "real"), a particular mode of human relationship
is legitimated. The film, in other words, is a cultural exchange
through which the dominant ideology attempts to maintain its
authority over the affairs of society while suppressing other ways
of understanding friendship. To place the emphasis on the "discourse" of *The Big Chill* and to merely inquire into its diegetic
status is to aestheticize and reduce to a more or less cognitive act
what in the film is basically a political practice. Such aestheticization and cognitive reductionism are themselves acts of consent
supporting the dominant social order.

The "tale" of the film is *not in* the text itself (it is not a positive entity): it is not determined. Therefore, it is not accessible
through an analysis of formal properties. The formal features of
the film are not, it has to be emphasized, autointelligible, instead
they act as a discursive apparatus through which the limits that
ideology sets upon reality are naturalized. Reading a film is thus
not merely conditioned by the immanent features and practices
of the film or by the reader but rather is shaped, for the most
part, by historically produced frames of understanding. It is not
so much the empirical viewer who finds meaning in the film, as it
is the structures of intelligibility that produce the positions of
knowledge that will make sense of the film for those who occupy
the desired subject positions. Those who do indeed occupy the
subject position of knowledge provided by the film are, in return,
placed outside all social contradictions and endowed with coherence and clarity. It is necessary to bear in mind that the authority
of the film in interpellating the subject does not derive from

itself or its immanent filmic properties (poststructuralist theories of the avant-garde notwithstanding) but from the dominant social arrangements that encourage the subject to occupy the positions of knowledge proposed by the film.

Moving beyond neotraditional narratological models of film analysis and focusing on the tale will make it possible to inquire into the ideological and political conditions authorizing the viewer of a film to chain together its various signs according to a (socio)logic that she is interpellated to understand as the "logic" of the real. The tale of a film, in other words, is a theory of reality generated by the dominant mode of production; and in the spaces of this theory, its politics should be interrogated. The tale of a film is made intelligible when the spectator consents to the dominant modes of subjectivities and employs the frames of interpretation provided by the existing ideology.

4

But the production of an "obviously" intelligible tale by the spectator-film-ideology nexus suppresses *another* tale—the tale that the overt one prevents from being told. Each film is therefore the narrative space of contestation and struggle among different tales that produce warring theories of the real. The hegemonic "tale" of the film, which is enabled and secured by the dominant "obviousnesses," is always different from itself; it is reversible and thus rather unstable. Along the line of some of Marx's writings, one can theorize the tale that "exists" (is historically recognized and sanctioned as the real) as an unstable effect of the conflict and contestation between the *actual* and the *possible* (Marx and Engels, 1975, 141–45). The obvious tale of a film is represented by the common sense as being an actual, already "existing" meaning in order to attribute to this hegemonic tale the authority of an inevitable and natural meaning. But the tale of a film is not an already existing meaning; rather it is a contingent construct produced under the conditions of certain ideological, economic and political practices. The framing ideology places the spectator in a position of intelligibility from which she understands the ideologically available (the commonsensical) meaning of the film to be its "real" meaning. In doing so the spectator equates the available (that is, the already existing) meaning with the "actual" and blocks the "possible." The film's other possible meanings—the utopian dimension immanent in all ideological discourses—are suppressed by this representation of the hegemonic tale as the sole meaning and thereby the "real" of the film. The cultural reality proposed by the film is thus perceived as the natural outcome of the world itself ("out there"), and the ideological operation of common sense in the construction of this reality is concealed. Both traditional film criticism and postmodern film theory participate in this repressive empiricism that equates the "actual" with the "real."

The suppression of the *possible* by reifying the *existing* is the effect of the idealist philosophy of empiricism prevailing in contemporary film criticism and theory. In this respect dominant film theory does little more than reinforce the ideological work of the contemporary mainstream film (whether realist or avant-garde). The mainstream film, for the most part, achieves its role in naturalizing the ruling social order not simply by offering films that "thematically" reproduce the "obviousnesses" of ideology but, more significantly, by the sheer "representation" of the "real" ("out there")—that is to say, by testifying to the existence of a real world whose reality is documented in the film as the film: its representationality as such. Mainstream film, in other words, is not so much "about" specific themes and topics (family, love, or, in the case of the avant-garde film, reflexivity) as it is about the existence of a real world *that is accessible to our senses and can be directly experienced.* By capturing the sights and sounds of this world (by testifying to the "obviousness" of *representation*), the film fetishizes a theory of knowledge that, more than any specific thematic, naturalizes the existing social arrangements and their contradictions: the theory of knowledge (empiricism) that equates the world itself with knowledge of the world. What we know, it implies, comes from the world itself as a result of our "experience" of it. Knowledge, in empiricist film theory and criticism is not a historical product constructed within social contradictions and thus the effect of class-gender-race struggles but the "natural" outcome of the world itself. What is visible (the surface tale of the film and the experiential world it represents), in short, is regarded to be the real itself.

My *renarration* contests this regressive empiricism that lends support to the social status quo by producing an "other" tale from the same (empirical) materials that the film offers and argues that the visible is not always seeable: that daily experience is not in and of itself self-evident and autointelligible but is understandable only in terms of the historical frames of intelligibility that in fact make sense of it. Because contesting empiricism is one of the most urgent tasks of a radical oppositional reading of film, I will discuss at length, in chapter 3, the politics and mechanics of the production of the "real" from the "actual" and reexamine the role of "experience" in the reproduction of the dominant social relations. Here, however, I would like to briefly outline the complicity of both traditional film criticism and postmodern theory with the project of empiricism and its politics.

Traditional film criticism reinforces empiricism by proposing that the knowledge of the world is derived directly from the world itself and consequently "experience" is the site of the real or truth. There is, according to traditional humanism, no mediation of "difference" or slippage between the consciousness of the experiencer and the experience. In spite of such variations as the histories of the experiencers, their social conditions, and their racial, gender, and class differences, experience, in essence, is a reliable "representation" of the real according to the empiricist philosophy of knowledge. In postulating experience as identical with the real, traditional film theory naturalizes two fundamental concepts necessary for the reproduction of dominant relations of production: the correspondence of the existing world with the real world and the inviolability of the individual as the receiver of knowledge of this world. Both these notions, as I have already indicated, are crucial to the ideological discourses that legitimate capitalism.

In postmodern film theory, the naive empiricism of traditional humanist film criticism is put in question by meticulous, immanent analyses that unearth the discourses actually involved in the construction and production of the world as it "really" is. Postmodern theory, in other words, to use Jean-Paul Fargier's metaphor, puts the material discourses of the cinema out of "parentheses" and demonstrates how what is assumed to be actually "out there" is in fact discursively constructed (1977, 23-35). In its critique of empiricism, postmodern theory shows the ideological operations of empiricism in reading films, but, in the last instance, it does not go beyond empiricism. It merely replaces one kind of empiricism (an empiricism of the senses and prediscursive reality) with another kind (an empiricism of discourse). The route to dismantling the ideology of the visible in postmodern theory is through the immanent analysis of the formal features of the film. It is the film itself that, in a self-reflexive move, doubles back upon itself and examines its own discursive practices, which found the grounds of its narrative. Empiricism, in postmodern theory and film practices, in short, is deconstructed by demonstrating that the film does not refer to an already existing world accessible to the senses but in fact points to its own materiality and involvement in the production of meaning (the world). Contrary to the traditional humanist view, film, in postmodern theory, is not considered to be "representational" (it does not refer to a world "out there") but is regarded to be "differential" (it acquires its meaning through the operation of its own signifiers that point to other signifiers of the filmic text and not to a preexisting signified called the *world*) and thus asserts the film's own "materiality." *Materiality* in postmodern film theory, however, is an "instrumental" materiality because what it signifies is merely the elements of its own discourses: the materials from which the filmic text-spectacle is made. As Marx has pointed out in his critique of Feuerbach, such a notion of materiality is ahistorical, mechanical, and nontransformative. Materialism in a radical political sense is, above all, the effect of social relations.

In opposition to both traditional film criticism and postmodern film theory, the politically radical theory needs to show that the visible (whether conceived as the "world out there" or as the immanent properties of the film itself) is not seeable without mediation. What is represented as visible in and of itself in the dominant discourses (what is held to be the "actual") is in fact made *seeable* (culturally meaningful although represented as naturally significant) by the mediation of the dominant ideology that posits one and only one meaning for it. Radical theory, by means of what I shall call *renarrating,* intervenes in the ideologically visible and demonstrates the *other* in the self-sameness of the visible. In other words, it shows that the visible can be made *seeable* in a number of ways depending on the historical situation and social contradictions that enable certain forms of social struggle. Radical theory destablizes the visible and shows that the empirically existing (the dominant visible) is traversed with the *otherness* of the possible. To articulate the possible, radical theory demonstrates that the empirical, far from being the real, is only an invention of the ruling class. To undertake its task, radical theory needs to produce "other" ways of seeing that break the fundamental laws of the bourgeois theory of looking, and in order to see, looks away from the empirical phenomena and, as I have already elaborated, refuses its "uniqueness" (Althusser, 1977, 13–69).

In demonstrating the reversibility and difference of the "existing" tale of a film, I have not taken the by now commonplace path of poststructuralism: I have not attempted to point to the everlasting gap in these texts between their argument and their tropes; between language and meaning; or between the signifier and the signified (Zavarzadeh, 1989). Such a route would lead back to a new formalism. Rather, I have shown the difference of a film from itself—its ideological insecurity, aporias, contradictions, and instability—by showing how the dominant and commonsensical "tale" of a film is in constant contestation with the film's latent tales. How, in other words, a filmic space is the site of the warring forces in culture between what social reality *is* under present ideological and economic practices and what it could *become*. To show this suppression of one tale by the other, I have renarrated these films in terms of their ideologically suppressed meaning: a procedure that offcenters a film's tales and indicates their historical contingency. A political reading of film needs to examine how the tale that is immediately recognized by the spectator and hailed by the dominant ideology is merely a tale of concealment: a tale that attempts to make the other tales of the film unintelligible. One way to allow other tales to surface is to use the device of renarrating to displace the overt tale.

Renarrating as a mode of "reading" is marginalized in formalist mainstream interpretive practices. Formalism finds this act to be a redundant reproduction of the film's story, a mere rehearsal of its plot. However, I believe that when the formalist mode of analysis disallows the rewriting of the film through a careful process of renarrating, it is attempting to aesthetically legitimate the political imperatives of the ruling social order: to prevent any recognition of the potency of the oppositional tales in cultural narratives by protecting the culturally dominant tale of the film as *the* (only) tale under the guise of aesthetic integrity. Such a strategy of containment, as I shall explain later, has profound implications for the production of cultural reality.

The function of a detailed renarrating of the tale of the film is to displace the film's narrative logic—an act regarded to be a violation of the artistic uniqueness and signifying integrity of the film. By displacing the film's dominant logic, renarrating demystifies the way that logic (which is itself an effect of existing frames of intelligibility) suppresses ideologically unfavored forms of understanding and organizing reality by making them unintelligible. In my critiques I have renarrated films to offcenter them and, in doing so, show the "other" tale that is not told. Renarrating a film reveals that what formalist criticism regards to be the unique and inevitable aesthetic logic of a film is instead the very general and quite common logic of ideology. By depriving a film of its "unique logic" one loosens the logic's grip on the narrative itself and takes away its ideological authority that is misrepresented as an aesthetic one. Through such a deaestheticization, the radical critic is able to inquire into the politics of the film as a discourse of culture—erasing the separate aesthetic space and interrogative immunities the dominant ideology offers works of art.

Renarrating, in other words, deprivileges the film as an aesthetic work and returns it to the general discursive domain of culture—this dehierarchization is the first step toward an understanding of film as an ideological and cultural act. This renarrating, of course, is itself made unintelligible by the dominant aesthetic ideology that rejects such writings about film and other arts for "not being specific enough" about the immanent formal aspects of the film in the sense that they do not accept the "uniqueness" of film as an individual aesthetic act. The reading of film as only one form of exchange and communication among others is resisted by film critics and theorists with the same conservative energy that the denial of "literariness"—the uniqueness of literature—has encountered among humanist and decon-structionist theorists alike. Because to violate the specificity of the film text is not only to put in question the centrality of what it actually stands for, namely, the uniqueness of the free subject (individual), but also to subvert another law of the capitalist eco-nomic regime: the intellectual division of labor that establishes independent zones of inquiry, each with its own unique identity (literariness in literature, visuality in film, legality in law, and so on), internal laws and rules of operation, the mastery of which is part of the professionalization of knowing in culture and the establishment of a disciplinary society with all its rewards (inclu-sions) and punishments (exclusions). My strategic refusal in this book about film to adopt the dominant modes of analysis in the discipline of "film studies" or to employ the methodologies legit-imated by it or even to "refer" and "quote" extensively from the scholarship of the discipline—privilege its authority—is an attempt to take film, as a cultural mode of exchange, back from the "professionals" and make it, once again, part of active ideo-logical struggles for social transformation. My bypassing of the "discipline," of course, will result in the delegitimization of my project by many film critics, theorists, and reviewers as well as other adherents of the discipline, who will place it in the zone of the unintelligible (illegitimate-marginal).

The political outcome of renarrating the tales of films is the display of the power relations and "logic" of exploitation in these films because the purpose of renarrating is not a simple reversal and substitution of one tale for another. The main goal of renarration is to bring to the fore the *contradictions* between the hegemonic tale and the "other" tale(s) and thus to produce (as part of an ideological struggle) the crisis that will show the dominant reading to be an "interested" reading and thus open to contestation and change. Renarration, in short, is a political weapon and not merely a hermeneutic enterprise. Recognition of the operations of power and the exploitation they conceal will enable those who suffer from them to resist them: the empower-ment of the powerless, in short, is the main goal of the political and antiformalist theory and criticism—the "ideology cri-tique"—I have practiced. I must add here that seeing films "other"wise (or even ideological struggle, for that matter) in and of itself, will not change the world, but it will help to produce counterintelligibilities that can denaturalize the existing social relations and thus become part of the larger project of a global revolution.

In renarrating the film's tale, it becomes clear that tales, as Wolfgang Iser has put it (in relation to a different set of issues), are not "told for their own sake but for the demonstration of something that extends beyond themselves" (1978, 123). This something is the focus of an ideology critique that moves beyond the dominant narratological analysis. Inquiry into this something beyond the tale, it should be emphasized, does not mean that the tale is an element of the film that can be cut off from the filmic text. At the same time, I believe the tale is a posttextual construct. Contrary to the views of mainstream film criticism, which regards all elements of the film to be essentially textual effects called forth by the rhetorical and tropic requirements of the text itself, the tale of the film is posttextual not in the sense that it is "extra" and thus nontextual. Rather, it is always a construct produced by the spectator, who is being interpellated by the dominant economic, political, and ideological practices of the culture—practices that do not necessarily work by the laws of textual-rhetorical difference. By posttextuality, then, I emphasize that the "meaning" of a cultural text such as film is neither in the text itself nor "created" by the sovereign viewer. It is rather the effect of the historical limits of cultural intelligibilities. In formalist theories, such as deconstruction, "textuality" (language) is understood as tropic slippage and "difference." In posttextual reading practices, the "difference" is seen not simply as the effect of inherent, and thus ahistorical, textual features but as the outcome of social contestations in labor relations and consequently in language.

Although all postmodern theories of understanding and interpretation—from the writings of Saussure and Levi-Strauss to those of Barthes, Foucault, Deleuze, Guattari, Lacan, Derrida, Lyotard, and Baudrillard—are based on a new understanding of intelligibility and representation as "difference," they do not address the relation between difference, intelligibility, and exploitation. Marxist cultural theory, on the other hand, has always theorized intelligibility as the effect of "difference" produced by the historical and material conditions of social life and thus has attended to the question of exploitation. In *The German Ideology,* Marx and Engels write that "language is the immediate actuality of thought" (1976, 446) and point out that the empiricity of the world "out there" is mediated through language, which is itself a historical product. However, what is significant in Marx's notion of language and signification for a postmodern radical reunderstanding of intelligibility is his emphasis on language as social—a point that, although hinted at by Saussure (1966, 14, 113), is suppressed in poststructuralism. In the same book, Marx and Engels also write that "language is practical, real consciousness that exists for other men as well and only therefore does it exist for me; language like consciousness, only arises from the need, the necessity, of social intercourse with other men" (1976, 44). In other words, they situate intelligibility in the social. The notion of intelligibility as a site of restlessness and semantic agitation is one that Marxism and poststructuralism share, but their understandings of it are radically different. For Derrida, for example, this semiotic excitement is the very characterization of textuality—the movement of difference. For Marx, the sign (intelligibility) is the scene of semiotic stirrings because it is the site of class struggle, the space where various social groups attempt to contest the established and assigned meanings of the sign in their struggles (consider the history of the social and economic struggles over *nigger, Negro, black, Afro-American, African-American* in the United States). The notion of the intelligibility of the sign as the site of social contestation is further developed by Volosinov-Bakhtin in *Marxism and the Philosophy of Language:* "Class does not coincide with the sign community, i.e. with the community which is the totality of users of the same set of signs or ideological communication. Thus various different classes will use one and the same language. As a result differently oriented accents intersect in every ideological sign. *Sign becomes an arena of the class struggle*" (emphasis added, 1973, 23).

Posttextuality, then, is a "meaning effect" produced in the nexus of global relations that endow the text and reader simultaneously with historical intelligibility. Historical intelligibility is thus inscribed, in the last instance, in the material conditions of social practices; and it in turn provides those practices with a "reason," an "explanation," and a "justification." The viewer, having been situated in a knowledge position in the act of viewing, makes sense of the textual signs given to her by placing them in a chain of signifiers that produce a tale according to the narrative schema and (ideo)logic of reality dominant in her culture (Zavarzadeh, 1985). This tale, which is made by the spectator in the act of viewing the film, is in fact a mark of her successful understanding of the film according to the dominant discourses of ideology and, therefore as I have already suggested, an indication of her cultural usefulness and reliability. If she fails to produce a tale, it is a clear "symptom" that she has not been able to respond to the call of ideology and make the film (and herself) culturally intelligible. Not all viewers, of course, are able to develop a tale out of each film they see; thus the familiar and common complaint by some viewers that "nothing happened" in the film: no narrative cohered and thus no map of knowing developed; nothing was made intelligible. The "failure" to construct the tale is the effect of a complex series of socioeconomic factors that determine the relation of the spectator to the symbolic practices of culture, and they include the exclusionary practices of the dominant intelligibility as well as the "resistance" of the spectator to the ruling codes and practices of social understanding. A film that is "perfectly" intelligible to members of one social class may in fact remain opaque or only partially intelligible to members of other classes. Whereas all view the same empirically "visible" film text, they do not all "see" it as they have different ideological frames through which they recuperate the signs of the film into a senseful tale. To the extent that their ideological frames prevent them from constructing a culturally meaningful tale—one understandable in terms of the dominant ideology—spectators are not awarded the final "pleasure" of viewing a film: their confirmation as culturally viable subjects. In others words, they remain unintelligible to themselves and become culturally unanchored (resistant) whenever they encounter certain symbolic products of culture.

Radical theory displays the class politics of intelligibility and helps produce the oppositional spectator, whose historical knowledge of englobing economic, political, and ideological structures enables her to go beyond the "pleasures" of the empirically visible and "see" the politics of the operations of intelligibility in cultural products. The oppositional spectator thus refuses to accept the dominant frames of intelligibility and resists constructing the (hegemonic) tale of the film. Of course, she ends up with an "unintelligible tale." But her oppositional tale produces a tale of counterintelligibility showing how that which is senseful in a culture is made to be that way. In doing so, she puts in question the solid and highly visible demarcations of ideology separating the senseful from nonsense. Sensefulness, in the oppositional tale of counterintelligibility, is shown for what it is: a reproduction of the dominant ideology. On the other hand, to construct a tale out of a film by means of the intelligibility offered by the dominant ideology to those who occupy the required subject positions is the mark of a successful operation of the culture's technologies of the self.

CHAPTER 2

PLEASURE, RESISTANCE, AND
THE LUDIC POSTMODERN

1

My focus in this book is on the ways in which films, as part
of the technologies of the self, are deployed in securing the domination of the ruling social order. It is necessary to make this
point clear because here, too, my position is at odds with current
film theory and criticism. Mainstream film theory, in its more
recent phase, following such theorists as Foucault, Deleuze,
Guattari, Lyotard, and the later writings of Derrida and Barthes,
has developed a populist "generic" brand of the "political"
(often called the *ethical* to emphasize the self-fashioning autonomy of the subject) for reading film; it places its primary emphasis
on the "resistance" of the subject as "agent" rather than on the
"domination" of prevailing social arrangements (Foucault, 1980,
1988; Deleuze and Guattari, 1983, 1987; Lyotard, 1987; Barthes,
1975; DeLauretis, 1984; Gallop, 1988; Silverman, 1988). Such a
political reading situates "resistance" in Foucault's word *everywhere* and thus in all the activities of producing and viewing
film—from the aesthetic counterforces within the filmic text
itself (how a film such as *Lost in America,* for example, deconstructs and thus resists its own ideology through its parodic elements) to the refusal of the spectator to go along with the subject
positions offered by the film. "Resistance" on the level of the
cinematic apparatus is considered to be focused largely on the
opposition to quattrocento optics, which theorists such as Mar-
cellin Pleynet see as code of specular vision producing dominant
ideological effects through the cinematic apparatus itself (1978,
159). I find such a ludic postmodern populist accent on "resis-

tance" to be itself an erasure of resistance and in fact an act of complicity with the ruling ideology.

Before interrogating the politics of ludic "resistance," however, it is necessary to, at least briefly, discuss the concept of "ludic postmodernism" because so far I have used the term *postmodern* in a general sense. Like all concepts deployed for culture analysis, "postmodernism" is not a stable one but a shifting site of social struggle. Even though one may consider certain local features of the contemporary as "postmodern," postmodernism is not an ensemble of free-floating, autointelligible lineaments. Instead, its meaning is the effect of a global frame of intelligibility in which various traces and marks are articulated. This frame of intelligibility is neither in the phenomenon itself, as empiricists propose, nor is it simply a matter of "writing," as textualists insist. It is rather produced historically through social struggles, and there are many contesting ways of constructing it. Following Teresa L. Ebert's reading of postmodernity (1990, 1–18), I shall name as "ludic postmodernism" that understanding of postmodernity which makes sense of it as a problematics of "representation" and, furthermore, conceives of "representation" as a rhetorical issue, a matter of signification in which the very process of signification articulates the signified. Knowledge of the "outside"—if one can mark such a zone of being—is, according to the ludic theory, traversed by rifts, slippages, and alterity that are immanent in signifying practices and above all in language. Representation, in other words, is always incommensurate with the represented as it is the subject of the law of "differance." Ludic postmodernism therefore posits the "real" as an instance of "simulation" and in no sense the "origin" of the "truth" that can provide a ground for a political project. Differance, in ludic postmodernism, is regarded to be the effect of the unending "playfulness" (thus the term *ludic*) of the signifier in signifying practices that no longer can acquire representational authority by anchoring the signifier in what Derrida has called the "transcendental signified" (1976, 20).

Contesting the understanding of "differance" as an effect of rhetoric, "resistance" postmodernism, articulates difference as the effect of "labor," focusing on congealed and alienated labor as private property. Labor, and not language, I argue is the practice that determines the regime of signification and the ensuing "representation" of the real. Language, and all other semiotic processes, are articulated by the division of labor. Difference, in short, is a "materialist" praxis produced through class struggle and not a "rhetorical" effect. I might add here that Ebert's reading of "resistance postmodernism" does not emphasize "labor" in the way I have done here since her reading of Marx's labor theory is more focused on those discourses of Marx that foreground the abstractness of labor under capitalism and thus the erasure of difference among the heterogeneous. She, in short accents Marx's notion of capitalism as itself a form of totalization. Whereas ludic postmodernism seeks its own genealogy in Nietzschean texts, resistance postmodernism is articulated in the writings of Marx.

Ludic theories essentialize resistance as an ethical imperative and consequently—as in all forms of ludic postmodern ethics—posit an ahistorical subject who overcomes the dominant regimes of subjectivities by virtue of his natural human abilities. These abilities, in turn, are mobilized by an equally ahistorical "human rights," often articulated in the form of oppositional pleasures. The subject of "resistance" in these theories, in other words, is the sovereign ethical subject who in his natural freedom ("human rights")—which is grounded in the ethics of resistance pleasures and guaranteed by body politics—takes charge of his destiny and transcends the historical structures of economic domination and political power. The appeal of the "ethical" (as opposed to the "political") in poststructuralism theories is identical with ethics in traditional liberal humanism. The "ethical," in Michael Levin's words, "does not require any particular stance on any public issue, be it pollution or apartheid. Honesty, industry and respect for others form the gyroscope that stabilizes an individual on his journey through life not an itinerary of policy positions" (15). To be politically engaged in a collective, transformative task, is, according to Levin, to have constraining, rigid, dogmatic "policy positions." Levin's humanist views confirm Foucault's notion of the ethic of care for the self as a practice of freedom (Foucault, 1987, 112–131).

Postmodern theories of resistance, following Foucault (1980), deny the repressiveness of power because, they argue, such a view of power is unidimensional and thus reductionist. In contemporary film theory power is thus seen as always activating a counterpower (resistance) and as such not only not dominating and repressive but in fact enabling: "Wherever there is power, there is resistance" (Foucault, 1980, 95).

In Foucauldian theory, there are no bipolarities: no plane of the "dominated" in contradiction to that of the "dominating," rather the two face each other on a single plane of the social as entities with movable and changing frontiers. The binaries of ruling and ruled, in other words, are done away with in ludic political theory that, in a mode of postmodern mysticism, theorizes the social as a site of monism in which the *many* simultaneously coexist in the *one*. "There is no binary and all-encompassing opposition between rulers and ruled at the root of power relations" (Foucault, 1988, 94). The ludic deconstruction of binaries is, of course, a postmodern reproduction of the ethos of the democratic pluralism that is the ideological underpinning of stateless corporate capitalism. The goal of Foucault's theory of power is to erase the binaries of powerful-powerless, dominant-dominated, subjugating-subjugated, and above all the category of (social) "class" (ruling-ruled) that foregrounds the social contradictions derived from the social division of labor. He consequently removes the concept of "class struggle" as the dynamic force of history and eliminates social transformation from the scene of the social. Writing from within conservative ludic postmodernism, John Fiske sums up the retreat from "class" in postmodern social theory: "One of the many debts we owe to Foucault is his insistence that power relations cannot be adequately explained by class relations, that power is discursive and is to be understood in the specific contexts of its exercise, not in generalized social structures" (1989, 179). As I shall argue later, this erasure of global economic and historical structures in favor of the local, molecular, and nomadic articulates the conservative ludic politics of postmodern film theory.

The world that emerges from the ludic theory of dispersed power is one in which, as I have suggested, there are no ruling or ruled classes because, in a world articulated by the playfulness of signifiers producing representations of reality, "class"—like all "concepts"—is an undecidable category and as such is in no sense a determining factor of subjectivity, representation, or the political calculus of power and exploitation. The ludic world, in contrast to the one theorized by radical theory, is a socially flat world in which everything affects everything else without any one having (explanatory) priority over the others. Each social entity has its own immanent laws of intelligibility and is self-determining. In its autonomy, it influences others and is reciprocally influenced by them on a democratic, open and equal basis. But, as James O'Connor writes in a rather sarcastic response to this ludic social analytics: "Of course everything affects everything else. But I affect my pet cat more than the cat affects me" (O'Connor and Cockburn, 1989, 37).

The ludic view that everything equally affects everything else emphasizes, as in the early works of Foucault, the notion of "domination" and "oppression" and posits multiple sites of domination and oppression in the social ranging from gender and sexuality to race, class, and the state. However such a schema is never able to answer the question, Domination for what purpose? Domination (by exertion of asymmetrical power) is always for the purpose of "exploitation"—a concept completely erased from the ludic analytics because it is closely associated with economics and class.

"Domination" is privileged in the ludic postmodern social logic because it blurs the social relations of production and conceals the antagonisms inscribed in them. It avoids positing the specific material interests that establish unequal relations between the "dominant" and "dominated" in terms of "class." "Exploitation," on the other hand, is a materialist concept: it situates the "exploited" and the "exploiter" in an antagonistic, conflictual material relation—that is to say, in a class relation. The welfare of the "exploiter," as Erik Olin Wright argues, is "obtained at the expense of the other" (1985, 65). As an analytical concept, then, "exploitation" foregrounds conflicts, antagonism, and class struggle. The erasure of "exploitation" and class allows ludic theory to construct a social world in which "domination" can be overcome not by class struggle and overthrowing the existing economic structures but through attaining "autonomy" (the Other of domination) by means of ideological struggle. As I shall argue shortly, the centrality of "ideological struggle" (and the marginalization of "class struggle") in ludic theory allows superstructural reform without ever transforming the relations of production and the material base. In short, ideological struggle—aimed at autonomy-liberation from domination-oppression—provides for an enlightened capitalism in which economic "exploitation" continues but with a human face: it grants every one "freedom" of speech and (ideally) access to the modes of signification without giving them access to the means of production.

In more recent versions of ludic political theory (Laclau and Mouffe, 1985; Aronowitz, 1990) that follow the later writings of Foucault, the concept of ideological struggle is made stronger by deemphasizing the notion of "domination" itself and consequently canceling the politics of liberation. Instead of "domination," Foucault (1980) proposes the category of "opposition" as there is no escape (liberation) from the oppressive bourgeois state, the family and other institutions. All one can do then is to "oppose" them and undertake local "struggles" in specific institutions such as prisons, city halls, abortion clinics, shelters for the homeless, alternative and nonrealistic film making, and different legislatures to fight for passage of individual bills like those on the environment. In other words, one works inside the system through the regular channels that the democratic bourgeois state itself provides for dissent. The political effect of this move is to relegitimate the status quo because "opposition" is always articulated in the terms set by the "dominant" power. The micropolitics of resistance is thus a form of affirmation of the system that reproduces on an "activist" level—in the Foucauldian manner developed by Laclau as part of a postpolitical "hegemony"— what Derridean deconstruction duplicates on the philosophical-literary level, through an "activist" immanent reading: both confirm the "inside."

The gradual erosion of radical political goals by changing the aim of political struggle from overthrowing "exploitation" through revolution to ending "domination" and then to a mere mobilizing of "opposition" through the ballot box is achieved by the deconstruction of the category of class, which explains "exploitation" and thus places conflictual and antagonistic material interests in full social view.

The ludic argument against the priority of certain explanatory concepts over others in the name of erasing epistemological "hierarchies" makes impossible the deployment of "class" as a prior social contradiction that is able to make intelligible other social contradictions under capitalism. The positing of the social as the space of "opposition" (and its Foucauldian accompaniment, "resistance") produces a notion of an autonomous, entrepreneurial individual that is central to the relegitimization of postmodern capitalism. In short, the removal of "class" from the scene of the social once again posits the individual as the source (agent) of social meaning and change and obscures the global structures of exploitation that in fact provide the necessary subject positions for continuation of the dominant regime.

Having removed "class" as the site of social struggle, ludic theory inscribes in its place the notion of "hegemony" as developed in Laclau and Mouffe's liberalist rereading of Gramsci (1985). Hegemony, in its ludic reincarnation, is the social space of a nonclass politics grounded on the local interests of agents as the basis of coalition—instead of collective "class struggle." "Class struggle" in radical political theory not only explains the dynamics of history but is also a radical practice through which political power is achieved. However, the purpose of acquiring political power through class struggle, it must be made clear, is to *abolish social class entirely*. Hegemony, on the other hand, is a configuration-coalition of diverse social groups around single issues for short periods of time to achieve political power—through electoral contests—to implement particular, specific, local goals within the existing class structures in advanced industrial democracies. Hegemonic coalition reduces the goals of socialism to a form of "radical democracy" and furthermore conceives of it economically as the regime making consumer goods available on a universal basis. It is, in other words, an ensemble of "strategies" aimed at "reforming" the dominant socioeconomic regime. Hegemony posits as the basis of postmodern radical liberalism and its allied notion of democracy a pragmatic, antifoundationalist "articulation" that politically constructs a new social formation out of dissimilar elements (Laclau and Mouffe, 1985, 149–193). The coalition formed out of this non-class hegemony is an apparatus of "ideological" and "cultural" struggle (as opposed to class struggle). Social antagonism—

which is marked in radical theory as the basis of the conflictual material interests of classes—is replaced in hegemony by a postmodern "monism." Thus, in a postmodern adaptation of traditional mysticism (Derrida, 1988), a new unitarism is posited as the political imaginary of ludic postmodern democracy.

In the ludic theory of domination and resistance, the dominated and the dominating share the same fate: both are divided by internal fissures (differance) and thus deprived of an "identity"—as either oppressed or oppressor. This division, as Laclau, Mouffe, and Foucault make clear, is postpolitical; that is, beyond the binary struggles between the dominant and dominated classes. Radical politics, in contrast to conservative postmodernism, has always insisted on keeping not only the difference *within,* as Derrida argues (1982, 1–27), but also the difference *between* social sites as the precondition for marking the "outside" as the place of revolutionary and emancipatory practices. As I have already suggested, what is regarded in dominant film theory to be the inside (the immanent laws of signification of the filmic text) is in fact the very terms of the dominant ideology masquerading as the inherent properties of the discourse. The ideological character of the "inside" will become clear only when it is subjected to a sustained critique not "in its own terms" but in terms of the political economy of the relations of production. However, in a ludic analytics, the dominated and the dominant, in their fissures and gaps, are equal: neither can "master" the other because the exploiter and the exploited, underneath their seeming powerfulness or powerlessness, are both in the same condition according to the postmodern social logic. In such an analysis, battles in which one gets scarred and loses are the same as those in which one is scarred and wins, since in both the combatants are scarred, marked and wounded! The social and economic consequences of the battle (improving the conditions of life for the winners at the expense of the losers) are occluded by foregrounding the process of war: its local, micropolitical, daily actions and agony and its constantly moving, unstable frontiers. The result is obscured— thus the opposition to "closure" in ludic theory.

The ludic social world "articulated"—in Laclau's sense—by hegemonic coalitions founded on ideological and cultural interests rather than on economic and class conflicts is a segmented world; it not only has no place for "class," it is void of "totality"; it is a-total. In other words, social totality itself, in ludic political theory, is put under erasure and rendered unintelligible. In his "Structure, Sign, and Play in the Discourse of the Human Sciences," Derrida provides an authorizing account for the dissolution of all concepts, as centered totalities, into the differential play of discourse. The "truth" of a proposition, according to Derrida, is not centered in itself and thus is not reliable because:

> the center had no natural site... it was not a fixed locus but a function, a sort of nonlocus in which an infinite number of sign-substitutes came into play. *This was the moment when language invaded the universal problematic, the moment when, in the absence of a center or origin, everything became discourse*... that is to say a system in which the central signified, the original or transcendental signified, is never absolutely present outside a system of differences. The absence of the transcendental signified extends the domain and the play of signification infinitely. (1978, 280)

In the same text he relates this observation on discourse to the impossibility of the total and regards any act of totalization to be coercive and totalitarian because it violates the principle of playfulness—the freedom—of the sign-discourse. Totalization of the social is impossible, Derrida maintains, not because it is empirically unfeasible and can never be completed but because of

> the nature of the field—that is, language and a finite language—excludes totalization. This field is in effect that of *play,* that is to say, a field of infinite substitutions only because it is finite, that is to say, because instead of being an inexhaustible field, as in the classical hypothesis, instead of being too large, there is something missing from it: a center which arrests and grounds the play of substitutions. (289)

The signifier, in other words, always "exceeds" and is never exhausted by the signified and systems of representation.

On the "foundation" of such a ludic difference, Ernesto Laclau argues that the social is not a determined totality but follows the logic of the "sign." Thus, in the absence of any intelligible totality or even originary "difference," the social is a series of conjunctural sites that are autonomous, autointelligible, and make sense without any necessary structural connections with others. Like signs the conjunctural instances may have connections with each other, but these connections are by no means necessary. The ludic social is, in Lyotard's terms, an ensemble of "language games" (Lyotard and Thebaud, 1985, 50–51) incommensurate with one another. The social, as a site of reversible differentiality, is a significatory (discursive) atotality; a series of autonomous localities in which each derives its own logic from its own immanent laws of signification. In other words, the social is articulated by the local laws of the incommensurable "inside" and not the global laws of an "outside" such as class or economics. In this ludic social, as Paul Hirst states, there is no such thing as class (1979). In this postclass ludic space, the subject is produced not by its position in the relations of production but through the intersection of incommensurate language games: the grids of intelligibility produced out of the intersections of slipping signs. The only viable politics in the discursive social is, as I have already suggested, the micropolitics of the signifier.

Hegemonic ludic politics, then, is a localist micropolitics; it proposes the social as, what Deleuze and Guattari would call "body without organs," an "assemblage" (1987) in which each entity is autonomous and linked "to concrete struggles of social agents" (Laclau, 1988, 16). To go beyond the "specific" and to posit a social totality as well as a social logic—which marks the connections among the diverse, differential specificities and singles out particular social contradictions such as "class" as prior to others—according to the ludic logic, is to "essentialize" the social. The ludic social analysis, in other words, is a species of rhetoric, and like all forms of rhetorical analysis, it is focused on the mechanics—HOW—a particular political, cultural, aesthetic entity actually works in concrete situations.

The politics of this social rhetoric produces such a wealth of contradictory, self-canceling, heterogeneous details that the only "reasonable" (nontotalitarian) conclusion to be drawn from the minute genealogical inquiries generating these vast details is that there can be no general theory of the social. This "resistance to theory" in Laclau and other post-Marxists is a reproduction, on the political level, of DeMan and Derrida's "resistance to theory" on the cultural and literary level: all place specific "experience"—the sites of the dominant ideology—under interrogative immunity from radical critique (Zavarzadeh, 1989). Any analysis that does not focus on the "vast ensemble of different operations and interventions that crystallize, however, in certain configuration—in what Foucault calls a *dispositif*" (Laclau, 1988, 21) is "essentialist." The consequence of such an erasure of theory is that the hegemonic rhetoric conceals the underlying logic of exploitation that traverses all seemingly heterogeneous social practices. There is , of course, nothing more "essentializing" than to "essentialize" "essentializing": to say, once and for all, that under all historical circumstances, "essentializing" is a "bad" argument. As progressive feminists are now reunderstanding it, essentializing is in itself neither good nor bad—there is no intrinsic truth in it. Under certain historical conditions, "essentialization" might be the only mode of (revolutionary) intervention in the dominant social arrangements, as in fact the history of progressive feminism shows. By the way, this heritage of radical feminism is now being rediscovered by some feminist thinkers who have not found the ludic politics of poststructuralism to be radically productive (Fuss, 1989).

Upon his release from prison, Nelson Mandela's very first words opening his first public speech to the collectivity of people, were:

> Mandela: Amandla!
> (Power!)
> People: Ngawethu!
> (It is Ours!)
> Amandla!
> Ngawethu!

In terms of Laclau and Mouffe's Foucauldian notion of "power" (1985, 93–145), Mandela's is an "essentialized" power. It is, in fact, theorized radically differently from Foucault's idea of "dispersed" power: it is a power in the hands of the ruling class and has to be "acquired," "seized," "shared." Furthermore, it transgresses yet another injunction of ludic theory: the erasure of binaries. Mandela's theory of power goes beyond the Foucauldian idea in that it assumes "binaries" and "opposition" (more essentialization) "between rulers and ruled" (Foucault, 1980, 94).

Binaries, essentialization—in radical politics are all historical constructs for revolutionary praxis in the hands of people. Binaries, in other words, are historical concepts produced out of the existing social contradictions and necessary for transformative politics. They should not be allowed to be read as metaphysical fictions and thus as epistemological categories deconstructed by rhetorical strategies. The dissolution of binaries in a ludic (mystical) monism blurs the boundaries of exploiter-exploited and obscures social contradictions in the interests of the dominant. In class societies there is a binary of the inside and outside, and one of the effects of revolutionary practice is to maintain the outside and not allow it to collapse into the immanence of an inside or its alibi—the undecidable zone of the inside-outside. Through the historically moving outside the immanent practices of the closed system of class society are subjected to transformation.

Apartheid is the product of social contradictions that cannot be erased by a ludic slogan—"Down with Binaries"—nor by attempting to resolve the many into the mystical monism of the undecidable. Its historical materiality can be foregrounded only as part of social dualisms, oppositions, and contradictions. Mandela and other revolutionary intellectuals are not the bureaucratic, instrumental, "specific," ludic intellectuals that Foucauldian micropolitics privileges.

Through terms ultimately put forth by the dominant power itself, ludic theory erodes "exploitation," cutting it down to "domination," and then further reduces "domination" down to "opposition." In doing so, it replaces the political (as the struggle over the means of production) with the ethical—the specific conduct of a particular individual in a concrete situation—as a strategy of self-fashioning. The ludic social is void of the social as collectivity; it is populated by isolated, autonomous individuals whose identity is defined by their civil rights, with no economic rights, and their political activity is organized into a pattern of congregation-dispersal around specific issues in a hegemonic "articulation." Because the hegemonic is a field of articulatory practices, *cultural* rather than *economic* struggles provide its ground. Endorsing this postpolitical, posteconomic view of social change in his "Triumph of Freedom" speech (delivered to honor the memory of Winston Churchill on June 13, 1989, in London), Ronald Reagan theorized "ideological struggle" as the cause of new world revolutions: "The communication revolution will be the greatest force for advancement of human freedom the world has ever seen." In other words, "freedom" is simply the effect of people speaking of "individual liberty." Laclau gives more nuance to this statement by stating that "the aesthetic dimension—the dimension of desire that is fulfilled in the aesthetic experience—is fundamental in configuration of a world" (1988, 22). Integral to the Foucauldian "genealogy," of course, is the mobilization of "desire" as the source of the "ethical."

2

This elimination of "class" and deconstruction of "domination"—by collapsing the "dominant" and the "dominated" into a new social monism articulated by "hegemony"—has had considerable impact on postmodern film theory. The space where the struggle over social totality and domination, and ultimately over the logic of social transformation, has been fought out most intensely in film criticism is the site of cinematic pleasure, particularly the theory of the "desire" of the spectator and its role in formation of the subject. Radical theorists such as Laura Mulvey (1975), who have theorized cinematic pleasure and the problematics of desire from a feminist point of view, have posited the patriarchal cinema as a political apparatus through which the female (body) is subjugated and fetishized as the object of the pleasureful male "gaze." The classic (Hollywood) film, in such a radical reading, is the unfolding of a narrative that tells the story of the "mastery" of the male over the female body for the pleasure of the male spectator. The trope of this "mastery" is "sadism." The female viewer of patriarchal cinema can share the (masculinist) pleasures of classic film only by occupying the subject position offered by "masochism." The dominant (sadism) and the dominated (masochism), in other words, are part of a political strategy in which binaries of desire are evoked for emancipatory practices: to critique the oppressive practices of mainstream cinema.

However, following the ludic Foucauldian line of rejecting global politics in favor of a localist micropolitics, some postmodern feminist film theorists have criticized this radical reading of patriarchy and its visual regime as "essentializing," "binarist," "totalizing," and thus "reductionist." In their attempts to provide a more "complex" theory, they have deconstructed "sadism" and argued that it is far from being a desire with a centered totality and a unitary identity; instead it is an undecidable pleasure traversed by its "other"—masochism. Sadism, in other words, is a differential desire, and as such its seeming coherence and identity is subverted immanently—from inside—by its other: masochism. Masochism is not only not the "inferior" other in the binary of sadism-masochism, but is the excluded difference that, through a subversive return, changes the entire immanent economy of the system of desire and provides new possibilities for resistance and new resisting subjectivities.

In her essay "Masochism and Subjectivity," Kaja Silverman (1980) follows Lacan and such neo-Lacanians as Deleuze in arguing that "masochism" is not a specific trope for female desire but rather marks a particular affective behavior that crosses gender boundaries. The history of the subject, regardless of sexual difference, is inscribed by moments in which, as Freud has argued (1961), it learns to experience pleasure in pain. However, in the patriarchal cinema, the female, according to Mulvey, almost exclusively is placed in the position of experiencing "pleasure" in pain. Silverman's reexplanation of this cinematic practice is that the woman is the trope, the figure, to whom man's desire (pleasure in pain) is transferred as in a "dream." The woman, in other words, is a stand-in for the man in taking pleasure in pain and loss: she acts out what the man experiences but cannot express because of the injunctions of the symbolic order—the Law of the Father—which inhibits such nonphallic, nondominating pleasures. "I go so far," writes Silverman, "as to say that the fascination of the sadistic point of view is that it provides the best vantage point from which to watch the masochistic story unfold" (1980, 5). The male viewer, in other words, is "sadistic" not to "dominate" the female, but to voyeuristically experience the "pleasures" of being "dominated." The "dominant" and the "dominated," in Silverman's ludic analysis, become indistinguishable and collapse into a gender monism—a-subjectivity and a-sociality—of desire as-for loss. In her reading, the man is not a coherent totality bent on mastering the woman, but a fissural construct marked, above all, by its own undecidability.

In the subversion of sadism, masochism becomes the trope for all the forces that free the subject from the constraints of culture in an ecstasy (*jouissance*) of transgression of such social boundaries as gender. If civilization is an act of ordering by writing—narrativization of nature—which is to say an act of domination by imposing homogenizing meaning over the heterogeneous experiences, then masochism, in the work of such contemporary theorists as Leo Bersani, is the trope of freedom from that narrative (mastery). Masochism, in Bersani's view, is nothing if not revolutionary because it unwrites the writings of culture, denarrates its narratives, and consequently, in a carnavalesque orgy of undecidability, offers *jouissance* to the spectator-reader by an "interpretive suspension between narrative and nonnarrative readings" (1986, 78).

In her reunderstanding of some of Josef Von Sternberg films made in collaboration with Marlene Dietrich, such as *Blonde Venus,* Gayln Studlar goes beyond the limits Bersani puts upon the subversive power of masochism and posits masochism as the force that completely unwrites the Oedipal scenario of subjectivity. By subverting "domination" (which writes male subjectivity in the symbolic order through suppression of his bisexuality), masochism takes the subject, according to Studlar, to a preoedipal moment of *jouissance* that is unencumbered by the forces of culture that have inscribed the subject as a gendered entity. This is, it must be noted, a purely aesthetic and nonpolitical moment because it subverts subjectivity (the inscription of the individual in the political economy of the relations of production) through the bliss of the erasure of culture and its taming subjectivity (1988).

This shift in theorizing desire and cinematic pleasure—from focusing on sadism as the trope of domination to masochism as the figure for the immanent subversion of that domination—is represented in ludic postmodern film theory as a move toward more complexity, a move that overcomes the nonproductive, reductionist binarism of radical critique through a productive and freeing deconstruction. In spite of the ostensible rejection of the concept of "progress" by poststructuralist theory, it is a move represented as "progress" from "false" to "true." The shift, however, is essentially a political one and has very little to do with the complexity of understanding desire or helping the social causes of feminism. It effectively renders unintelligible the distinction between the dominant and the dominated by positing the dominant as a form of dominated and the dominated as a species of the dominant: both are consequently represented as undecidable categories and as such unreliable grounds for any political action toward revolutionary practices aimed at overthrowing the dominant—patriarchal capitalism. Deleuze emphasizes the undecidability of the two when he writes of the "pseudo-masochism in sadism" and the "pseudo-sadism of masochism," the inscription of the "same" by the "other" (1971, 109).

The politics of such a move to represent sadism as uncertain—always already contaminated by its opposite—is to make "certain" that the status quo is kept intact. If uncertainty is the regime of truth that marks all representations (knowledge), it follows that there is no foundation upon which to begin the project of a new world free from exploitation and domination. Exploitation, in such a scheme, always already deconstructs itself—there is no need for intervention from an "outside" (revolution).

Furthermore, by removing the concept of domination, ludic theory also removes any understanding of patriarchy as a social totality of global structures of economic and political exploitation. Patriarchy—in its naturalization in theories of desire as masochistic-subversive—becomes itself an effect of differance: a conjunctural construct composed of isolated, autonomous, resistance localities. Masochism, in other words, in the last analysis, is a resistance to and subversion of patriarchy through a pleasurable return to the aesthetic by means of the "disavowal of phallic power " (Studlar, 1988, 16). It is a postpolitical practice that renders patriarchy, as an economic and political structure, undecidable. The shift from domination (sadism) to masochism as markers of desire, to be more precise, is a shift from radical politics and revolutionary practices to reformist ludic pleasures that overcome cultural subjectivities and, in a moment of *jouissance,* deliver the spectator to a presexual (pregender) utopian freedom. This is utopia as escape from global socioeconomic structures to local semiotic practices, from class struggle to ideological struggle. The suggestion that theorizing desire according to a Deleuzian model is freeing for feminism and feminist film theory, as Studlar's book indicates, is an alibi for reinscribing a conservative understanding of the politics of spectatorship.

The majority of feminist film theorists, however, have taken a middle course in this contestation over the construction of desire in ludic postmodernism and attempted to "mediate." Teresa de Lauretis, for example, in positing double identification and "double desire" (1984, 103–157)—the pleasures of experiencing both sadism-dominating and masochism-being dominated— retreats to a pragmatic "solution" that avoids the political economy of subjectivity and viewership and in the name of an empirical, localist activism reduces patriarchy from a global structure of domination to sites of differential practices and conjunctural politics. According to her, feminist film theory should no longer focus on interrogation of patriarchy but instead work on production of a specifically feminine "vision" (1987, 127–148). This move, of course, is now part of the common sense of ludic postmodernism in which a global revolutionary politics aimed at overthrowing exploitation is abandoned for a reformist, nomadic, flexible politics at the micropolitical level. The consequences of such a retreat has been to posit the social in a postpolitical series of localities that have no necessary relation with each other: the environment, feminism, gay and lesbian movements—all withdraw into an "inside" bent on constructing a feminine vision, a green vision, a gay vision. All thus end up assisting the status quo to continue its regime of truth and maintain its global logic of domination that underlies all these seemingly autonomous and resisting localities.

In ludic postmodern theory the immediate site of desire and its subversive "resistance" as an ethical imperative of self-fashioning in violation of the law of the Father is named the *body.* The "ethics" of resistance, in other words, is situated in the "sensory" and articulated as an antipolitics that, following Baudrillard and Lyotard, regards the postmodern as the end of the grand conceptual narratives of political economy and the time of the micropolitical or, in other words, the experiential, regional, local, "body" politics. The fetishization of the "body"—as the site of the intensity of experience beyond the reach of history—finds its perhaps most romantic expression in the dedication of Jane Gallop's *Thinking through the Body* (1988): "For Max," (the newborn), "Who as yet thinks only through the body. May he never lose that." In the discourses of ludic postmodernism, "politics" is an exemplary instance of totalitarian "conceptuality." The micropolitics of the body, on the other hand, is politics without concepts: the local politics of material experience. However *material* in these theories, as I have implied, means the immediate elements of the medium of the political, that is to say, the discourses that articulate subjectivities and thus produce the micro-political. It is, in other words, a materialist politics only in the sense that, for example, focusing on the "photochemical reality" of film makes the film maker a "materialist film maker" (LeGrice, 1977, 35). An idealist materialism isolates single issues and their mode of enunciation from the global structures of the political economy.

In the (discursive) politics of ludic postmodernism, "domination" is seen primarily to be a condition brought about by instituted, predetermined meanings or, in Lyotard's words, "cultural policy" (1984, 76), which erases "difference" and by "totalizing" becomes "totalitarian" (1984, 81–82). The subject's "resistance," then, is basically a resistance to the "cultural policy's" discursive suppressions and therefore takes the form of a semiotic "war on totality" (Lyotard, 1984, 82): a subversion of the preordained meanings that restrict his ethical autonomy. The totalizing-totalitarian regime of meaning against which the postmodern subject rebels is the modernist theory of signification in which a regulated correspondence is established between the signifier and the signified; the meaning of the signifier is thus always exhausted by the concept (signified) to which it corresponds.

The "resistance" that recent film theory highlights is the ethical war against this totalizing semiotics: a resistance, in other words, against a *system* of representation and an opening up to what Barthes called *The Third Meaning*. By contrast with the first two meanings—"communication" and "information"—the third meaning is a "significance" that "cannot be conflated with the simple *existence* of the scene" and thus "exceeds the copy of the referential motif," nor can it be "conflated with the dramatic meaning of the episode" (1977, 53). In short, it cannot be accounted for by the narrative, or even by textual difference, but is immanent in certain images that hail the reader through the very presence of his body (56–65). This bodily meaning is, of course, the kind of "meaning" that Lyotard calls the *unrepresentable* in his postmodern moral lesson: "Let us wage a war on totality; let us be witness to the unrepresentable; let us activate the differences and save the honor of the name" (1984, 82). This resisting "meaning"—what Barthes calls "significance"—is produced not by concepts but by sensual pleasures.

In *The Pleasure of the Text*, Roland Barthes establishes a typology of intense bodily experiences in which "pleasure" (*plaisir*) is distinguished from "bliss" (*jouissance*). Pleasure is cultural in the sense that it confirms the subject in its identity acquired through daily practices. This identity is often an oppositional one that contests the dominant identity, but the terms of this opposition are those already inscribed within the cultural. The pleasure of this "resistance" then is the pleasure of affirming one's autonomy within social subjectivities. *Jouissance,* on the other hand, is an abandoning of subjectivity (cultural identity) altogether in a moment of ecstasy that takes the subject back to "nature"—the body in its presocial state before culturally produced subjectivities were inscribed on it. As a negation of subjectivity, *jouissance* is also a transgression and annulment of ideology. In a sense, for Barthes, the intense bodily experience he calls *jouissance* is the entry into the postpolitical. To experience *jouissance* by breaking the molds of subjectivity and ideology is to "resist" cultural policy in a much more radical way than through "pleasure" (*plaisir*). It goes beyond culture and reaches the plenitude and presence of nature. This is a moment very similar to the one Silverman, Bersani, and Studlar posit as the effect of the masochistic subversion of sadism—which in their schema stands for the forces of male subjectivity.

The ecstasy of the postpolitical, above all, is physical. It is achieved mostly, for Barthes, by "reading" and "writing" through the body or bodily reading-writing. This corporeal reading-writing—unlike conceptual ones—does not produce or find total meaning, rather it creates "excessive" signification by fore-grounding the concrete (the experiential and the bodily):

> If it were possible to imagine an aesthetic of textual plea-sure, it would have to include: *writing aloud.* . . . *Writing aloud* . . . is carried . . . by the *grain* of the voice, which is an erotic mixture of timbre and language, and can therefore also be, along with diction, the substance of an art: the art of guiding one's body. . . . *Writing aloud* is not phonological but phonetic; its aim is not the clarity of messages, the theater of emotions; what it searches for (in a perspective of bliss) are the pulsional incidents, the language lined with flesh, a text where we can hear the grain of the throat, the patina of con-sonants, the voluptuousness of vowels, a whole carnal stereophony: the articulation of the body, of the tongue, not that of meaning, of language. A certain art of singing can give an idea of this vocal writing; but since melody is dead, we may find it more easily today at the cinema. In fact, it suffices that the cinema capture the sound of speech *close up* (this is, in fact, the generalized definition of the "grain" of writing) and make us hear in their materiality, their sen-suality, the breath, the gutturals, the fleshiness of the lips, a whole presence of the human muzzle (that the voice, that writing, be as fresh, supple, lubricated, delicately granular and vibrant as an animal's muzzle), to succeed in shifting the signified a great distance and in throwing, so to speak, the anonymous body of the actor into my ear: it granulates, it crackles, it caresses, it grates, it cuts, it comes: that is bliss. (1975, 66–67)

Jouissance in Barthes's text is the trope of a superstructural-ist politics: the ludic politics of the signifier that privileges an "ideological struggle"—directed and controlled by the upper (middle) classes who have access to modes of signification (media, culture industry, universities, publishing networks, and so on)—over "class struggle." The notion of ideological struggle has acquired great prominence among the professionals of ideol-ogy, such as film theorists, critics, and other disseminators of films and film knowledge, in ludic postmodernism because of the commonsensical belief that the new forms of deploying capital rely more than ever for their effectivity on the strategic uses of ideology. In fact the very notion of politics and political struggle is so rearticulated in ludic postmodernism as to render "ideological struggle" identical with emancipatory practices by erasing revolutionary "class struggle."

The tenet of postmodern superstructuralist politics is perhaps best articulated by one of its precursors, Bakhtin. In his framing of the logic of signification, he writes that intelligibility is produced "Not from the thing to the word, but from the word to the thing; the word gives birth to the thing" (1986, 182). Bakhtin's ludic politics is the trope for the global reversal of the relation of "production" and "consumption" in the ludic logic of the social. This ludic logic also informs such other local reversals as Baudrillard's positing of "exchange value" as the producer of "use value," Roland Barthes's shift in the relation between denotation and connotation, and Foucault's articulation of "genealogy" as the discourse of immanence; it also shapes the central principle of Derridean "differance" that traverses all binaries and marks them as the effects of a protoform (archewriting). In fact, the popularity of Bakhtin's ludic politics among film theorists (Stam, 1989) is one of the symptoms of the "cold war," during which time his writings were deployed as the grand strategy of containment for radical practices.

Superstructuralism, thus, is the regime reversing the relations between the material base and cultural and political productions by privileging politics and culture over economics. It is the archelogic of ludic postmodernism. Through its philosophical and cultural practices, such as the production and dissemination of films, it produces the social frames of intelligibility that most effectively construct the political and economic "obviousnesses" needed by advanced capitalism under the sign of the postmodern. In his address to the joint session of the United States Congress on February 21, 1990, Czechoslovak President Vaclav Havel announced the death of socialism and the triumph of capitalism by appealing to the ludic logic of the superstructuralist common sense when he declared to the cheers of his ecstatic American audience: "consciousness precedes Being, and not the other way around as Marxists claim."

Radical politics, for ludic postmodernity, is not so much a

matter of providing access for all to the means of production (economic democracy as the foundation of rights) but rather access to the means of signification (semiotic democracy). In spite of ludic superstructuralism's ostensible erasure of all forms of determinism, it still sees "culture" as the determinant of intelligibilities; thus radical politics is rearticulated as a "resistance" to cultural "meanings" by the (free) ethical agent. The most "radical" form of this intervention, according to ludic deconstruction, "obscures" (renders "undecidable") the established meanings of the old common sense—the bourgeois common sense that no longer is historically relevant to the unimpeded movement of capital. This jettisoning of the traditional (humanist) common sense, in the name of a "radical politics," in other words, is itself a subtle maneuver to remove from the scene of philosophy those frames of intelligibility that have lost their economic relevance to the relations of capitalist production. Barbara Johnson formulates the major premise of superstructuralist radicalism when she writes, "Nothing could be more comforting to the established order than the requirement that everything be assigned a clear meaning or stand" (1987, 30–31). In the writings of Foucault, Derrida, and particularly Lyotard, then, "radical politics" becomes a matter of a local obscuring of the "obviousnesses" of the dominant common sense, thus problematizing its "certainty" about the real, rather than globally transforming the existing social arrangements and providing access for all to the means of production. Lyotard goes so far in this "obscuring" of meaning as to equate any coherent collective cultural meaning with "cultural policy," and he regards "cultural policy" as a form of "totalizing" and the effect of its underlying totalitarianism.

In the antitotalitarian, democratic ludic politics of postmodern film theory, "parody," "pastiche," "irony," "pun," and their archewriting—"laughter"—are used as devices through which the connection between the signifier and the signified is deferred and the "obviousness" of "cultural policy" (established meanings) is "obscured." Obscurity is thus considered to produce a radical effect because it empties the world of ready-made meanings. However, the way the emptied world is charged and made to resignify is politically of significance.

By privileging ideological struggle as an obscuring of cultural meanings, a "joyous" politics locates the site of change in the superstructural series. Cultural meanings, life-styles, modes of thinking and representations-images, in other words, can all be "changed" through the intervention of the professional of ideology, and in this change, *jouissance* is a subversive device: it renders the old verities ridiculous, empty, and pathetically backward. However, and this is the genuinely reactionary politics of *jouissance*, such superstructuralism, by proposing the culture as autonomous, allows the economic to remain intact. Whereas cultural meanings are laughed out and emptied and new modes of thought are emerging in the "new age," the old regime of economic exploitation continues. Thus, today, in the 1990s, the integration of a few high school "proms" in Georgia is taken as a mark of change and heralded on the front page of *The New York Times* (May 14, 1990, A–1), while in the same state of the "union," the rate of black unemployment is twice as high as that of whites, and the majority of black people still live in abject poverty.

3

The resistance subject reads the texts of culture not for their "meanings" (totalizing concepts) but for the experience of their semantic "excess"—the "significance" of the signifier that is not exhausted by the "signified" and in fact is so uncontainable that it deconstructs the concept-signified and turns it into another signifier—another instance of "excess." The film text's surplus of meaning, displayed in "parody," "pastiche," and the "carnivalesque," is a playful commentary on the processes of signification in the film itself as well as a "resistance" to the "seriousness" (non-pleasure) of the bourgeois reader who—through a confining, linear, and conforming reading that locks the signifier into the designated signified—constructs solemnities upon which the official culture is established. To experience *jouissance* —by inflicting fissures, wounds, splits, and gaps on the text—the "excessive" reader shatters the bourgeois solemnities and the "domination" that accompanies them. The solemnities of truth are associated in postmodern theory with phallocentrism and in fact such theorists as Lacan, Felman, Barthes, and Cixous equate

jouissance not only with freedom and the autonomy of the subject but also with the feminine and its struggles to deconstruct
mastering patriarchal seriousness (Cixous, 245–64).

The practice of "excessive" reading is enabled by strategies
of rhetoric (thus the resistance against a separation of "rhetoric
and politics" in ludic postmodernism) and is rooted in the idea
that bourgeois culture is based on utilitarian—conceptual and
assigned—meanings (hence the hostility of the bourgeois to
"rhetoric"); and to resist the utilitarian meaning by the nonutili-
tarian—the experience of *jouissance*—is, in and of itself, liberating. Rhetoric in postmodern film theory is understood not as the
"outside" of film and writing, but in fact, as the logic of "textuality," which is the film itself, and textuality, as the movement of
"difference," is a resistance to the idea of the political that
argues for global transformative practices. Such a notion of the
political, in ludic postmodern theory, is considered to be unviable because it assumes that such concepts as class, economics,
and gender exist outside the rhetorical movements of the textual
organization of the discourse. However, in the actuality of the
postmodern, these concepts are mere "tropes" whose meta-
phoricity has been forgotten. There is, in other words, no politics
outside the law of difference.

Difference in postmodern film theory, as in poststructuralism, is theorized in a Derridean manner and has become a mode
of textual dogmatism that limits the play of difference to the
ahistorical effects of a "trope" undermining the identity of the
discourse's "argument," thus revealing it to be a metaphysical
fiction void of any claim to grounded knowledge. Rhetorical difference, in short, displaces the modernist difference *between* two
self-same objects by substituting the difference *within* the object
itself; in doing so, it foregrounds the unsuspected fissures that
distance the object from itself and thus deconstruct its self-mastery. Class struggle, for instance, emerges in the politics of ludic
postmodernism not as the struggle *between* classes but as that
struggle *within* a class that puts in question the very identity of
the class and therefore its ability to engage in any emancipatory
practice. As I have already suggested, difference, far from being
the panhistorical effect of textuality, is a historical and material
construct produced through class struggle. Specifically, it is an

articulation of the labor relations at any given historical moment: "difference" is alienated labor, the congealment of which, in the form of private property, constructs social "difference."

The resistance formulated in contemporary film theory is an exclusively "cultural" resistance. Although ludic film theory rejects the Frankfurt School—especially the idea of popular culture as the producer of "false consciousness," arguing that it is a logocentric modernist project of enlightenment—ludic notions of resistance are directly related to the theories of agency and opposition proposed by such thinkers as Adorno, Horkheimer, and Marcuse. What is proposed as the bodily experience of *jouissance* in postmodern film theory, for example, is basically a structure of negation that has its roots in Adorno's nonidentitarian dialectic. In Adorno, the subject acquires agency and the ability to resist the dominant through access to the negative dialectic whose "logic" is "one of disintegration: a disintegration of the prepared and objectified form of the concepts which the cognitive subject faces, primarily and directly" (1973, 145). To point to another connection between ludic thought and its putative "other," the surplus meaning that, according to Barthes, the resistance spectator finds in her "excessive" reading of the film text and that serves as the energy for negating the set meanings of the text, is in fact a reunderstanding of Marcuse's notion of "surplus repression"—a repression that exceeds the repression required by the reality principle and, according to Marcuse, becomes the source of revolutionary changes.

In both ludic postmodern film theory and the modernist theory of the culture industry, "resistance" is more an idealistic, ahistorical force than a social and materialistic entity. It is, in fact, an ideological device used to relegitimate the autonomous subject of free enterprise. In postmodern thought the autonomy and freedom of the subject are established by appeal not to a Cartesian consciousness but to the naturalness of the body as the source of *jouissance* or, more generally, "experience" (De Lauretis after Foucault). The "body" and "experience" are, in spite of the Derridean overtone in the writings of the theorists of "resistance," finally new transcendental signifieds that exist outside the play of signification (Gallop, 1988, v); they are considered autointelligible and as such the ground for ethical undertakings such as the deconstruction of totalizing meanings through "excessive" readings that are a new Hegelian negation and surpassing. In modernist theories, the freedom of the subject to act derives from the pansocial forces of the instincts (Marcuse) or from a subject that, through negation, cuts himself loose from constraining concepts (and even from himself) and becomes an unencumbered floating self-reflexivity (Adorno) who is an instance of "resistance" to the dominant power. The myth of "excessive" reading as a feminine form of unmastering is of course just that—a myth—because "laughter" and "parody" are in fact pleasures of mastery: what is presented as the pleasures of unmastering (the subversion of phallocentric truth) is in fact the deep pleasure (*jouissance*) of mastering a new form of truth—the postmodern truth of the body as an oasis of nature in culture.

(Post)modern bourgeois thought needs the category of "experience" in order to construct a world of autointelligible empirical essences that will more effectively conceal the global logic of domination by proposing resistance as immanent in the subject. "Resistance," as posited in ludic theories, is hardly more than a form of "spontaneity-ism"—the subject's natural rebellion against domination by mobilization of body: physical rights to autonomous pleasures. This stunning naivete becomes more clear in Foucault's question (which echoes Camus's romantic notion of "resistance and rebellion"): "What enables people . . . to resist the Gulag? What can given them the *courage* to stand up and die in order to utter a *word* or a *poem*" (emphasis added). It is quite clear that for Foucault "resistance" is a matter of "experience" ("courage") and *jouissance* (the "poem" as a discourse whose significance exceeds its social meanings) that establish the subject as the subject of human rights (resisting the Gulag). In *Subculture: The Meaning of Style,* one of the exemplary instances of the micropolitical as resistance, Dick Hebdige uses *style* to designate what Foucault calls the *poem.* It is through "style," for example, that "punk" musicians display their "courage" and resist the domination of mainstream music (1979, 1–19).

By breaking through social subjectivities, *jouissance* deconstructs ideology. Because ideology has become a highly contested concept in postmodern theory, it might be helpful to examine its main deployment in contemporary discourses and briefly inquire into the quarrel of ludic postmodernism with the radical theory of ideology.

Depending on how *ideology* is articulated with economic and social class structures, the concept of ideology produces different political effects. To stage the conflict between ludic postmodernism and the concept of ideology, I propose a fourfold schema to account for the main understandings of ideology in contemporary discourse.

1. Theories that see ideology as a historical system of social intelligibility that naturalizes the economic interests of the ruling class by producing a political imaginary ("false consciousness") for the "subject." This political imaginary then interpellates the subject within a social zone in which the social contradictions of the relations of production are reversed and the interests of the dominant class are seen as logical, universal and inevitable and thus as part of the natural order of the world: the way things are and ought to be. This, I would argue, is essentially a Marxian—as distinguished from a marxist—view. In Marxian radical theory, ideology can be overcome only through a revolutionary restructuring of economic practices and not by an ideological struggle that at most will reform semiotic (not economic) social relations.

2. Political theories that regard ideology to be an ensemble of practices that are, as in the Marxian view, closely related to material conditions and the mode of production but not specifically tied to the interests of one single class (the ruling class). For such theorists as Lenin and Gramsci, proletarian (and other) ideologies coexist with the dominant ruling class ideology at any given historical moment. Thus the "proletarian ideology" does not produce "false consciousness," quite the opposite. Ideology in this sense, then, is a generalized understanding of the world related to the class position of the subject: it can be emancipatory (proletarian ideology) or oppressive (bourgeois ideology).

3. In the writings of Althusser and others, Lenin's expansion of the notion of ideology—to include other modes of

intelligibility than the ruling one and reverse social relations—loses its specific class ties and its involvement in
class struggle. It becomes instead a set of material practices and forms of knowing shaping the horizon of cultural
intelligibility. Ideology—which in Marx's theories is part
of the knowledge and practices justifying the economic
relations of exploitation in class societies—becomes a
postclass and panhistorical process: ideology is eternal, it
has no history in the sense that all societies, as a condition
of their existence, secret ideology. Although Althusser
himself maintains a notion of class, in the form of specific
ideologies, his theory provides a new frame for the complete depoliticization of ideology. Under the pressures of
ludic discourses, ideology after Althusser becomes completely depoliticized and innocuously descriptive and can
be characterized by such statements as "ideology is not a
system of true or false beliefs and values, a doctrine, so
much as it is the means by which culture represents beliefs
and values." As such, it becomes a ludic dogma that there
is no "outside" to ideology—a notion implicit in Lenin,
becomes more overt in Althusser, and finally assumes the
status of a postmodern truth in contemporary cultural
criticism.

4. The ludic pronouncement on ideology as grounded on
the experience of *jouissance* that, however, goes much
further than a depoliticized Althusserian reading. It is
most clearly articulated in the writings of Gilles Deleuze
and Felix Guattari. In *A Thousand Plateaus: Capitalism
and Schizophrenia,* they write: "There is no ideology and
never has been" (1987, 4).

The radical notion of ideology is thus the repressed concept
in the discourses of ludic postmodernism. Ludic postmodernism—as the regime of difference and reflexivity—reads (radical) ideology as a mastering mode of understanding: one that
attributes "difference" to the "other" and thus erases it within
itself to construct an identitarian truth and its corollary, a self-
same falsehood. The concept of ideology, in other words, is seen
in ludic discourses as another repetition of a familiar logocentric

story. Of course, this view is itself a repetition of a familiar story: Mannheim's narrative in which the radical theory of ideology is regarded as being interested in examining only the opponent's position and not its own. Ideology, according to Mannheim, protects its own "truth" by constructing a coherent "other." In other words, the radical concept of ideology, in this view, provides a unified account of the world from the perspective of a privileged subject (the proletariat) whose own position is never put in question. In fact, Mannheim anticipates the ludic notion of ideology as the all pervasive discursive horizon of cultural intelligibility—and not as class device for reversing social contradictions—when he writes that ideology "cannot, in the long run remain the the exclusive privilege of one class...it is no longer possible for one point of view and interpretation to assail all others as ideological without itself being placed in the position of having to meet that challenge" (1972, 66). Mannheim, clearly, demands that ideology be read reflexively so that its reading of the world include itself. The ludic postmodern reading of ideology is reflexive: by inscribing the "other" in ideology, it deconstructs the radical political use of the concept in Marx's texts, among others, as identitarian.

Jouissance as the experience of the excess (of meaning) is also the mark of the inner contradictions of the dominant ideology. The surplus meaning, in other words, shows the difference of the ideology from itself and foregrounds its lack of mastery (domination) over its regulated meanings. For such feminist theorists as Teresa De Lauretis (1984, 1987) and Catherine Belsey (1985), as well as the contributors to Elizabeth Weed's *Coming to Terms: Feminism/Theory/Politics* (1989), the excess of meaning is the site of intervention and change because, in this surplus meaning, ideology is shown to be other than itself and the seams, folds, and aporias of its contradictions appear. Unlike what it is for Barthes, *jouissance* for these feminists, as well as for Constance Penley (1989) who is somewhat closer to Barthes, is not simply the effect of the ineffable but the instance in which ideology is shown to exceed itself and be deconstructed by its own difference: at such moments the patched up discourses of ideology come apart under the pressure of their own excessive differences. In these spaces of ideological "otherness," human agency and resistance emerge, and a localist, regional, and particularistic "experiential politics" develops. Although the genealogy of this mode of politics includes the traditional "personal is political" brand of local politics, it is not identical with it, rather it has its more recent source in Foucault and his notion of the "specific intellectual" (Foucault, 1980, 109–33), who wages a war against totality and intervenes in the systems of representation from within (immanently). The "excess" of meaning in the film, according to contemporary film theory, shatters its own ideology, the conventions of film genre and other codes of viewing, because as a "remainder," the "excess" is not easily absorbed and normalized by those conventions. It thus deconstructs, from within the film itself, the subject position that is ostensibly posited by it. The "excess" therefore acquires the revolutionary force of dismantling the conservative (normalized) relation between the viewer and the film and consequently developing new modes of subjectivities in culture at large. In ludic theory, ideology self-deconstructs, and there is no need for an intervention from the "outside" (revolution) as radical politics proposes.

Thus rather than overthrowing ideology by revolution as in radical theory, ludic postmodernism deconstructs the "truth" of ideology by indicating its implication in its seeming opposite, "falsehood." Such a move ultimately is founded on a theory of language derived from Saussure. In *Course in General Linguistics,* Saussure writes, "In language there are only differences *without positive terms* (emphasis in the original, 1966, 120). The philosophical and political ramifications of such a theory of the sign are many, but perhaps the most important, at least in Derrida's radical reading of it, is the notion that no self-possessed, identitarian concepts can be said to be "present" to themselves and, as such, self-standing and without intertextuality. Seemingly positive, coherent, and unitary concepts, such as "nature," "truth," "goodness," according to Derrida, are part of what he calls the (Western) "metaphysics of presence" and its affiliated regimes of logocentrism and phallologocentrism. Each of these putatively self-possessed concepts is an instance of "differance": its excluded opposite is not in its "outside" but is, in fact, inscribed in its "inside," thus undermining its claim to coherence. This is, of course, another way of saying that the boundaries of inside-outside are also part of the regime of logocentrism.

The coherent concept, in short, like the (linguistic) sign, is internally divided and marked by the "trace" of other signs—its identity is enabled by its intertextuality and not through a direct participation in the "reality" that it is said to signify. "Nature," for example, cannot be conceptualized without its binary opposite, "culture"; and in this sense it can be said that "nature," far from signifying a moment of plenitude and fullness, is constituted by its excluded "other"—culture, by what it is not supposed to be, by its own "absence." As such it is not a "decidable" category whose meaning is "present" to itself, rather it actually means through its supplementary relation with Culture. Culture, in other words, is the "differance" of "nature" from itself—the nonpossession of reality it seems to signify—and this differance is banished to its "outside" that marks absence and fallenness. By the same token, culture is also a differential concept whose meaning is not in itself but falls between itself and its other—nature. Thus both nature and culture, like all other categories of intelligibility, are "undecidable." It is important to remember that the purpose of ludic, Derridean deconstruction is not a simple reversal of nature-culture, truth-falsehood, but a destablization of both. In short, like a linguistic sign, all seemingly self-coherent concepts derive their meaningfulness not from their own positivity but through their supplementary relation with other signs and concepts that are always "present" in them by their "absence."

Ludic postmodernism thus reads the "truth" of the radical theory of ideology—its proposal that the social is produced by the historical interests of the ruling class but represented in the dominant ideology as the transhistorical and universal truth derived from the very structures of actuality—according to its notion of supplementarity and trace. Such a radical "truth," according to the ludic view, is not an instance of "positivity" and self-coherence but is constituted by its excluded "other" (the falsehood of bourgeois ideology). As such it is not a self-constituted and self-identical truth that can provide a reliable ground for such political and social actions as "revolution." The truth claimed by the radical theory of ideology, in ludic terms, is an undecidable truth.

To disregard the rhetoric of truth—its textual difference

and tracefulness—according to ludic postmodernism, is to "essentialize" truth and become "reductive." In her reading of Alfred Hitchcock's films, Tania Modleski (1988) provides an exemplary instance of such a (self-)deconstruction of the truth (of patriarchy) by its binary "other." Her argument is grounded on the notion of "excess" in ludic theory: a view of "meaning" in which signification of the signifier is never exhausted by the signified—the sign always already slips and "overflows" what it is taken to mean. In radical readings by feminists, for example, Hitchcock's films are marked by their misogyny and phallologo-centrism—the regime of the truth of the phallus. They are narratives of "mastery" (sadism). In contrast, Modleski argues that such radical readings are reductive because Hitchcock's films always "exceed" themselves and in that "excess" show that what is taken to be their "truth" (the assertion of patriarchy) in fact is a species of "falsehood" because the films themselves are much more "complex" and self-reflexive.

For example in *Vertigo,* Modleski finds that Hitchcock's patriarchal ideology overflows itself and, in an act of self-deconstruction and auto-erasure, becomes differential and "undecidable": it loses its masculinist self-mastery and by doing so indicates that its "truth" is nonunitary, incoherent, and contradictory. Its "sadism" is inscribed by "masochism" and its "masochism" is traversed by "sadism." In the "excessive" staging of a self-possessed masculinity symbolized in Scottie's obsession with Madeline, Scottie loses his "self-sameness" and becomes "other" than himself and part of the "otherness" of the woman. According to Modleski, "It is as if he were continually confronted with the fact that woman's uncanny otherness has some relation to himself, that he resembles her in ways intolerable to contemplate—intolerable because this resemblance throws into question his own fullness" (1988, 92). In other words, patriarchy is not unitary, it is not exhausted by the meaning (exploitation on the basis of a repressive gender division) that the radical theory of ideology attributes to it. There is always an "other" (redemptive?) "remainder" in it that "exceeds" the binaries of gender (man-woman) and becomes other than itself—an instance of protogendered archewriting—that cannot be fixed in a "decidable" meaning. Patriarchy as the putative regime of gender division, in one word, is "undecidable." The "uncanniness" of woman for man is allegorized in a dreamlike sequence in the film, which Modleski analyzes as an instance of the film's immanent deconstruction of its own patriarchal ideology. After Madeline has been to Scottie's home, he follows her, the next day, in his car:

> She leads him on an especially circuitous route, while the camera, continually cutting back to his face, emphasizes his increasing perplexity. To his great surprise and puzzlement they wind up back at his house, where she has come to deliver a note. Scottie's pursuit of the mysterious other, then, inevitably takes him to his own home, just as Freud has shown that the uncanny, the *unheimlich,* is precisely the "homelike," the familiar which has been made strange through repression (1988, 93).

The political implications of such a deconstruction are extremely significant. In short, if patriarchy is undecidable—if all the man-woman–male-female categories melt away in a moment of excessive signification—then it cannot possibly be the object of a radical critique and intervention. Critique and intervention are possible only when their object can be drawn clearly and has a definite "identity." If the identity of patriarchy is, as Modleski claims, always already at odds with itself and "different" from itself, then it would mean that it is not stable and fixable; it is, in a sense, constituted by its seeming other and intertextual. Such a "textualization" means that patriarchy not only is not a unified, identitarian category, it is in a sense actually produced by "women" who, by the same token, are themselves deprived of a unitary identity and thus are in no "secure" position from which to critique and overthrow patriarchy because they are always already "within" it; and patriarchy, in the same manner, is not their other but inscribed within them. Women as well as men are "undecidable." Given the "fallenness" of both concepts—their lack of self-possession, truth, and unitary coherence—neither has access to an outside and nondifferential truth in order to "master" the other.

Although Modleski at one point in her book emphasizes the need for political critique (11) and even insists that the concept of "sadism" should be maintained in analyzing the desire of the spectator and not completely replaced by the aesthetics of the trope of masochism, she nonetheless offers a reading of *Vertigo* that follows the ludic logic and is a neither-nor equivocation (12). Such a reading leaves things as they are: it reinforces the status quo in which the already dominant preserves its domination from the contestation of the "other" by claiming that it is its own other and as such is in an exemplary position to critique itself from within. The final outcome of such a deconstruction of the outside is the substitution of reform—the immanent critique of ideology through its own immanent excess of signification—for radical transformation. If man is always already self-differentiated (Scottie in *Vertigo*) and, through recognizing his own otherness, is "redeemed" from his self-possession and coherence by woman, then there is no ground to argue for the erasure of a gender division that exploits on the basis of a clear (decidable) division of people according to their gender. What gender division?

Like all ludic readings of the "truth" of the radical theory of ideology, Modleski's critique is founded upon a privileging of "paradox" in ludic interpretive practices. A "paradoxical" reading demonstrates that what seems clear from a "simplistic" point of view (for instance, a patriarchal or classist one) turns out, upon "textualization," to be both more and less than itself. Such readings, which by now are canonized in ludic discourses as "complex" readings, in the last instance, are a political alibi for the ruling social order. For instance, in the reading just briefly outlined, such a "complex" (complicit) reading "shows" that Hitchcock's view of women is not as "simplistic," "reductive," "essentialist," and thus oppressive as some radical feminists have proposed in their critiques of the dominant ideology. Hitchcock, in other words, is a complex figure who exceeds politics, economics and other such "reductive" entities and can be understood fully only through the regime of textual signification in his films. Such a reading, in the name of paradox, parody, and pastiche—complexity—places the most blatant instances of social exploitation and their naturalization in films and other texts of culture under interrogative immunity and grants them free play under the sign of immanent resistance.

The notion of immanent (self-)deconstruction of ideology—a reading of ideology against itself enabled by its own inner

contradictions—is highly popular among postmodern film theorists. Such a view simply carries out the program of (post-)struc-
turalism by showing how ideology, like any other text, is at odds
with itself, void of self-mastery, and therefore not capable of
being as "dominating" as it is made to be. In fact, in its contradictions, it is even enabling, as a Foucauldian culture critic states:
"Ideology functions not only to limit human action but also to
enable it" (Giroux, 1983, 145). But locating "resistance" and
"agency" in the fault lines of ideology reduces "resistance" and
human agency to a mere ideological struggle and thus brackets
the global economic and sociopolitical structures of domination.
Furthermore, it installs a "reformist" politics that, in the last
instance, supports the dominant social order.

As a deconstructive reading, an immanent critique of ideology simply "reforms" the internal relations of inequality among
the constituents of the system but keeps its enclosing structure
intact. Briefly, in ludic film criticism an immanent deconstructive
reading is a double move: after the initial dehierarchization of
unequal binary terms—male-female in the gender system, for
example—these terms are, in a subsequent move, not discarded
but reinscribed in the system. The equilibrium of the gender system, based on a binary in which the first term is implicitly prior
to the the second one, is disturbed by showing that the first term
acquires its firstness through violently expunging its own "difference" from itself and representing it as the "otherness" of the
second term. By returning this erased difference to the first term,
an immanent critique demonstrates that the term in fact exceeds
itself and is other than itself—is in contradiction with itself—and
thus deprives it of its (false) privilege of "identity" and self-
coherence. After such an operation in which the hierarchical
relation between the two terms is deconstructed, both are seen
as traversed with difference (which is the inscription of the third
"proto-term") therefore both are ontologically and epistemolog-
ically marked by "undecidability": they are now, in a sense, made
"equal."

The relation of male-female, which was initially hierarchical
in the dominant gender system, is now on equal terms. However,
the gender system of patriarchy itself and its global structures
are kept intact! Deconstructive readings based on the inner con-

tradictions of the laws of signification of a system, in short, merely update the regime's discourses that have lost their legitimacy
for a nuclear age. To return to the example of the gender system,
deconstructive readings democratize the feudal relations
between males and females by deploying new discourses that
legitimate the same old ideological effects necessary for reproducing the dominant social order (the gendered subject, for
example). Adjusting the system—reforming it through local critique—is necessitated by the pressures of capitalism itself: in this
case the need for an expanded labor force in which "independent" women can play a role.

Yet, after a deconstructive critique aimed at displaying the
contradictions of its discourses, the system remains the same
(Brunett and Wills, 1989, 139–171). It is just a "reformed" system.
A more radical deployment of Derridean differential reading
goes beyond a simple destablizaton of binaries and attempts to
open up one system (e.g., gender) to others (e.g., class, race).
However, because deconstructive reading is a detotalizing regime
of intelligibility, this "opening up" amounts to little more than a
collage of systems: adjacency without global connections. Consequently, as long as resistance is conceived as a regional, local, and
thus micropolitical practice, resistance to one aspect of the social
(in one locality) becomes in fact a legitimization of another locality of the system. In a sense, any form of local resistance is complicit with the system since a resistance against local aspects of the
system is, at the same time, based on the acceptance of the legitimacy of the system itself and acts on the "unsaid" assumption
that the problem to be contested lies in the isolated wayward
effects of the system and not the system as such. However, only
through a global understanding of the social—the relational practice of a macropolitics aware of the political economy of localities
in their interdependence—can transformative change be effected
and the regime of domination overthrown. Thus the localist,
experiential politics of rupture (*jouissance* and or as "contradictions"), which sets out to "radically" deconstruct the repressive
solemnities of "cultural policy" and its underlying patriarchy,
ends up supporting, through regional reforms, the very global
structures of domination it had designated as the solemnities of
bourgeois culture and tried to dismantle.

The idea of "excess" as resistance to the dominant has frequently been used in ludic film theory to justify some of the most conservative film practices. The reading of such reactionary film makers as Hitchcock, Ford, and Preminger as agents of "resistance" in some "liberal" circles is based on the interpretation of their works as instances of (radical) "excess." The textual systems in their films, it is assumed, are never exhausted by their "meanings." Perhaps one of the most celebrated cases of such justification is the reading provided for Douglas Sirk's films. Sirk's reactionary naturalization of patriarchal capitalism in such films as *Written on the Wind,* for example, is normalized by a reading that focuses on the film's immanent formal features that produce a "remainder" not absorbed by the conventions of its genre (melodrama) and thus becomes an "excess" that comments, through strategic irony, parody, and pastiche, on its own procedures and ideology. In other words, it transcends its own limitations (Willemen, 1971). Such view of film as an aesthetic entity that overcomes its own ideological limits by virtue of its own immanence (textuality), of course, is an entirely familiar theory in conservative humanist film criticism. The convergence of the old and the new in the effects they produce from their immanent readings, once again, points up the ideological collusion between traditional and ludic film criticism and theory in reading texts of culture in such a fashion as to always produce the ideological effects necessary for producing and maintaining dominant subjectivities. Producing a radical text by an "excessive" reading of Sirk's film goes beyond the film as the ostensible object of analysis and serves as a civic allegory through which citizens are assured that the established system itself (as exemplified in a film) "resists" its own abuses through the immanent operations of the system and thus "reforms" itself from within. The ideological function of an "excessive" reading and its underlying project of resistance by *jouissance* is as I have indicated to render any intervention from outside the system—in other words, revolution—redundant. The popularity of the idea of resistance by *jouissance* in postmodern theory is precisely because it is an ideological alibi: a lesson in systems maintenance through which the dominant class relations and exploitative social order that they underwrite are resecured and the intervention from outside the system is represented as violent and hermeneutically "unsubtle." In such ideological moves and assertions of the specificity of film as a system that has to be read in terms of its own inner capacity for reflexivity and thus as a system that doubles back upon itself and reforms itself, dominant film theory marginalizes ideology critique as disrespectful of the film's immanence and thus as crude "external" misreadings. However, what dominant film theory, in its political anxiety, rejects as "crude" is itself an intervention in the bourgeois subtleties that legitimate the rule of one class over others through the privileging of the formal and the immanent. The subtle and the "aesthetic" in ludic film theory, as Stephen Heath's classic "excessive" reading of *A Touch of Evil* (1975) suggests, "always already" surprises the political.

Resistance (i.e., transformative resistance), however, *is* a "crude" historical intervention from "outside" the system itself: one in which the exploited rid themselves of their exploiters by obtaining access to the means of production and not simply to "free expression." Radical theorists and critics should be prepared to go beyond the institutionalized hermeneutic "subtleties" of the bourgeois academy and its accompanying culture industry and become "crude." "Crude" enough in fact to be part of what Walter Benjamin, in his reading of Brecht, names the *progressive intelligentsia*—those involved in "liberating the means of production and hence active in the class struggle" (1973, 93), words that have strange echoes in ludic theories of resistance through *jouissance!* Resistance and agency as revolutionary practices are, in short, produced not by pleasure (*jouissance*) but by "knowledge": knowledge of the global structures of the social contradictions that in fact construct what is commonsensically perceived as experience (of *jouissance*) because, historically speaking, there is no human "experience" as such but only "experience effects." As Marx has argued, "Men make their own history, but they do not make it just as they please; they do not make it under circumstances chosen by themselves, but under circumstances directly found, given and transmitted from the past" (1978, 103). Resistance and agency, in other words, are produced through knowledge of the determining global structures of historical forces; the kind of knowledge, in fact, that contemporary film theory as well as ludic postmodern theory in general reject as "totalizing" and therefore (by the logic of a pun) "totalitarian." One of the reasons for dismissing "global" ("totalizing") intelligibilities in poststructuralist theory is that such a mode of "reading" is indifferent to the specificity of local and regional phenomena. In other words, it is assumed that in these discourses the "global" is a "formula" applied to the "local" without any accounting of its specific materiality—it is "decided" even before the analysis begins. On such "logical" grounds, of course, the "local" mode of understanding is as "formulaic" and thus totalitarian as the global because the regionalist analytic of poststructuralism also *begins* with a decidable knowledge that the only appropriate mode of knowing is the "local." The "local" of poststructuralism is, in other words, as abstract (indifferent to *this* local) as what it attributes to the global analytics.

What is treated as "resistance" in ludic film theory is itself a strategy of containment that reproduces and protects the dominant system's enabling structures by introducing reform (local critique). Engaging the subject-as-spectator in local, micropolitical resistances gives him the illusion of agency and thus recruits him all the more effectively as the (free) agent of the structures of domination. The emphasis on resistance by means of *jouissance* is a strategy distracting attention away from domination. Focusing on "resistance" obscures the logic of domination that underlies seemingly different, local, and heterogeneous practices of postmodern patriarchal capitalism—from the naturalization of intimacy to the theory of the arts. Domination is terminated not by the spectator's micropolitical and local resistance nor by what I call an *immanent semiotic coup d'etat* ("excess") in the film text legitimated by a totalitarian poststructuralism. Rather domination is terminated by class struggle—a subject on which contemporary film theory is dead silent because it follows Lyotard and other ideologues of late capitalism in regarding the postmodern to mark the end of such "grand narratives" as class struggle and the demise of global transformative politics. Radical critical theory, however, produces new ways of seeing and thus constructs a new understanding of the postmodern: a postmodern that Teresa Ebert calls resistance postmodernism (1990).

My foregrounding of the structures of domination that

underlie various "experiences," institutions and practices of capitalism should not be taken to mean that I believe all films and other texts of culture produced at the present moment or all theorists and critics are equally complicit in reproducing the existing social relations. Rather, my point is to make a distinction between the institutionally authorized "resistance" of a localist politics—practiced by a "generic" Left in the academy and culture industry—that ends up protecting the dominant social relations and a revolutionary politics of transformation of the existing relations of production.

To be more precise even though somewhat repetitious, the currently popular notion of the "political" is based on a harmless idea of politics put forth by poststructuralism. This "generic" politics, which is merely a panhistorical ethical "attitude," regards the political to be simply a matter of the film's discursive self-consciousness, a doubling back upon (an ethical inspection of) the formal procedures for representing the real in the film: a self-reflexivity that renders the "meaning" of a text an "undecidable" and contingent effect of the rhetorical tensions between containment and excess. The underlying assumption here is the canonic poststructuralist notion that the function of a "radical" reader is to differ by deferring the fusion of the signifier and the signified—to make problematic the meanings of texts of culture. According to such a view of the political, then, all formally self-reflexive films (the popular genre of the ludic avant-garde) are "radical." In these films, for example, the continuity editing that marks the classic Hollywood film is subverted so that the material discontinuity of the film is displayed as a means for showing the arbitrary connection of the signifier with the signified, thus deconstructing the logic of representation: the ideology of the visible. The idea of the political as a concerted effort to subvert the easy movement of meaning in culture has lead to privileging those films and cultural texts with a high degree of formal reflexivity. Moreover, the popularity of these avant-garde texts and their perception in the ludic postmodern common sense as "political" has in fact not only obscured the political economy of emancipatory transformation but consequently naturalized the status quo. Thus, before moving to other issues, I would like to inquire into the politics of self-reflexivity and the privileging of the formalist avant-garde in ludic theory.

Ludic postmodern theory represents itself as antiempiricist and opposed to the traditional humanist notion of the subject as a free and unitary agent. However, what it rejects in the open, it quietly relegitimates through more sophisticated discursive maneuvers. Privileging formal self-reflexivity is one such ludic device for reinscribing empiricism and positivism in contemporary discourses because without them the bourgeois knowledge industry cannot operate and fulfill its ideological role in capitalist economy—the production of the free subject and the naturalness of the way things are. Self-reflexivity retrieves the self-presence of the "real" through reference to the experience of the subject of the physical (*jouissance* or body) and the empirical (immanent formal properties of the film text). In his ludic postmodern manifesto of the "radical" avant-garde, *Abstract Film and Beyond,* Malcolm LeGrice writes that the aim of a truly self-reflexive film is to produce an experience in which "action on the automatic nervous system seeks to create a nervous response which is largely preconscious, the psychological reactions sought being a direct consequence of physical function" (1977, 106). Positivism-empiricism-subject, to which the ludic postmodern opposes itself, thus return to its discourses through the resurrection of the body-physical-experience all by the alibi of self-reflexivity. The experience that LeGrice posits as the mark of the successful self-reflexivity of a film and the *jouissance* that Barthes theorizes both produce the "body" (physical) as the securing source (the transcendental signified) of cultural reality. In short, they cut off the meaning of experience from economic, political, and ideological practices and regard it as autointelligible.

Their claim to the radicality of self-reflexivity is, of course, based on the dogma that formal self-reflexivity will not allow the spectator to identify with the characters of the film or take its fiction as "real" because the formal negotiations in the film will keep the spectator aware at all times that he is a witness not to the real but to a fiction (about the real). Self-reflexivity, it is assumed, produces active subjects of resistance who will not go along with the fraudulence of "identitarian" politics and the regime of "realism" in the Hollywood film. It is politically significant that such an "active" subject is privileged not only by avant-garde film makers and theorists such as LeGrice and Peter Gidal (1976) but also by such conservative theorists as David Bordwell (1985, 29–47). The active and resisting subject produced by this mode of formal self-reflexivity is indeed nonthreatening to the dominant social relations because his "activism" focuses on the *process* (discursive self-reflexivity, formal problem solving). Such "activism" (resistance), in other words, acts through cognitive contemplation to construct the subject as self-present, autonomous, and free and at the same time to divert attention away from the question of the socioeconomic effects and consequences of the "process," of the *jouissance* of excess. Here I would like to question the basis of the ludic avant-garde's claim that formal self-reflexivity in film is in and of itself a (politically) radical intervention in systems of representation and thus in reading texts of culture and the construction of social reality.

The laying bare of fictional and narrative devices is far from being the exclusive mark of the avant-garde; it is in fact a common feature of many Hollywood films that postmodern theorists have rejected as politically reactionary. In her *The Hollywood Musical,* Jane Feuer demonstrates that the "direct address" as a device of "distanciation" of the signified is deployed not only by such avant-garde film makers as Godard but is also the staple technical apparatus of such musicals as *An American in Paris:*

> When a character in Godard addresses us directly, he breaks the narrative surface, and this makes us aware that we are watching a created fiction, not a world of dreams whole in itself. The Platonic ideal of a Hollywood film is one in which the audience perceives even the celluloid stock as the stuff of magic and the story as transcending its origin in light and shadow, the narrative of musical films exemplify this classical pattern. But the musical numbers regularly and systematically violate the smooth surface. The goals of musicals and those of Godard must surely be opposed. But—as in the case of direct address—their methods are identical. How can this be? (1982, 35–36)

Rather than facing the political implications of her own analysis, which denies the panhistorical, transsocial, and inherent "radicality" of any (anti)narrative device, Feuer attempts to save the radicality of self-reflexivity by arguing that the self-reflexivity and excess of the musical is contained by other narrative devices such as the presence of audience in the film itself, a technique routinely used in musicals. Her analysis, however, shows that contrary to the claims made for the inherent radicality of the effects of self-reflexivity and its various formal devices, they are not in and of themselves radical—they can be found in all kinds of films and their presence in such reactionary films as musicals indicate that they are not exactly apparatuses of revolution. In fact one can go further and point to the fact that postmodern popular culture (commonly regarded by postmodern film theory as oppressive and reactionary) has become "self-reflexive" in almost all its representations. Such self-reflexivity not only pervades contemporary advertisements but also marks, for example, such popular "talk shows" as those by David Letterman and Arsenio Hall. The formal self-reflexivity of these cultural products in no way changes their ideological effects; on the contrary, it enhances those effects by updating their modes of articulation.

In his "Film Work 2," Thierry Kuntzel marks the main features of an avant-garde film: it subverts the traffic of conventional meanings in culture by means of its immanent formal features and thus achieves radically new forms of signification; forms that, unlike the traditional Hollywood narrative, will not constrain the spectator by coercing him into ideologically desirable subject positions. The subversive film is one in which "the initial figure would not find a place in the flow of narrative, in which the configuration of events contained in the formal matrix would not form a progressive order, in which the spectator/subject would never be reassured...within the dominant system of production and consumption, this would be a film of sustained terror" (1980, 24–25). Tania Modleski in her "The Terror of Pleasure: The Contemporary Horror Film and Postmodern Theory" shows that recent "horror film" not only uses the formal devices of the avant-garde but produces the effects that Kuntzel outlines as the signs of the "radical" film. The horror film, like the avant-garde text "exceeds" itself and overcomes traditional "closure" by formally and self-reflexively remaining "open-ended"—a device that offers the audience *jouissance* by subverting its expectations and, significantly, at the same time keeps the (financial) possibility open for countless sequels as with such successful films as *Friday the Thirteenth.* Another formal similarity between the horror film and the avant-garde text is the treatment of "character" and the construction of "plot." Unlike the traditional narrative, the horror film does not have any psychologically developed character or causally developed plot, and when, in Modleski's words, "villains and victims are such shadowy, undeveloped characters and are portrayed equally unsympathetically, narcissistic identification on the part of audience becomes increasingly difficult" (161). In other words, these films, like the avant-garde film text prevent the spectator's identification with the "character" and require a mode of *anti*narcissistic identification that "the audience delights in indulging" (161). The effect of such formal devices in popular culture and especially horror film is that postmodern popular culture no longer offers the containing and harmonizing experience of cultural identification that Barthes named *pleasure* (1975), in contrast with a radical and subversive *jouissance,* and instead, like the avant-garde, it offers the spectator the experience of *jouissance* (bliss).

Jouissance, which is offered as radical politics in poststructuralism, is, of course, a strategy reinforcing the idea of the sovereign subject. The ideological effect of *jouissance* (bliss) is not only (re)produced in the theories of poststructuralism and in the performatics of the cult of "bliss" in the horror film but also in the gnomic texts of the petty bourgeoisie. Joseph Campbell, a prophet-celebrity of this class, sums up (his) wisdom of myths in the aphorism, "Follow your Bliss": a crypto-fascist enjoining that secures the free subject outside the reach of collective practices and the social (Brendan Gill, 16–19).

The adversarial aspects of the horror film, however, are not limited to its counternarratival effects and formal self-reflexivity. Its products are as antibourgeois as any avant-garde film: it opposes such cherished bourgeois institutions as "the individual and the family," which "are *dis*-membered (like the narrative itself) in the most gruesomely literal way" in the horror film (Modleski, 160). Formal self-reflexivity and antibourgeois content then are not in and of themselves politically radical. In fact, as I have already pointed out, resistance and subversion of this kind are authorized by the dominant ideology itself as ways of articulating internal discontent and thus instituting reforms that protect the structures of domination. The attack on the family and the unitary individual, for example—which is the common theme of the avant-garde and such products of contemporary popular culture as the horror film—is a necessary adversarial intervention at this moment of history. The culture of late capitalism has outgrown both the unitary self and the nuclear family. It needs more dispersed, more "differential" subjectivities and structures of socialization, and the subversive avant-garde and adversarial popular culture are, in fact, doing the work demanded by the dominant ideology. In other words, they are helping to produce a ludic postmodern split self and a postmodern metonymic family that is more responsive to the needs of transnational capitalism.

The politically transformative has to be sought elsewhere. The radical film may or may not use self-reflexivity as its mode of articulation. In the Brechtian tradition, radical film may deploy self-reflexive devices, but the purpose of such a practice will be a political (and not formal) self-reflexivity: a practice that defamiliarizes the familiar and turns it into a social and historical construct that, in Brecht's words, "calls for explanation" (1979, 125). Whether self-reflexive or not, a radical film cannot be content to be simply antibourgeois in the manner of poststructuralist theorists or formalist avant-garde films; that is, to merely shatter bourgeois solemnities as textual products and to regard such a deconstruction as a mark of transformative change. Rather radical film (or theory) has to be, above all and always, anticapitalist. It has to go beyond mere ideological and superstructuralist struggles. It has to assist in transforming the social relations of production. Resistance to capitalism in order to transform it cannot be carried out through "excessive" representation and *jouissance*. A radical film must produce "knowledge" and not merely *jouissance;* and the most urgent knowledge is class consciousness.

This form of knowledge or class consciousness, however, is not hidden in a (radical) text—knowledge is *produced* and not *found* in texts of culture. This book is an attempt towards the production of such knowledge. However, instead of locating such knowledge in "radical" or "avant-garde" films, which situate

themselves as the "other" by virtue of their techniques and the-
matics, I have sought to produce oppositional knowledge out of
the common films of popular culture in the 1980s. These common films might be called "trivial" films: films that constitute the
main frame of visual and discursive intelligibility for most people
and are seemingly innocuous texts dealing with the mundane
and the routine of daily life. They reify daily experience and
reinforce the "naturalness" of existing reality.

But why address the "trivial"? Because to ignore a trivial
film such as *Desperately Seeking Susan* on the grounds that it is
formally uninteresting and philosophically vacuous is to confuse
its aesthetic and intellectual worth with its ideological "uses."
The vacuity of the trivial film is not a matter of directorial or
scriptorial neglect that can be explained in terms of individual
"errors" and ineptitude. *Desperately Seeking Susan*'s formal
naivete, its sheer intellectual emptiness are part of the social
contradictions and thus highly significant. The vacuity of the trivial film, in other words, is a structure of knowing: a form of
understanding the world that displays the operation of ideology
in its attempt to explain away social contradictions. In the spaces
of the trivial film the dominant ideology reproduces the reigning
ideas and "obviousnesses" and repairs the damages that the discourses of common sense have suffered in their conflicts and
clashes with antihegemonic discourses. The "trivial" film, in an
uncanny way, speaks the "unsaid" of the dominant social relations. Ideology proposes a way of seeing: the director-producer-
actors of the trivial film are ideologically situated in a position of
knowledge and subjectivity from which is seen only that which is
necessary for the reproduction of existing social relations. They
"see" on behalf of the ruling class. The trivial film, in other
words, is unable to see what, in fact, it actually encounters; it
stops at the "visible" that it represents as the "seeable" and the
"real." In this ideological blindness its historical insight resides.
The trivial film opens up a space for recycling those discourses
required to legitimate the practices that enable the existing set of
representations to endure. In the cultural space articulated by
the trivial film, the dominant ideology reproduces itself and constructs and maintains those subjectivities needed for the perpetuation of the status quo. Through such films, the dominant ideolo-

gy offers the spectator a position of intelligibility from which he can make sense of himself as a continuous subject in spite of the changing historical situation.

At times of crisis, like the present, when the continuity of the subject (the subject position of "wife" in *Desperately Seeking Susan*, for instance) is threatened by the intervention of oppositional discourses, the trivial film acquires immense significance. By reproducing traditional positions of intelligibility, *Desperately Seeking Susan* helps secure the old subject positions needed for the prevailing family arrangements. This is why the trivial film cannot be ignored; its political uses in culture indicate the operations of the larger frames of intelligibility and their connections within the dominant economic, political, and power-knowledge relations. To transform these relations, it is necessary to intervene in the circulation of "obviousnesses" disseminated by the trivial film because, through such an intervention, the speculary relation of people with the historical and contradictory discourses of the social may be changed and the continuation of hegemonic representations interrupted. Only a sustained ideology critique of the trivial film, such as I have undertaken in the following chapters, can disclose the political function of the trivial film's vacuity and conceptual innocence in repressing "other" possible social arrangements.

4

Tales of films then are, in a double sense, tales of intelligibility: they make sense not only of the film but also of the viewer (the subject). Both the film and the viewer are thus inscribed in the relations of (re)production because intelligibility is historical and the effect of the socioeconomic relations legitimated by the discourses of ideology. The film participates in the culturally significant act of the circulation of ideology: the film shows the reader how to recognize and, above all, "experience" the real in culture. The (mainstream) film especially lends support to the dominant ideology in those areas where the meanings required for reproducing the relations of production have, for various reasons, lost their potency. By engendering tales—providing domains of intelligibility—films (re)secure those meanings for ideology. In *The Big Chill,* for instance, the culturally necessary modes of intimacy (such as marriage), endangered by the development of alternative modes of intimacy in the 1960s and after, are powerfully resecured and reinstated. The (hegemonic) tales of intelligibility produced by films, in other words, resecure the "real" that is losing its legitimacy under the interrogation of oppositional ideologies. Tales are thus a necessary part of the ideology through which the hegemonic theory of the real works.

The optics of the tale, what the tale makes visible, is of great significance in the ideology critique of film because what the tale sees is what ideology requires the viewer to see: the domain of intelligibility and thus obviousnesses that the dominant social arrangements need to continue their hegemony without contestation. Tales, taken together, form the cognitive environment of a culture and provide the patterns of perception, organization, and interpretation of daily practices for people in that culture; they demonstrate, in concrete form, how to make sense of experience.

The ideology critiques that follow inquire into the modalities of this secure plenitude of the imaginary, which is achieved in filmic tales that reproduce the dominant social relations in the spaces of historical lack and noncontradiction and attempt to point out the politics of this plenitude. They argue that the bourgeois film—as exemplified by the common, that is the "trivial," films of the 1980s—erases historicity, political alterity, and social difference, reducing them to a mode of sameness and obviousness. Ideology critiques intervene in this process by changing the relation between the spectator and the film—the text of culture—and resituate the viewer in an oppositional relation to the prevailing mode of seeing and "subjection."

In my ideology critiques I have undertaken what might be called *transgressive readings:* a mode of reading that substitutes a subversive critique for subservient and appreciative interpretation. The transgressive readings that my ideology critiques offer are not close readings, which maintain fidelity to the film text (a reproduction of empiricism), but rather are ways of unveiling the operation of ideology and power (demonstrating the ideology of the empirical as a guide to the real). They thus attempt to provide space for the political struggle to change the prevailing economic and power relations. My readings then are a mode of intervention, which I believe is the ultimate goal of any radical critique, and are opposed to interpretation as explication and close reading as appreciation. The discursive task of ideology critique is to make the "unsaid" of the text part of its "said"; thus to decenter the "said," locating it in the cultural unconscious, and to point up the economic, political, and ideological practices that construct and maintain that unconscious. Politically transgressive readings are not simply instances of disagreement over aesthetic judgments about a film, but are contestations over the dominant tale of the film, that is to say, struggles over what version of reality will (or should) prevail. When such a reading produces an "other" tale from the film, it is demonstrating the "possible" inscribed in the "existing" and points toward the practices that will realize the "possible."

However, dominant film theory marginalizes ideology critique on the grounds that such "readings" reduce the meaning of the film by imposing a "closure." Since the emergence of ludic postmodern theory in the late 1950s, the most favored mode of reading cultural texts has been those that approach the text as a reversible plurality whose meaning is to be found in its very "process" of structuration and not in the (ideological-economic-political) effects and consequences of structuration. This theory of meaning and signification leads to what I have called *process activism*—a theory whose ideological purpose is to produce the reader as the autonomous subject who can, as a mark of freedom, endlessly construct and generate meanings. There is very little difference between the subject-as-process-activist in ludic theory and the traditional humanist subject who was the author of all meanings. The difference is that the traditional free subject grounded her freedom in her consciousness whereas the new subject founds it upon her "body," which is capable of experiencing rupture in the form of the *jouissance* of excess. The final outcome of both theories is the same: meaning is, ostensibly, posited as reversible (nonbinding), undecidable (nontotalizing), and "open" (amenable to new "playfulness"). The qualities attributed to meaning in ludic theory are the characteristics associated with bourgeois democracy: the construction of meaning in ludic theory, in other words, is an allegory of "human rights" and the economic legitimation of free enterprise. In these theories, *jouis-sance* (the experience of freedom through the empirical body-text) provides the ground for an open-ended, reversible, and undecidable meaning that is out of the reach of history. Meaning is thus plural in the sense that it is not determined by any other entity except the subject who can perceive many configurations in the text, all of which are equally valid as long as they produce *jouissance* (the ultimate mark of the freedom of the subject). To approach meaning normatively—to ask questions about its polit-ical and economic effects, as ideology critique does—is, in ludic postmodern theories, to limit the play of the signifier and impose a totalitarian "closure" on it. As long as meaning is plural, the film cannot be marked for its politics and economics, as, for example, "reactionary." It is always already (panhistorically) "other" than itself because there are other "readings." The notion of meaning as plural, reversible, and undecidable then is, in one sense, a maneuver to give interrogative immunity to those films that actively render support (in terms of their historically specific meanings) to the dominant class relations.

We can gain a more precise sense of the politics of meaning and the limits of "excessive" reading by a closer examination of some of the debates in film theory over these issues. For exam-ple, in her essay, "Women, Realism and Reality in British Films, 1943–53," Sue Aspinall argues that the British melodramas pro-duced in this period failed to represent the reality of women at that time, and she relates this failure to economics and the politi-cal: the structures of ownership and control in the British film industry. The class structure and relations of productions, in other words, are seen as directly involved in the meaning of the films (1983, 292–93), and the films are themselves marked as reactionary since they have performed a consensual function and "helped to resolve an ideological crisis in the post-war period" (293). John Hill's equally critical, "Working Class Realism and Sexual Reaction: Some Theses on the British 'New Wave'," also uses a detailed analysis of class relations to reach the conclusion that, contrary to commonsensical readings, the realist films of the early 1960s are "far from being 'progressive'" (1983, 310) and were in fact reactionary in their solution of sexual and fami-ly issues: "By and large, such films end by reproducing an ideology of marital and procreative sexuality.... These films also affirm the need for male regulation of female sexuality within the marriage institution" (310).

In contrast, Andrew Higson, writing from within the ludic postmodern problematics, uses the essays by Aspinall and Hill as a site to assert the class values legitimated in the films these critics reject as reactionary, but he does this by marginalizing the very mode of analysis (ideology critique) they deployed as totalitarian. His "argument" appeals to the ludic common sense dominated by the theory of meaning as an undecidable process of structuration. In terms of this common sense, the very gesture of marking a system of meaning as "reactionary" is, in and of itself, "proof" of theoretical coercion and totalitarianism. Aspinall and Hill argue that their tutor texts have historically effective "meanings"; that is to say, they have political and economic consequences that go beyond the reader's *jouissance* and naturalize certain class interests and economic and social practices. Rather than addressing this issue—the historicity of meanings—Higson, following the lead of Derrida, Lyotard and Barthes, appeals to the ahistorical plurality of meaning. Thus Aspinall's and Hill's readings are unacceptable to him because they are "closural" and, like any ideology critique, a mark of the "desire for a text to be *either* 'progressive' *or* 'reactionary', and a refusal to pay attention to the permanent and productive tensions, the play of containment and excess, in the film system" (1983, 87). The italicized *either-or* in Higson's text is meant to signal to the "subtle" reader that Hill and Aspinall are "crude" readers; totalizers whose readings are totalitarian and disrespectful of the "permanent" (panhistorical) reversibility of the text. Through the alibi of the aesthetic, the complexity, and the richness of the layered meanings of the film text, Higson's critique performs a political function: it rejects marking as "reactionary" those texts that in fact have legitimated the dominant class relations.

The proposition that meaning is "undecidable" is, in the last instance, a proposition that legitimates an ahistorical mode of understanding cultural texts. It offers an interrogative immunity to texts of oppression because, from the position of the "resistance" reader (the subject of *jouissance*), no text can be marked as *either-or;* every text, to use the poststructuralist platitude, is *both-and*. *Both-and* foregrounds the permanent "unre-solved tension in the film-viewing experience for the spectator," a tension that, in Higson's words, "works over the ideological stresses of the period" and sets the film text free from the reach of history (88). The logic of reading texts of culture as *both-and* is the logic of domination that conceals itself as an aesthetic prin-ciple by appealing to unsaid assumptions of both-and as the very logic of democracy and free enterprise. There are, in other words, no "reactionary" films, no "progressive" films—there are only films! And films should be read not in terms of their ideo-logical consequences (the structures of domination they inscribe) but in terms of their structuration—the sheer joy of being an active witness to the process of their signification. *"Party Girl* has an idiotic story," writes Fereydoun Hoveyda. "So what?" he continues and goes on to resecure the ideological in terms of the formalism of his own time. "[W]hat constitutes the essence of cinema is nothing other than *mise en scene....* What is immedi-ately striking in *Party Girl...* is the graceful ease with which it unfolds, the perfect unity of its aesthetic, and the uncluttered immediacy of what it has to say" (1986, 123). In other words, it is the "process" of signification that matters, and only a spectator who is capable of responding to the "process" can appreciate the uniqueness of the film. This gesture is repeated by David Bord-well, in terms of a "new" formalism in which he conceives of the spectator of the film as forever "active" in the processes of signi-fication but, curiously, as in Hoveyda's theory, always "cued" by the text itself (1985, 29–47). This double inscription of the spec-tator posits him as "free" but still subject to the laws of the "text" (the authority of the free market)—a freedom, in other words, whose main purpose is to allow the subject to freely sub-ject himself to authority, the authority of an open and reversible proliferation of surplus meaning.

The contestations among Higson, Aspinall, and Hill also point up the problem of "aestheticization" not only in film theo-ry but in ludic theory as well. Higson rejects the ideology cri-tiques made by Aspinall and Hill because they offer "very little visual analysis" of the films they discuss. In other words, they are not respectful of the aesthetic specificity of films and treat them just like any other general text of culture. The emphasis on specificity—visual analysis in film—is, as I suggested before, a means for leading the critique away from the historical, economic, and political consequences of the film and focusing it instead on the immanent features of the film. Thus in place of critiques that unveil the global structures of economic and political domination legitimated by the film—critiques that are complacently dubbed as "reductionist" in the new common sense—the reader must offer ever more "subtle" visual analyses that substitute a Barthesian *jouissance* for "knowledge" and a Deleuzian-Bergsonian "ineffable" (*Cinema 1: The Movement-Image,* 1986) for class consciousness.

The text, in ludic postmodern theory, is, to repeat, treated as an open-ended ensemble that continually defers, through the movement of textual difference, the linking of the signifier and the signified and thus avoids "closure." "Closure," in ludic postmodern theory, is almost equivalent to the act of "interpretation" itself because interpretation is theorized as a limiting mode of understanding—thus the substitution of "reading" for "interpretation" and the call for going "Beyond Interpretation" (Culler, 1981, 3–17). In terms of Susan Sontag's *Against Interpretation,* which marked the postmodern turn away from interpretation, reading, as opposed to interpretation, should be an instance of *jouissance* and sensuality (body-experience). Interpretation ruins our sensual capability; to interpret is "to impoverish, to deplete the world—in order to set up a shadow world of 'meanings'" (1967, 7). It is to avoid interpretation that the ludic postmodern text becomes a "parody" (10) and as such serves as a subversive act. Radical art subverts its own ideological contents (interpretive elements) and resituates itself by virtue of its own formal features: in Bergman's *Winter Light* and *The Silence,* the beauty and visual sophistication of the image subverts before our eyes the callow pseudo-intellectuality of the story and some of the dialogue. (The most remarkable instance of this sort of discrepancy is the work of D. W. Griffith.) In good films, there is always a directness that entirely frees us from the itch to interpret" (11). Ostensibly Sontag's uninhibited desire for "presence" ("directness") is at odds with the ludic notion of textual mediation, but in actuality Sontag and Barthes (who institutionalizes antiinterpretation) both seek the sensual and the experimental

that is beyond the reach of history. The opposition to "interpretation" in postmodern theory is, in the last instance, an opposition to history—to the fact that meanings have determined historical consequences.

The politics of Sontag's opposition to interpretation
becomes more clear when she picks up the texts of Marx as one of
the major targets of her attack on interpretation. Marx's writings,
for her, are "elaborate systems of hermeneutics" that are "aggressive and imperious theories of interpretation" (7). The attack on
Marx is because of his insistence that there is no "meaning" without "explanation" and "interpretation"; that is, no meaning without the mediation of history and structures of subjectivity. Even
such an "obvious" direct experience as "revolution," for him (to
the dismay of the "process activists"), has no meaning in itself: it
has to be interpreted; that is to say, historically evaluated in terms
of its consequences. For Sontag such a view impoverishes "revolution" because it reduces the "excess" of "revolution." Revolution—for her as well as for other theorists of meaning as *jouissance,* process without closure, such as Barthes, Lyotard,
Baudrillard, Foucault, and Derrida—is basically a "May '68" or
Woodstock (Fall of the Berlin Wall) Party-type moment of
"excess" whose main effect is to offer *jouissance* to the revolutionary: a noninterpretive immanent rupture and "surprising"
slippage. Instead of hermeneutics the ludic postmodern culture,
according to Sontag, needs "erotics" (14).

The move against interpretation—which was later updated,
relanguaged (Sontag's vocabulary was embarrassingly loaded
with humanist sentimentality), and institutionalized in postmodern theory, mostly through Roland Barthes's *The Pleasure of the
Text*—marginalizes ideology critique as a totalizing closural
interpretation. To avoid "closure" the focus of reading is shifted
from the "product" (the final result) of reading to its "process."
However, the injunction against "closure" is a subtle strategy of
containment that, in the name of openness, democratic participation in the production of meaning, and the plurality of meaning
itself, actually installs a regime of monism (only "process"),
oppression (the "other" of process), and avoidance (the consequences of process). As long as the text is proposed as a
reversible process in, for instance, Barthes's *S/Z,* Lyotard's *The*

Differend, or Derrida's *The Post-Card,* the reader will never have to face such final signifieds (consequences) of the reading as racism, sexism, classism, and Eurocentrism, upon which the entire process of signification under patriarchal capitalism is founded. The war on totality is waged, ultimately, to regulate the political economy of signification and focus it on local and process politics, which violently excludes the consequences of process. The "product" of the process, the regimes of understanding that it sanctions, the forms of reality that it legitimates, and the modes of social and economic arrangements that it enables are all assigned to the "outside" of the process, and the product itself is represented as the "transcendental signified" (Derrida, 1976, 44–65).

Process, it should be clear by now, is an ideological alibi, a means by which the historical effects of reading are excluded from the "play of signification" so that the political responsibility of the reader can be rearticulated as an "ethics of reading" (Miller, 1987, 1–11). In such an ethics of reading, the process of self-fashioning the individual subject—set free from what Michael Levin calls "policy positions" (15) through the "excessive" reading generated by process—displaces the political, collective subjectivities that are always the historical products (signifieds) of reading texts of culture. Diverting attention away from the consequences of reading and toward its process makes it possible for the reader to avoid drawing connections among the seemingly heterogeneous "meanings" produced by the seemingly heterogeneous "processes" of reading. Each reading and its unique process is, to use Barthes's term, "received" as a singular moment of *jouissance* or, as Brunett and Wills put it, an "event" (1989, 139). Consequently, to seek connections among the seemingly heterogeneous and thus to be able to read "productively" has been made equal to totalizing and to being totalitarian in the dominant theories of reading. (It is worth noting here that what is proposed in vulgar postmodernism as the production of meaning is in fact a mode of consumption; the reader consumes the text by choosing—"producing"—meanings that give him the "highest" *jouissance.*) However, by focusing on the "process," the reader actually engages in a more pernicious kind of totalitarianism: he hides his situationality in a processing "omniscience" and speaks the truth of the process as process—a pan-historical form of understanding founded upon its own imma-nence. The injunction against interpretation and-as closure, in other words, is a refusal to face the historical and public conse-quences of the process of reading as free play. It is a refusal to face the fact that "process" closes off (is closural of) its own his-toricity and social consequences and as such achieves "mastery" by an exclusion that it does not acknowledge as part of its own historical limits.

Anti-interpretation refuses to recognize, for example, that Derrida's "argument" (in his *The Post Card*) for an unhindered reading that is not responsible to any outside metaphysics but only to its own immanent economies is, in the end (its product), an argument for deregulating, *privatizing,* interpretation. His call for the deregulation of interpretation performs, on the cultural level, the same political task, on behalf of the ruling class, that Reagan-Bush-Shamir-Mitterand-Thatcher-Kohl-Gorbachev do on the economic level. They all institute a practice ("deregulat-ing") through which the private entrepreneur, whether in the domain of reading or banking, is free from the pressures of a pub-lic (historical) scrutiny that places individual practices in a global relation with each other as well as with other social practices and "regulates" them in terms of their consequences for collective needs and desires. What Reagan or Thatcher rejects as "big gov-ernment" is an ideological alibi for naturalizing the "human rights" of the autonomous subject to assert his or her freedom through unregulated economic practices in the free market. What Derrida's "process" reading (an everlasting and unconstrained playfulness of signs in which signifiers refer to other signifiers in a chain of signification that never leads to a final signified that might "regulate" their play) rejects as "logocentrism" (big gov-ernment = big meaning) is also an ideological alibi. Institutional-izing "playful" reading (Brunett and Wills, 1989, 91–96) relegiti-mates the free, enterprising individual—Foucault's "specific intellectual" and Derrida's (playful) reader—who can assert her (ethical) freedom by making any and all meanings provide her with the "highest" *jouissance* ("benefit") without being con-strained by (public) questions concerning the consequences of her reading for the social collectivity. *Social collectivity* itself is seen by Foucault and Reagan as part of the "gulags" of the "evil empire" of totalization (the universal intellectual).

The call for deregulation, however, is itself a historical practice: it is issued when the entrepreneur of "meaning" or "banking" is highly confident and able to act with sureness as his enterprises expand and colonize successfully. The ideologically significant point here is that, at the first sight of trouble, big government (closural interpretation) is called upon to rescue the "free" enterprises: the Chrysler Corporation, savings and loans, and Paul De Man's "playful" Nazi readings. In their essays on the DeMan case, for example, Derrida and Miller—to mention only the two most vocal among De Man's many "defenders"—suddenly put aside their demands for deregulated, playful (mis)readings and ask for a reading that is based on "facts," is "correct," and avoids being "misinformed," "distorted," and "irresponsible" (Miller, 1989, 334–35). Such a "correct reading" is always already possible because "the fact" is out "there" (Derrida, 1989, 128). Derrida goes even further. Now that the "local" (texts of Paul De Man's wartime journalism) has turned out to be extremely damaging, he suddenly recognizes the limits of the regional and appeals to the concept of "totality" ("what he was, thought, wrote, taught" in their totality) as the necessity for our knowledge and judgment. In short, there is a return to "regulated" discourses and interpretation at times of trouble when the apparatus of (playful) reading is appropriated and deployed by "the Other." But this revival of regulation is not limited to discrete entities and concepts. Derrida grounds his text about De Man's Nazi writings in that most regulated of all frames of intelligibility—a chronological narrative—and gives it "presence" by the "speech" (telephone calls) of intentional "subjects" who are fully aware of their purposes and through their teleological activities establish their self-same identity: they plan to take "advantage" of a colloquium that is to be convened in Alabama to discuss (defuse?) the effects of De Man's wartime journalism on contemporary reading practices (1989, 147).

The telos of a discourse acknowledges its historicity thus giving it its own "closure"—situating it within sociohistorical and institutional limits. And that is what "closure" is: a recognition of the limits of a discourse. One can either foreground the "clo-

sure" of one's reading—accept its interestedness and thus situationality—and be self-reflexive about it or posit a "closure" in
the recesses of "process," "undecidability," and "reversibility."

However, the readings offered by Sontag, De Man, Barthes,
Derrida, and Lyotard are "closural" in yet another way. They
generate a far more pernicious closure that does not see its own
closural strategies and is unaware of its own historical limits. In
the readings of these interpreters, a process reading is offered as
a radical reading that daringly gets rid of the "safety" of "closure." The "dangerous" risks of a process reading are taken in
full safety, however, because their outcome is always already
guaranteed by "textuality" itself. If, as vulgar postmodernist theory claims, ideology critique places a "closure" at the end of its
narrative of cultural texts, then ludic, blissful, erotic reading
begins with a closure: before reading even starts the reader
"always already" knows that the meaning of the film or text is to
be found in its immanent operations, in the "text" itself. "Meaning," in the most radical form of process reading, is a text and, as
Barthes states, the text "is held in language, [and] only exists in
the movement of a discourse" (1977, 157). To be more precise,
the meaning of a text in process theory is endless, unpredictable,
and surprising combinations in language. However, this is only
an apparent "openness" because these linguistic combinations
are all subject to the laws of intelligibility of language and as
such are always already determined by these laws (they are closural). This is one reason why all process readings are pre-
dictable repetitions of and variations on one Reading: a Reading
that finds in all texts of culture, from Plato to Mallarme, panhistorical (linguistic) tropic slippages that are mastered by the violence of the logocentric desires for presence.

"Closure" of meaning is part of the political, economic, and
ideological struggles over the signs of culture. A radical reading
not only marks its own closure but also foregrounds it as an indication of its own engagement in these struggles. It has, in other
words, a political self-reflexivity about its own closure and closural effects in the political economy of cultural signification.
Clearly such a closure is very different from the "natural" closure that traditional humanist film criticism imposes on its discourses. Traditional closure is a mark of nostalgia for the resolu-

tion of social contradictions that cannot be resolved in practice. Radical and politically self-reflexive closure, on the other hand, is a heightening of these contradictions and a marking of the socioeconomic struggles over the construction of the real in culture. By its own self-reflexive closure, radical postmodern discourse takes a position and indicates its own engagement in class-gender-race struggles. Process reading, on the contrary, contains the struggles over meaning through an everlasting deferral of "closure"—by bracketing the outcome of reading. The refusal of closure, in other words, is a refusal to confront or contest the conclusions and consequences of the text (which historically make them intelligible) and instead deals with their process of signification. This mode of reading, for example, allows the fascist text (Celine's writings, for instance) to have the impact of its conclusions on the reader while placing those conclusions under interrogative immunity by diverting attention away from them and toward the formal(ist) process of signification. Closure designates the historical sites of social struggles over the real and by doing so places in public discourses the issues that are, at any historical moment, at stake in setting the socioeconomic agenda. In contrast, by bracketing closure and transferring the site of intelligibility from the *knowledge* of telos (closure) to the *pleasure* of undecidability (operations), a process reading conceals the economic instability of the real. This instability is foregrounded in the contesting closures of texts of culture and thus represents the way things are as the way they ought to be. In "process" reading, meaning is posited as the effect of textual playfulness: like play it is open, aleatory and, above all, voluntary. The political outcome of such a conservative move is to reinforce law and order under a very benign representation. To participate in play, it should be remembered, one must first accept the rules of the game and their syntax (law and order). The representation of meaning—which is based on rules—as open and playful, in other words, teaches the player-subject how to cope with the closure of his or her life in a regulated capitalist state.

CHAPTER 3

THE POLITICS OF REALITY

1

In renarrating the tales of contemporary films through the transgressive readings of ideology critique, what is at stake, as I have already suggested, is the construction of social reality. To renarrate is to activate the "other" and thus to destablize and show the contingency of the "existing." Renarration as a reading strategy, then, is a political act that calls attention to the construction of the real and furthermore opens up a space for contesting the existing. To inquire further into the relation between the "existing" tale and its "possible other" and to understand the urgency of seeing films politically, we need to investigate, at some length, the production of the "real" in culture.

Films, like novels, paintings, and even music, are often regarded as reflections, reports, or at the least interpretations of reality: interpretation in the sense of a representation of something prior to and independent from the very historical process of sense making and understanding; in short, interpretation as an external and additional act. Such a commonsensical view of the relation between the arts and reality has important political implications. By regarding films or other forms of art as reports, interpretations, or reflections of the real, such attitudes assume that reality is a "natural" order and exists independent of films: that there is something "out there" which is autonomous; and films are merely statements, of varying degrees of accuracy, made about it. The tale is taken to be the tale of the "real" and not a tale of the way in which the real is made intelligible. In fact most of our "debates" and discussions about the films we have seen are based on the notion that, through our independent and unique consciousness, we have direct, individual access to that autonomous reality and know beforehand what it is like. It is this "beforehand" knowledge of the nature of the real that in fact gives us the authority to judge a film as good (faithful to our knowledge of the real) or inferior, that is to say unreal (distorting our knowledge of the real).

The camera (or any other device), however, does not simply capture "the real." What it grasps is in Claire Johnston's words " the 'natural' [naturalized] world of the dominant ideology" (1974, 28). It should be by now clear that my argument in this book is that what is assumed to be "out there," *naturally* in the world itself, or "in here," *mentally* (in the mind of the artist, reader or spectator), is in fact put "out there" or "in here" by such diverse discourses of ideology as film, novels, paintings, conversations, jokes, food recipes, and so on. And the function of ideology, as I have discussed in connection with radical theory of ideology, is to explain away and thus naturalize class rule. Films, then, do not so much "report," "reflect," or even "interpret" (in the conventional sense of the word) the world "out there" or "in here" as they do in fact "produce" it and produce it historically; that is to say, within the frames or intelligibility available to a culture at a particular moment. These frames of intelligibility and models of sense making are themselves engendered by the material relations of production in that culture. "Reality," in short, is not "natural" but "constructed." However, unlike the new orthodoxies of poststructuralist film theories, which regard this "construction " of reality to be the effect of the internal signifying activities of the film itself, I argue that reality is "constructed" by a society's political, economic, theoretical, and ideological practices (including signifying activities such as film making and film watching). Ideology participates in the construction of cultural reality by providing a (seemingly) coherent and integrated view of life and a sustained theory of reality for members of a culture, thus making available to them a battery of "obvious" answers that give the historically contingent world a look of naturalness and permanence. By representing the historical as natural, ideology facilitates the perpetuation of the dominant social arrangements and thus guarantees the continuation of the ruling asymmetrical power relations which provide the basis for exploitation under capitalism. By ideology, to repeat, I mean the structure of (mis)representation that explains away social contradictions in the interest of a particular class. In other words, ideology is an ensemble of images, narratives and practices that place the subject in a position of knowledge from which social contradictions that are produced historically are seen as "essential" and thus as "natural."

To take a simple example of the way ideology (and not "nature") constructs reality, when a film posits a "character" as "feminine," it is not simply depicting a female who is already "naturally" feminine. Rather it "produces" the woman as feminine by endowing her with traits that are ideologically desirable for an ideal femininity in a historical society. In doing so it relies on what I have called *historical limits of intelligibility*, what is regarded as "sayable" and thus as "obvious" and "sensible." What is rejected as "odd" or "extreme" is that which contests the "sayable" as the natural. The limits of intelligibility, which are set historically and through social contestations and contradictions, aim at erasing these contestations and contradictions and representing the constructed cultural reality as a seamless natural one. Ideology critique reads the texts of culture against their limits and shows how seamfull they indeed are. The seams are the weak links of ideology—the sites of crisis. Capitalist patriarchy, for example, requires an idea of femininity that reproduces its relations of production and thus perpetuates itself without any serious challenge to its fundamental social norms. The "normal" woman (as feminine) is articulated in contemporary films (one of the many discourses of ideology), for example, as emotionally warm, as physically slim, as intellectually accommodating, as morally sensitive and caring. None of these traits are in themselves and "by nature" definitive of femininity and all are in fact political attributes required for maintaining asymmetrical power relations and thus the exploitative gender relations between men and women in patriarchal capitalism. These traits, however, are not produced in a material vacuum: a society "desires" that which is historically necessary for its reproduction and can be made intelligible to its members. For instance, slimness—as a mark of the individual's control over her body—becomes moralized-aestheticized ("truth and beauty") and used as a trait of femininity only in a culture that valorizes "control" (as necessary for instrumentalizing nature and accumulating cap-

ital). Such a culture thus produces supporting ideological discourses to naturalize control as a sign of natural femininity. To
be "slim" one has to have "control" over oneself. However, the
same cultural regime that privileges control, in moral and aesthetic terms, also (for its own reproduction) requires that people
consume (relax the control). The moral and aesthetic discourse
of control is thus "supplemented" by the discourse of pleasure
(as marker of success). "Slimness," in short is the "crisis" site of
a social contradiction. As a site of contradiction, "slimness"
might also be an appropriate space to further clarify the politics
of what in the dominant discourses is called *local resistance.* The
person who refuses to go along with the imposed norms of "slimness" and "resists" them in the name of her own power to negate
and surpass (the norm of the social) is not so much "resisting"
the dominant discourse as in fact responding to the hail of the
ruling ideology, which calls upon her in her other subject positions: the subject position of the pleasureful subject who consumes (relaxes control) as mark of her own autonomy and social
power. "Slimness," in short, is a global, political, and economic
category (crisis moment of contradictory structures of domination) and not a local, aesthetic one. As such it cannot be "resisted" regionally and in isolation from those global structures that
construct socially necessary subjectivities. By constructing slimness in its text as a mark of ideal femininity, film identifies the
slim female with femininity itself rather than one possible (ideological) version of it.

Film, in other words, locates the spectator in ideologically
produced frames of meaning in terms of which he makes sense
of specific representations as not only feasible but natural. The
spectator of Jean-Jacques Beineix's *Diva,* for example, is placed
in a position of knowledge from which he "immediately" recognizes Cynthia as "feminine" (as having the traits necessary to
make her nurturing, vulnerable, accommodating and passionate)
while he rejects the policewoman in the film as definitely
"unfeminine" (as lacking these traits). Neither character is in
herself, inherently (by nature) either feminine or unfeminine.
The discourses of the film render the urgencies and interpella-
tions of ideology plausible and thus construct one as feminine
and the other as unfeminine. In doing so, the film provides the

spectator with a model of understanding: a grid of intelligibility according to which he can identify the woman in terms of the prevailing cultural codes of femininity and thereby contribute to the survival and perpetuation of the existing social arrangements. Femininity—as the effect of the correspondence between a female and ideological attributes—is thus not already "out there" in nature; rather it is put there by ideology through such cultural discourses as film, which represent the "out there" as having derived directly from the structure of the world itself and thus prevent any interrogation of the processes involved in the ideological construction of the real.

What we are taught to think of as the "real" is the accumulated residue of all the things that have been put "out there" by films, novels, paintings, music, and other acts of ideological meaning making in culture that are themselves historical articulations of social contestations. Films (and other works of art) are *related* to reality, but this relation is not one of reflection, reporting, or even interpretation. Rather films are related to reality because they actually participate in the cultural act of producing the real. Furthermore, they do so along with other art forms and discourses of culture, but all suppress their own role in the production of reality for political reasons, which I will discuss. Consequently their construction of reality is represented as a neutral reporting or an objective interpretation of an already existing reality.

An important question here is why the role of films (like that of any other art form) in the production of the real is concealed, and why films are usually perceived as being reports, reflections, or interpretations of the real rather than its active producers? The suppression of the productive role of film in constituting the real is ideologically and politically necessary: through such suppression the alliance of dominant interests (the hegemonic class, gender, and race groups), whose values and ideas constitute the cognitive environment of a society, manages to represent its interested view of reality as the real itself and thus endow it with inevitability. Moreover it attributes that real to the very structure of the world instead of acknowledging the real as an effect of the particular social relations this alliance has with the rest of the people as part of the dominant economic arrangements. The political and economic interests of this alliance, in other words, are furthered by representing the real as nonconstituted, as the inevitable outcóme of the "natural" organization of reality itself while denying it is produced by a culture's specific historical relations.

To understand the process involved in the production of the real by various acts of meaning making, which are all ideologically motivated, it is important to distinguish between the *actual* and the *real.* My discussion, it should be clear is about the constitution of the "real" and not the ontological status of the "actual" (the nature of "being"). Therefore when I state that the signifying practices mediate the economic, political, and ideological series in a culture and produce the real, I am not saying that they produce the actual in the sense of creating trees, snakes, tables, or the physicality of male and female persons. Instead, signifying activities (languages) are grids by means of which the undifferentiated continuum of nature is differentiated, and through such segmentation the various parts of nature become known as trees, snakes, tales, and male and female. Human beings, for instance, as long as they are part of the continuum of nature, remain undifferentiated from each other and the rest of nature. They have no meaning, no reality since they do not play any role in the organization of cultural life and do not take part in social and economic arrangements. Reality, in other words, is a cultural and not a natural matter. However, as soon as actual individuals enter the domain of culture (which is before they are even born), they are differentiated by its symbolic order, its codes of gender; they acquire meaning as specific kinds of "masculine" or "feminine" persons. They become culturally "real" and from that point on participate in the cultural negotiations and organization of the social.

The transformation of the actual into the real takes place through a culture's various languages or discourses, which produce differences out of the sameness of nature. Without language (differences) there will be no (cultural) reality. Film is one such language in those cultures with access to film-making technologies. Through its various practices and discourses, such as film, a culture endows actual individuals with the cultural attributes of masculinity and femininity, thereby constituting them as gendered subjects in that society. Language, as I have already suggested, acts as a historical and social entity. The role of film in this process of engenderment, incidentally, indicates that signifying practices are part of the material organization of a culture and are effects of its mode of production.

A culture that has no access to film technology is not able to use films as part of the meaning-making activities by which it changes nature into culture. It will have to rely on other means of communication to make the components of nature intelligible. It is, of course, inevitable that in our century such societies will come into contact with more advanced, film-producing countries and end up importing films. However, to understand and enjoy these imported films, the consuming culture will have to make sense of the world in an essentially alien language. It will have to interpret the real in terms of the unfamiliar codes underlying the communication process of imported films. The conflicts between the codes of the alien films and the modes of intelligibility of the native culture often lead to confusion regarding the established reality and a dissembling of traditional modes of making sense. Such a dissembling in turn opens the way for what is nothing other than a mode of colonization that might be called (post) coloniality: a form of domination befitting the late capitalism of the Age of Information; one that exploits by redrawing the map of the real according to the interests of the owners of the ruling technologies and their culture. This is why for some time now the Third World and the First World have been contesting the flow of information with the Third World calling for a "new information order." This contestation is, in the last instance, a struggle over intelligibility, over the means of making sense and, ultimately, over the meaning and boundaries of the real in the contemporary world. What is the real? Is it what the technologies of the First World make of nature and posit as the given reality, or what the Third World, by its own frames of intelligibility, produces from the actual and proposes as the real?

Access to film-making technologies should not be taken literally: many societies have access to film-producing technologies but are unable to make the texts of their films an effective part of the construction of the real simply because their texts are marginalized by the film and information texts of more powerful economic interests. This mode of neocolonialism attempts to make the world intelligible in terms that legitimate the dominant economic interests of transnational corporations and can be clearly seen in the post-World War II expansion of the U.S. culture industries. In this period, American news agencies such as the Associated Press and United Press International displaced other news agencies, including such European ones as Reuters, and became the main providers of international news. In this period the world has been largely constructed ("reported") through the eyes of Americans. Also in this period "Hollywood films," according to Herbert J. Schiller, "with considerable assistance from the Motion Picture Export Association, saturated the world's movie screens." Along with the news and movies, "American television programs, replete with images of U.S. products and services, became the staple fare of viewers the world over."

Against such a one-sided flow of representations, images, and ideas Third World nations called for a new information order. Their call has been recuperated by the American media as nothing less than the violation of free enterprise and the restriction and censorship of the "free flow of information." But the "free flow of information" is not neutral, rather it guarantees the domination of Western images and representations of reality throughout the world. In 1973, in one of the earliest protests against this interpretation of "freedom," the Group of 77 and the Non-Aligned Movement issued a statement in Algiers that in part reads: "It is an established fact that the activities of imperialism are not confined solely to the political and economic fields but also cover the cultural and social fields, thus imposing an alien ideological domination over the peoples of the developing world" (Schiller, 1985, 248). This contestation indicates, among other things, the close connection between that which is called the real in each culture and the material means and conditions under which the actual is turned into the real. The boundaries of the real are not fixed. They vary according to the frames of intelligibility, and these frames, as I shall argue, are themselves effects of historically determined modes of production.

The encounter with the actual is part of the material processes themselves. Making sense of this encounter locates the actual in the cultural and endows the natural with significance for a particular group of people, who by virtue of this shared significance are brought together as members of a culture. The issue here is *the constitution of the real* and not *the existence of the actual:* to confuse the actual with the real is to bypass the politics of meaningfulness. When Marx observes that "the *entire so-called history of the world* is nothing but the creation of man through human labor" (1974, 100), he is addressing the question of the construction of the real in culture. History (the real) is produced by human labor: the site of meaning is not nature, but nature transformed into social product, into the real. To substitute the actual for the real and tie language (or signifying practices) to the actual is precisely to postulate meaning as natural, given, inevitable, and thus unchangeable. Such a move is a strategy of containment: it is part of the dominant ideology's effort to mystify culture by representing it as nature and offer the real as actual so that culturally constructed values are put forth as immutable natural givens (Nichols, 1981; MacBean, 1975). In this way they are placed beyond interrogation and class contestation. The assumption here is that we have to adjust to these given values rather than attempt to change them since they are, like the laws of nature, unchangeable and universal. They are, in other words, part of the order of things. If meaning (the real) is produced through cultural practices, it is important to examine this process a little more closely.

For the sake of clarity and simplicity, we can use the example of a language (English) as a signifying system through which the actual is transformed into the real for (English-) speaking persons. To do this we have to first extend the idea of "renarrating" that I have so far used in connection with such texts as films. I have argued that in renarrating a film, the tale that is obvious is obscured and the *other*—nonempirical—is made seeable as part of a "possible" reorganization of the film's economy of signification and its political economy of the real. Renarrating, I have suggested, is a mode of intervention in the "existing"—a way of producing a different story (the "real") from the same empirical materials. Renarrating can be equally effective in obscuring the obvious "problematics" of theory and in producing from its discourse an*other* problematics. The discourses of Saussure, Hjelmslev, and Eco, for instance, can be renarrated so that through them the problematics of the real can be rearticulated with the difference of "practice" and not simply that of the "formal" (difference). We can conceptualize this process by employing some of the concepts of Ferdinand de Saussure and, following him, Louis Hjelmslev. Each signifying system (in this example, the English language) is composed of two planes: the plane of the signifier (expression) and the plane of the signified (content). These two planes are in turn constituted by two strata: the stratum of "substance" and that of "form." The two terms are easily misunderstood since, as Roland Barthes warns us, "each of them has a weighty lexical past" (1968, 40). "The form," according to Barthes, is "what can be described exhaustively, simply and coherently (epistemological criteria) by linguistics without resorting to any extralinguistic premise." The "substance," to continue Barthes's exposition, "is the whole set of aspects of linguistic phenomena which cannot be described without resorting to extralinguistic premises"(1968, 40). Because both "form" and "substance" exist on the plane of expression as well as the plane of content, a four-term analytic scheme emerges:

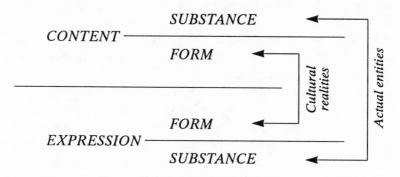

SIGNIFYING SYSTEM

On the plane of expression, substance (in a language) is all the sounds that the human speech organs can produce. Using the International Phonetic Alphabet, some are transcribed as

θ d b ə s t x

These "phones" are physical ("actual") events, and as such are nonlinguistic (noncultural) entities that belong to nature, to acoustic actuality. They acquire cultural "reality" if and only after they have been given a form by the phonological system of a language. The substance, "phone" (an actuality of sound), acquires form and becomes a "phoneme" (a culturally meaningful part of language) and in being enformed by the phonological laws of a language (cultural codes) constitutes a part of the cultural reality. In English [s], [b], [o] are "real" sounds (phonemes) in the language, while as far as the English sound system is concerned [x] is a substance, that is culturally nonexistent (mere physical actuality). However, [x] is "real" (a phoneme) in some languages, including modern Persian.

Although the features of substance and form on the plane of expression are fairly easy to determine and demonstrate, their characteristics on the plane of content are much more complex. The substance of the content is described by Saussure as "the whole mass of thoughts and emotions common to mankind independently of the language they speak—a kind of nebulous and undifferentiated conceptual medium out of which meanings are formed in particular languages by the conventional association of a certain complex of sounds with a certain part of the conceptual medium" (Saussure, 1966, 111–12; Lyons, 1968, 56). Such a description of substance, like some other aspects of Saussurian theories, is psychologistic. We can reduce the psychologism of Saussure's idea of the substance of content and provide a "material" basis for it by theorizing the substance of content as the undifferentiated continuum of all perceptual, conceptual, and physical "events" that the human sensory system is capable of producing and responding to. Like the substance of expression in language, which is composed of all the sounds that human speech organs can produce, the substance of content is an effect of the materiality of the human sensory system and, as such, a natural and actual entity. In perceiving a cardinal flying against the sky, in responding to the darkness after sunset, the human nervous system responds to an actual event. This event is then made intelligible by being situated on the historically specific set of cultural grids that differentiate the entity "cardinal" from all other birds and also from the "sky." Depending on the occasion, the intelligibility of the event can be increased by describing it as "beautiful." "Cardinal," it might be said, has a more or less clear "referent," whereas "beautiful" derives its "sense" from belonging to the semantic field that in English also includes "lovely," "attractive," "pretty," and so on. The meaning of "beautiful," in other words, is the effect of a sense relationship in this particular semantic field in English. The substance of such terms as "beautiful" then is more a sense relation among various members of a semantic field in a given language than it is a referable physicality. This, however, does not mean that terms such as *cardinal* (which have a physical "referent") are in themselves any more accessible to us through the "referent" (rather than through the "sense") than is *beautiful,* which is more obviously a cultural term. Both terms acquire form and thus intelligibility from the cultural grid on which they are placed. Both entities are, in other words, intelligible as cultural terms rather than as actual or natural categories.

To make this last point about entities like "cardinal" a little clearer, it may be helpful to examine color terms in various languages and to investigate their differences. Like "cardinal," color terms seem to have a clear referent: they are assumed commonsensically to be physical phenomena and as such directly accessible to the viewer without cultural mediation. Modern linguistics, however, proves otherwise. Color terms in various languages are not merely different labels for the "same thing" (language is not a mere nomenclature), but are signifiers that enform the color spectrum and thus make it culturally intelligible in different ways.

Because colors have physical existence, it is convenient to think that language merely reflects that existence and what is actually "out there" is present to us in all its fullness. However, this is far from being the case: we understand colors not because we respond to them directly through our sensory organs, but because the responses of our sensory organs are made meaningful for us by the language. Different languages make sense of this physical continuum in startlingly different and dissimilar ways, thus putting in question the commonsensical view that nature is in itself intelligible. The English word *brown,* for instance, "has no equivalent in French (it would be translated as *brun, marron,* or even *jaun,* according to the particular shade and the kind of noun it qualifies... there's no equivalent to *blue* in Russian—the words *goluboj* and *sinij* (usually translated as 'light blue' and 'dark blue' respectively), refer to what are in Russian distinct colors, not different shades of the same color, as their translation into English might suggest" (Lyons, 1968, 56–57)

The role of culture in turning the actual into the real is made even clearer when we examine the color terms in languages, such as Hanunoo, having a system of color terms that, unlike those of Western languages, are not based entirely on hue, luminosity, and saturation, which are often considered to be the three dimensional substances that underlie color terms. In "Hanunoo Color Terms," H. C. Conklin has demonstrated that the four main terms of the Hanunoo color system are based on lightness, darkness, wetness, and dryness (1955, 339–44). The distinction between "wetness" and "dryness" is not simply a matter of hue (green versus red); "a shiny, wet, *brown* section of newly cut bamboo" is described by the term that is often used for light green. According to Conklin, not only is color in its technical sense not a universal, "natural" category, but the very opposition of terms by which the substance of color is determined depends on culturally important features (Lyons, 1968, 431).

In *Pertinence et pratique,* which forms the basis of Umberto Eco's interesting essay, "How Culture Conditions the Colors We See," Luis Prieto calls these culturally important features "pertinent" points according to which a signifying system makes the world understandable. These points of pertinence are themselves effects of practice (culture) not nature. In his exposition of Prieto, Eco provides a simple example of how practical purposes (daily practices determined by social arrangements and not by the actual) produce pertinent categories according to which we endow meaning and significance to our world, make sense of it. If, Eco writes,

> I have on a table before me a large crystal ashtray, a paper cup and a hammer, I can organize these pieces of furniture of my limited world into a twofold system of pertinences. If my practical purpose is to collect some liquid, I then isolate a positive class whose members are the paper cup and the ashtray, and a negative class whose only member is the hammer. If, on the contrary, my purpose is to throw a missile at

an enemy, the the heavy ashtray and the hammer will belong to the same class, in opposition to the light and useless paper cup. Practices select pertinences. The practical purpose does not, however, depend on a free decision on my part: material constraints are in play, since I cannot decide that the hammer can act as a container and the paper cup as a missile. Thus practical purposes, decisions about pertinences and material constraints will interact in leading a culture to segment the continuum of its own experience into a given form of the content. To say that a signification system makes communication processes possible means that one can usually communicate only about those cultural units that a given signification system has made pertinent. It is, then, reasonable to suppose now that one can better perceive that which a signification system has isolated and outlined as pertinent. (1985, 163)

Through the determination of pertinences the natural order is intervened into, disrupted, reorganized, and turned into culture. What Eco and Prieto do not inquire into is the role of "power" and "exploitation" in the constitution of "pertinence." Eco merely refers to "material constraints" and seems to understand these constraints in a purely mechanical sense (the constraints, for example, that a hammer cannot act as a container). But daily practices, motivated by power in culture, are processes aimed at transforming various constraints: scarcity of resources, for example, can lead to the exertion of power to obtain them through exploitative acts of imperialism and colonialism. Also, through the exercise of power, points of pertinence are set in a culture by directing daily practices toward goals that legitimate exploitations of the ruling classes in a culture. This is done through the operation of ideology that, in a sense, is the practice in a society through which pertinences are naturalized for an entire culture. In Wim Wenders's *Paris, Texas,* which will be discussed in detail in this book, the film (the signifying system) posits the family as the pertinent point for making the world meaningful. Inquiring into the family, it further assumes blood relation as the pertinent feature according to which a genuine family (people with blood ties) are distinguished from a pseudo-family (people united by affection and choice, e.g., adopted children). The daily practices that determine such a pertinence are themselves shaped by economics of patriarchy that is, in the last instance, a system of power for the maintenance of exploitative gender relations in society.

The form of content, then, segments the substance according to the principles of pertinence established by material practices, which are tied to obtaining and maintaining power in a culture—the power to own and operate the means of production. The content of a language is more an effect of the pertinences that a culture accepts as necessary coordinates for making distinctions rather than a space in language in which the actuality of nature shines through. "What is content?" asks Eco in response to the problems involved in inquiring into the relation between substance and form, actuality and culture. His answer is helpful and should be quoted in full here. Content, according to Eco,

> is not the external world. Expressions do not *signify* things or states of the world. At most, they are *used* to communicate with somebody about states of the world. If I say that ravens are black and unicorns white, I am undoubtedly uttering a statement about a state of the world. (In the first instance, I am speaking of the world of our experience, in the second I am speaking about a possible world of which unicorns are inhabitants—the fact that they are white is part of the state of affairs of that world.) However, a term like 'raven' or 'unicorn' does not necessarily refer to a 'thing': it refers instead to a cultural unit, to an aspect of our organization of the world. (1985, 162)

Pertinences, however, it should be emphasized, are not given once and for all. They change as a result of historical transformations taking place in the political, economic, and ideological practices of a culture. Until recently in the English language, for example, the pertinent principle according to which women were differentiated and addressed was the principle of "belonging." According to the pertinent feature of "belonging," women were separated into "Mrs." (belonging to a man) and "Miss" (not yet belonging to a man and thus available to interested men). Transformations in contemporary technologies and the increasing need for an educated, skilled labor force to develop, produce, and manage them expanded the recruitment of women for various positions. The increased presence of women in the workplace, particularly in positions of some responsibility and authority, then resulted in such changes as the legislation of anti-sexist laws and a shifting of the pertinent features in terms of which women have been distinguished. The two-term system (Mrs. or Miss) was modified and a three-term system in which "belonging" is somewhat blurred has emerged. In the new scheme women continue to be marked as belonging to a man (Mrs.) or as traditionally minded and not yet belonging to a man (Miss). But the addition of a new term allows for women to be categorized according to the more egalitarian and liberal of not-belonging and not wishing to belong to a man (Ms.). The substance of the form (femaleness) has not changed; what has changed is the mode through which that substance is made part of culture and thus turned into the "real." It is not the substance that determines meaning, it is the frame of intelligibility that recognizes segments of the substance as real and suppresses other segments as unreal or nonvisible.

The changes in the forms of address for women in English indicate a rearrangement of the system of pertinences under pressure from economic practices. This reordering of pertinences is transmitted and naturalized by ideology. As I have suggested before, part of the operation of ideology is to conceal the categories of culture in terms of which meaning is produced as ideological practices aim at representing the relationship between language and actuality as a direct unmediated one. Such a direct relationship gives language the authority of the actual by representing it as inevitable and necessary. Culture uses various modes of signification such as film, painting and fiction to suppress these mediating terms and naturalize the process of communicating values that ultimately legitimate the reigning order of things. The arts, and other acts of communication, naturalize cultural values and attitudes by constructing what might be called the *cultural inventory of representations.* These images, narratives, and problem-solving schemes instruct the members of a culture in a concrete manner on how to read and respond to the various texts of their daily life and, consequently, how to relate to the world around them and understand the conditions of their existence as social beings. The arts use various strategies of representation, particularly those that might be called *realistic,* to subdue and in many cases suppress their own discursively constitutive role in constructing values. They offer values and attitudes not so much as effects of signification but as reflections of the actual, as representations that go beyond the reach of the process of signification.

2

The world that emerges from empiricist theories of knowledge equates the *real* with the *actual* and exists outside the economic, political, and ideological practices of culture in a more or less "natural" state of objecthood and immanence. Both traditional (humanist) film criticism and ludic postmodern film theory, in their different ways, are empiricist theories that locate the "real" beyond the reach of mediations of the social. Given the official differences said to exist between the two and the (in)famous quarrels between them, my statement may at first seem to be obscure. However, as I have suggested before, both traditional film criticism and ludic film theory propose that knowledge is immanent to the object of knowledge and not an effect produced through class, race, and gender struggles. The difference between the two is in the way they name the object and the site of knowledge. In traditional film criticism the "object" of knowledge is the world "out there"—the world of common sense in which the individual with his inherent unitary consciousness and identity conducts his daily life. In ludic theory the natural world of common sense and its given meanings are deconstructed and shown to be a very "unnatural" world of constructed discourses that produce sliding, unstable, precarious, and nonunitary positions of subjectivities: that which traditional film criticism regards as "natural" turns out to be an effect of "language" in ludic postmodern theory. However, in its "de-construction" of the natural, ludic theory keeps the immanence of the new object of knowledge (language or textuality) intact and out of the reach of historical intervention. The subject acquires its subjectivity (its ability to utter "I") by entering language and the symbolic order produced by language—both of which are considered formal, panhistorical systems of differences (Lacan, 1977). In other words, ludic postmodern theory simply replaces one ahistorical world (of commonsensical, natural meanings) for another (of textualized meanings held in language). Both theories regard "knowledge" to be immanent in the object of knowledge and therefore equate knowledge with "experience" (of the object of knowledge).

Consequently, traditional film criticism regards the "meaning" of the film to precede the film text and reside in the natural world of common sense that is the referent of the film and determines its significance for the viewer. In ludic postmodern theory, on the other hand, the textual organization and articulation of the signifiers—their internal differences—provide a meaning effect that makes sense of the film. The traditional empiricism of film criticism is thus displaced by the ludic postmodern empiricism of the "trace," to use Derrida's term (1981). In both, knowledge (meaning) is asocial: it lies either in the natural world or in the formal structures of language; it is, in short, immanent and not produced by economic, political, and ideological practices.

The ultimate goal of empiricism—whether the empiricism of common sense or the empiricism of the trace—is to represent the "real" (made in social struggles) as the immanent world of "actuality"—whether the actuality of natural-common sense or of the textual—and consequently to posit the "experience" of that world as its "truth." *Experience* could be natural daily experience (in traditional criticism) or textual-aesthetic experience (*jouissance* in ludic theory). The political importance of such a move, it should be clear by now, is that the experiencer (the person) is privileged as the knower who knows because he has direct, and thus "authoritative" and incontestable, access to the truth residing in the object of knowledge itself. Such a view, in its traditional as well as ludic versions, represents the world as autonomous and self-regulating: it is organized according to its own internal laws and is thus ("naturally" or "aesthetically") complete and beyond intervention. All we can do is adjust to it. The techniques of "close" reading, which are the dominant modes of understanding and analysis in both traditional film criticism and ludic theory, are marks of this acceptance of the world as it is. No close reading "changes" (intervenes in) the object of study—it merely attempts to "know" it better, in other words, to get adjusted to it through "appreciation." These theories then support the status quo by accepting the "existing" as the "real" and considering the visible tale to be the (only) tale of the film. To point up the politics of this mode of knowing, "profit," in the empiricist view, is derived from the "commodity" itself (the empirical object). In *Capital 1*, however, Marx demonstrates that "profit" is the effect of a *structure* of exploitation (the surplus value) and not the outcome of the visible (commodity itself). Similarly, the "truth" of *Diva* is neither in the viewer's "experience" of the "character" (traditional criticism) nor in its "textual articulation" (ludic theory) but in the abstract (invisible?) *structure* of gender politics in late capitalism.

Experience, far from being the means of access to truth, is itself produced by ideology: there are no "experiences" only "experience effects"; in other words, the effects of social structures. Empiricism represents experience as autointelligible— something whose meaning is in itself and does not need to be "interpreted" in terms of "external" references and criteria. "Experience," E. P. Thompson declares in his manifesto on contemporary empiricism, *The Poverty of Theory*, "walks in without knocking at the door, and announces deaths, crises of subsistence, trench warfare, unemployment, inflation, genocide" (1978, 201). "Inflation," in other words, is not a concept produced in economics (an ensemble of knowledges historically produced through social struggles) to "explain" structures and practices in the political economy but a self-evident reality, the truth of which is directly accessible to the experiencer—the free subject or individual. The meaning of experience, however, does not reside in itself; it is in the historical frames of intelligibility that situate the subject in a knowledge position from which she understands or interprets her experience. Of course, one of the roles of dominant ideology is to erase these other surrounding frames of understanding so that experience is represented as self-evident and at no time mediated by the economic-political-ideological series. Positing experience as truth is an attempt to erase these historical structures and thus produce the subject-of-truth as a free, panhistorical agent. By locating truth in experience (of the existing), film theory puts forth the dominant tale (which is empirically available through common sense) and suppresses the other tales that are not visible in the discourses of common sense. Experience, in other words, fixes and stabilizes the tale, whereas ideology critique provides the necessary knowledge of the *structures* of experience and demonstrates that the stable is "stable" only through operation of the supporting assumptions of the dominant ideology.

Radical film theory thus regards experience to be a site of the dominant ideology and attempts to offer different understandings of experience through counterhegemonic readings. In doing so it constructs other modes of seeing films and produces other cultural products that contest the empirical given and see the "other" tale in the visible one. To understand how an "experience" of something, in and of itself, does not explain that thing but is itself interpreted in terms of frames of intelligibility, one has only to consider that the "gap" between the "American dream" and the daily realities of the lives of millions of Americans, for example, can be "experienced" in a number of ways. Traditional film criticism does not see any "gap" at all in its interpretations—just different degrees of fulfillment caused by the "natural" dissimilarities and singularities of free people who have equality. Ludic postmodern theory, however, sees a "gap" but interprets it as "difference," a difference that is equally "natural" because it is constitutive of the social "difference" *within* the subject and is the condition of possibility of the social. The social is, in other words, the subject of the laws of differential textuality. In neither of these modes of seeing films is "difference" understood as related to social "conflicts." Radical theory, on the other hand, recognizes that the gap is neither "natural" nor a manifestation of a transhistorical "difference" but is historically produced out of social contradictions that can be eradicated under other possible social arrangements. Each of these modes of understanding, therefore, makes sense of the "experience" of the gap differently. Through its writings bourgeois film criticism and theory places the reader in a position of knowledge requiring him to adjust to and accept the "gap" as the necessary condition of possibility of a differential social order. Radical theory, on the other hand, uses the "gap" as the symptom of social contradictions through which class consciousness can be developed in order to remove the gap—to transform social exploitation and inequality.

Radical film theory is important because, among other things, it is involved in the ideological struggle to provide discourses that make sense of the gap—differences—in emancipatory ways that lead to the displacement of the existing structures of exploitation. Radical film theory seeks to make the viewer, whose life is fraught with the contradictions of capitalism, aware of the gap as a historical effect and to enable her to erase it by erasing the social order that underlies it. Through making "other" sense of daily experience radical film theory can intervene in the discourses of the dominant ideology.

However, dominant ideology tries to render radical theory unintelligible by positing it as "extreme" and "unreasonable" discourse while reifying daily "experience" as empirically valid, self-same, and, in and of itself, a reliable conduit to truth. It does so by producing a set of cultural "obviousnesses" that enable the dominant representations of the real in a culture to be assured continued existence without the requirement of "proof." The notion, for example, that wifehood and motherhood are a "natural" part of being a woman or the idea that "experience" is the ultimate test of truth are among such obviousnesses. In constructing the obvious, ideology postulates a world that has always already been there and will always already be there. In other words, ideology puts forth a world of eternal truths: unchangeable, inevitable, and natural. The "obviousness" of ideology situates the individual in a position of intelligibility within the social arrangements from which she either does not see the constructedness (unnaturalness) of the dominant social order—the fact that the existing social arrangements are the effect of asymmetrical power relations—or if she sees the social as constructed, she considers it to be "obviously" fair and just. She will, therefore, come to regard the prevailing social organizations as the place within which she has to live her life—the place, in other words, to which she has to get adjusted—rather than treat them as the site of contestation and change. The discourses of ideology are aimed at removing social contradictions and thus eliminating social struggle as the source of history and the production of cultural reality. Such a view of social and cultural reality is necessary to maintain the reigning social organizations and the class relations they legitimate as well as to explain the prevailing socioeconomic hierarchy and their fundamental exploitative practice: the transference of wealth away from its producers to the owners of the means of production.

Films are among the many discursive devices that ideology uses to construct and circulate the culturally obvious. Wim Wenders's *Paris, Texas,* for instance, is based on one cultural obviousness of contemporary common sense: the "fact" that the family is the most important aspect of life and that a true and genuine family is based on a blood tie. By representing the family as a biological and natural unit, the film suppresses the social constructedness of the family. It offers this form of the family as an eternal and unalterable given even though it is the effect of certain historically specific arrangements. This move to mask the cultural as natural and disguise the real as actual is one of the most important functions of ideology because through such an operation the world of culture is endowed with the authority and certitude of nature—a certitude that supports the workings of the prevailing economic regime. Moreover, the representation of existing social relations as natural is one of the processes a society undertakes to reproduce the conditions of its own production. The obviousnesses engendered by ideology play a central role in these reproductive processes. In opposition to these ideological obviousnesses, radical film theory and criticism produce a countertale to demonstrate that the seemingly natural and given is in fact constructed, and since it is constructed, it can be de-constructed and remade under the sign of different social arrangements. Referring to the ideological discourses that represent the empirical as the real, Claire Johnston declares that the "cinema involves the production of signs" and "the sign is always a product"; what the seemingly impartial camera records is not the real but "the 'natural' world of the dominant ideology. . . . The 'truth' of our oppression cannot be 'captured' on celluloid with the 'innocence' of the camera: it has to be constructed, manufactured" (1974, 31). Ideology critique "constructs" the "truth" of our oppression.

CHAPTER 4

THE CULTURAL POLITICS OF INTIMACY

1

The horizons of private life in postmodern culture are set by the discourses of intimacy—the state of plenitude and presence in which one person, in completeness and without "difference," is accessible to another. Intimacy, however, like all modes of cultural intelligibility, is a social construct and produced in response to the needs for the particular modes of subjectivities necessary for reproducing the dominant relations of production. Through naming and thus recognizing certain kinds of relating to others as *intimacy* and by implication designating other modes of relating as *indifference* or *hostility,* the reigning ideology organizes the historically available relationships along socially necessary lines. In doing so it privileges a specific set of values that then becomes part of the complex ensemble of social strategies of intelligibility used to construct and circulate what it regards to be "the real."

Intimacy, contrary to this commanding common sense, is the effect of the intricate political operations involved in interpellating subjects, and modes of intimacy vary not only from culture to culture but quite significantly within the same culture from one class to another. Intimacy is therefore neither universal nor "natural." Discourses of ideology, however, represent intimacy as inevitably "natural" and thus as private, asocial, personal, and, most important, transdiscursive—they mark it as situated outside the cultural series. This ideological representation of intimacy is politically critical because if intimacy can be represented as outside the reach of history and culture then, it follows, those who are intimate with each other derive their relationship not from a given historical and social situation but by virtue of their own panhistorical individuality. They are, in other words, free subjects whose freedom is "given" and not implicated in the discourses of culture or in social and political modalities. Intimacy is thus the ultimate sign of their sovereignty as individuals; it signals their freedom. In fact intimacy is made to appear so private in order for it to be taken as "natural" as the personal seems to be: I am what I am (a "natural" and transhistorical fact) and, because of what I am, I have certain types of relations and particular forms of intimacy (which are also "natural" and transhistorical).

These forms of intimacy, however, are always already limited by the historical situation in which the subject is located and thus by the subject positions available. One "chooses" one's intimates not "freely" but in an overdetermined way from within the constraints of class, sex, race, and religion, to mention only the most significant ones. However, to acknowledge these constraints is to see the operation of economic, political, and ideological practices in the production of intimacy. Furthermore, it is to become aware that intimacy in late capitalist societies is far from being a mark of individuality and freedom, rather it is one of the most apersonal and socially overdetermined modes of subjectivity in postmodern life. Intimacy is one of the social apparatuses of intelligibility necessary for the operation of the existing social arrangements. It produces "free" individuals who are then recruited by the dominant economic order, which is maintained by such notions as "free enterprise," "entrepreneurship," "originality," and, most important, "competition."

The limits of the "freedom" of the individual, however, immediately become clear as soon as she enters the domain of the social, and discovers the extent of her embeddedness in the social "collectivity." Such a sense of social solidarity works against the fundamental notions of "free enterprise" and its accompanying "free market" based on "competition." To background this social solidarity, the discourses of ideology designate the social as secondary and privilege "intimacy" as the site for manifesting true and authentic selfhood. What, of course, makes the dismissal of the social as the site of difference, absence and lack—secondariness—so commonsensically possible in postmodern culture is the ideological organization of the social in late capitalism. The social is represented as the space of the "role" not the "self," the site of "division" not "unity" where, in short, one is not a "true" person but is involved, as in the (false) fictions of the theatre, in playing a game. Such a representation of the social as essentially and universally nonpersonal, false, and thus a form of "absence" erases the historical specificity of the social in contemporary society and gives intimacy its particular features.

Postmodern intimacy is (historically) specified above all as the "other" of the social: it is the moment of "unitariness," "presence," "noncompetition," and contrary to the social, noninterrogatory, and "supportive." It is basically emotional and affirmative instead of analytical and inquiring. Under such terms of familiarity, one does not "know," rather one "feels" the other. Such a relationship prohibits any form of critical reflexivity about the relationship and forbids any investigative attitude toward it. In contemporary intimacy, supportive relationships prevail—whether in the appreciation of art in the aesthetic domain, the worship of God in the religious space of culture, or parent and child interactions in the realm of the family. In each the emotional is privileged while the analytical and interrogatory are suppressed. This denial of the interrogatory is necessary for the security of the dominant ideology and the view of reality it propagates: the ideological and its common sense survive only in the sphere of the emotional out of reach of social interrogation. An interrogative attitude in a relationship is thus represented as a form of aggression, a mode of hostility: the hostile, it is understood, is not suitable for intimacy and its user will be relegated to (punished by) "loneliness."

The assumption underlying such a view of intimacy is that closeness is a moment of plenitude, presence, and pellucidity: an instant in which intimates are free from the mediating forces of culture and society and directly present to each other's consciousness, feelings, and perhaps bodies. An interrogative intimacy (almost a paradox in postmodern culture) is represented in the dominant discourses as aggressive and hostile, but it actually seeks to reground relationships by exposing the political presuppositions and assumptions about intimacy and demystifying the expectations and frames of intelligibility each intimate brings to the association. It points out that private intimacy, which is postulated by dominant culture as the embodiment of similarity, transparency, closeness, and plenitude, is but an exemplary instance of difference, opacity, distance, scarcity, and gaps. It is not the "other" of the social in capitalism but in fact its mirror image. It reveals that opacity and gaps are inevitably inscribed in any relationship in culture, which is a set of conflicting discourses attempting to "explain" its social contradictions. People in contemporary culture are not only incomprehensible to one another but also to themselves. Clarity and transparency are only ideological constructs projected onto intimacy to hide the unavoidable opacity of people produced by the contradictory practices and discourses of a consumer society. A truly interrogative intimacy inquires into the production of codes and the way these codes form and shape intimacy. It is a form of political knowledge of the situatedness and historicity of the relationship as well as of the people involved and regards intimacy as a mode of social collectivity and thus an effect of the social. Through interrogation, intimates locate the politics of intimacy, and instead of forming atomistic relationships, they achieve what Sartre calls the "fused group" (*Critique of Dialectical Reason*).

The privatization of intimacy—whether in the domain of "friendship," "love," or "family," to take three main instances in postmodern culture—is ideologically, politically, and economically necessary. Through such privatization of intimacy, the subjectivities needed by the prevailing organization of the social are produced and maintained. In this space of emotional transcendence the individual who is "exhausted" in the daily competition of the marketplace is "repaired" and restored as part of a viable labor force. Intimacy, in other words, is itself a mode of production: not the production of "things" but the production of that force which produces things—the all-important labor force that is competent, competitive, and consenting to the social relations required for the reproduction of the prevailing economic order.

2

Through various ideological manipulations of its story, *The Big Chill* de-socializes intimacy and presents it as an affectivity that is, in the last instance, personal, private, and in fact a statement against society itself. The outdoor world (and one may take the "outdoors" to be a metonymy for the "outside") according to Michael is a "giant toilet," a place in which to piss and nothing more. Although Michael's statement may seem on the surface to state his urban sensibility and to contradict the close intimacy that Harold, Sam, and even Nick show with nature, a closer look reveals that all three "intimates" of nature have more of a "feel" for nature—an "instrumental" relation with it—than an "understanding" of it. They use the "outdoors" for their own private purposes: for the pursuit of health and fitness, as the site for their houses, or as a mark of sheer social status as in the exclusive ownership of waterfront property.

The question of intimacy determines the film from the very opening scene: the first sustained monologue of the film is a eulogy given by the pastor of the church. In his eulogy he states clearly that he did not *know* Alex, the friend who has committed suicide and whose death is the occasion for the regathering of his friends. He does not know, but he continues to talk about Alex, and since his view is external ("outside"), he talks awkwardly and even offensively. For instance, he describes Alex as a brilliant man who somehow lost hope and went astray, making his life a "seemingly random series of occupations." The pastor's social talk about Alex is immediately juxtaposed with the private and emotional talk given by Harold who begins by declaring, "I *knew* Alex." The nature of Harold's "knowing" is unique in that it is "intimate" and based on a sense of presence, fullness, and identity. The film makes this point clear by substituting Harold's intimate gestures for the pastor's professional intonations and manners. Immediately after starting to talk, Harold is reduced to inarticulateness and openly cries. Indeed crying becomes the mark separating those who knew him from those who did not; the camera makes this point quite clear when focusing on the different faces.

These two modes of relating—the pastor's external view, his not-knowing, his lack of intimacy, and Harold's internal, intimate knowing—become the paradigms of knowledge of the other in the film and the means for distinguishing Alex's intimate friends from those who did not know him, as well as for differentiating among those who did know him. Based on this affective, internal ("inside"), and intimate knowledge of Alex, the film establishes a hierarchy of private intimacies with him. In fact these two modes of relating to others become modes of knowing the world: one authentic and reliable, the other merely ceremonial and superficial. Among those "not-knowing"—those having a distanced and external understanding—the greatest contempt in the film is reserved for Karen's husband, Richard, who several times declares to his wife and her friends that Alex was "their" friend and that he "did not know him." Richard is not only external to Alex's life but, it turns out, to the life of his family as well. Karen is miserable as a result of the external relationship he offers her and ready to leave him for her old friend, Sam, who like her is one of the circle of Alex's intimates. She "knows" Sam whereas she does not know her own husband; as a symbol of her not-knowing, she is unaware of such private aspects of her husband's life as his insomnia. Alex's mother, on the other hand, unlike the pastor or Richard, literally "knew" Alex, yet she is not among his intimates (and thus "inside")—there is no private knowledge on her part of her son. Throughout the funeral her face is affected by the grief of a loss, but not the loss of an intimate. She is obviously shown as sorrowful over the loss of her son, but it is the "universal" sorrow of a mother: nothing in her face indicates the intensity of an internal, personal ("inside") knowledge of Alex. Among the friends who are gathered to mourn Alex's death there is clearly a hierarchy of intimacy based on who was most personally engaged with Alex and knew him most intimately. Sarah who had an affair with him is the only one shown in an anguished moment of uncontrollable weeping while in her shower, where Alex committed suicide. Her husband, Harold, is next in the hierarchy of intimacy. Not only did he continue to stay closely "in touch" with Alex after their student days but as a gesture of this personal knowing let Alex live in a farm house he owned as well as use his country estate in which Alex killed himself.

The relationship between Alex and Chloe, the young woman he was living with at the time of his death, is perhaps most ideologically revealing of the construction of intimacy as a private affair in the film. The subject position that the film provides for the spectator enables her to produce a "take" from the film in which the real is represented as a tiered entity: with an "inner" circle of "intimacy" and an "outer" layer of secondary and thus derivative sociality. In producing such a tale from the film the spectator assures herself that she is a coherent individual and at the same time an integral member of her culture, fully aware of its codes. The film, in other words, offers the spectator a position of intelligibility, and in return the spectator consents to the organization of the real in the manner proposed by the dominant ideology.

While riding in the funeral procession, Chloe expresses her regret that she has to ride in an ordinary car and not in the limousine. Those in the car with her at first think she desires to be included with Alex's family and most intimate friends, Sarah and Harold, in the limousine, but it turns out that Chloe longs to ride in the limousine only because she has never been in one before. Alex's friends, particularly Karen and Meg, are critical of her apparent indifference and lack of concern over Alex's death; they consider Chloe's knowledge of Alex to be external ("outside"): she did not really know him. However, she seems to have a completely different view of her relation with Alex. She is convinced that she has had the most authentic relationship and an unquestioned intimacy with Alex—an intimacy that is so unshakeable she does not find it necessary to use the social signs of sorrow, like Alex's mother, to indicate that she is sorrowful. Her claim to the most authentic intimacy with Alex rests on the fact that she knew him most personally, privately, directly, and with total "presence" yet she was in fact unaware of his *social* side. She declares to Alex's friends, whose claim to his friendship is, ostensibly, a historical and social one rooted in the fact that they all went to the same university together and were involved in the social and political causes of the 1960s, that "Alex and I made love the night before he died; it was fantastic." Sex is the moment of plenitude, the mark of private intimacy; the social is the distanced and thus external mode of knowing: the immediate presence of the body and not social mediation is what shapes the individual. Chloe knows Alex, and she is not going to be intimidated by Karen who pressures her for some clue about Alex's motives in killing himself.

Through her defiant statement and gestures of indifference

to the public signs of sorrow shown by Alex's previous friends, Chloe distinguishes herself from these people, all of whom she considers not to have known Alex because, like the pastor, they knew him only externally, through social associations. Alex's friends, however, are determined to prove her wrong: wrong not in her premise that a friendship based on a social collectivity is external, functional, and unreliable, but in her interpretation of their relationship to Alex and to each other. They have all gathered in Harold and Sarah's home not merely to mourn Alex's death but also, as Meg's symbolic act of "collecting addresses" indicates, to reaffirm their intimate friendship. The grounds for such a reaffirmation, the film clearly shows, is not social collectivity, social causes, or social concerns (of the 1960s) but personal and private affiliations.

The film is quite unambiguous about the fact that, although social causes might have been an initial point of contact, their true friendships developed through their own personal and private memories and desires. "Do you remember . . . " is the opening line of many of the exchanges in the film, and it is completed, more often than not, by such private reminiscences as "when in our senior year we decided to buy that piece of land outside Saginaw?" It is the archive of the personal that grounds the relation. All who have assembled on Harold and Sarah's country estate make it clear how far they have moved away from the social ideas that they owned when they were in college, nonetheless they are still friends in spite of such distancing from the past. They cynically joke with Meg, for example, rather than remonstrate when she describes her clients during her time as a public defender as the "scum of the earth." Now a successful corporate lawyer, she has renounced the social cause of justice to which she was once committed and instead seeks to fill the emptiness of her life by having a child. Nor are the friendships jeopardized by the confrontation between Harold and Nick, who is stopped by the police for reckless driving and drug possession but is not arrested, the film emphasizes, because of Harold's standing in the community and friendly relations with the police. Nick accuses Harold, the one-time protestor, of becoming a successful entrepreneur—"Mr. Cooper," the wealthy owner of the "Running Dog" athletic shoe company—and a "friend of cops." Harold, on the other hand, announces that "I am dug in here," refering to his affinity with the land and the community and his distance from the past, and adds that "I don't need this shit," condemning Nick's juvenile belligerence to the police and his success. The others in the group have similarly coopted their past ideals for success. Sam, who has become the celebrity in a TV detective series, diffuses the confrontation and amuses the policeman by attempting one of the stunts from his show—a running leap into his car—with disastrous results. Not only is he no longer attached to social causes, he is not even engaged in work that deals with the serious affairs of life. He is a sham, an actor creating entertaining illusions for which he is well rewarded. Similarly Michael has abandoned his attempts to write a serious novel and is now a hack journalist for a popular photo-magazine like *People*. He is now eager to be a successful entrepreneur and spends the entire weekend trying to recruit his now wealthy friends as investors in a club he hopes to open. Karen has likewise given up her ambitions to write poems and short stories. Now married to a successful advertising executive, she longs to leave him but cannot because she has accepted the role of a responsible mother; and mothers, according to her, are not free to do what they want. All, in short, have dramatically moved away from the social ideals that were based on the notion of collectivity. They make fun of that past and are quite uncomfortable with its remnants: Alex's unexplained death and Nick's odd, unfriendly behavior. The subject position ideology offers to the spectator here is one of confirmation of an individuality anchored in itself and its own desires.

The film resolves or at least hints at resolving the problems of this residual past represented by Alex and Nick. Alex, it turns out, was far more interested in his image in the world than in his commitment to social causes. In his papers is a newspaper article about his winning a scholarship that he turned down—an act that for his friends has always represented his refusal to compromise the social ideals of the past—but that, according to Chloe, he regretted not accepting. He has kept the article all these years as well as his draft registration card as mementos of the moments of public visibility of an isolated, individual self. There is no evidence of his commitment to social and political causes. The Alex they now come to know was a private person, even narcissistic, enamoured of his image in the newspaper and in the personal moments that Chloe describes.

Nick is at first presented in the film as a remnant of the past all the others have denounced. He is the last one to arrive at the funeral and most of the time is deliberately silent and seemingly distracted. His quiet antagonism toward the others in the group and their new thought forms and life-styles is pointedly revealed in a self-interview he conducts in front of a video camera he has found in Harold's house. In the interview he clearly rejects the values now cherished by all the other friends of Alex: a goal-oriented life with a set purpose. In answer to a question he has posed for himself, he declares that he never finished his Ph.D. dissertation in psychology because he is not hung up on "completion." With his rejection of the "completion" of projects, he rejects the foundational value of bourgeois life and its corollaries. Not only is he socially and culturally maimed, he is also sexually incapacitated. From the perspective of the other friends, he is a nonperson, a person contesting all that they have come to value in life. The tension between him and the others is manifested in the scene in which he confronts Sam. It is significant not only in its local values, in that it reveals the differences between him and Sam as the symbolic representative of all the other friends who have moved away from social causes, but also because it unveils an important facet of the nature of intimacy depicted by the film.

The enabling myth that has brought these friends together is the sense of a shared past, the conviction that they knew each other collectively. In his confrontation with Sam, Nick contests this myth and directly tells Sam, who claims that they are friends and have known each other for a long time, that they only had brief encounters in the past and these are not significant enough to give Sam the grounds for his claim to friendship. "You don't know me," Nick concludes, rejecting Sam's (and everyone else's) myth of the past as a collective friendship.

As the film unfolds it turns out that within the assembled group the shared pasts are of a private nature: Sam has desired Karen who was infatuated with him; Sarah and Alex had an affair; Nick and Meg were close; and, of course, Harold and Sarah are now married. These pockets of private and personal connections —not a collective intimacy—are the foundation for the network of relationships displayed in the film.

Nick's contestatory relationship with the other members of the group, however, does not last long. His interrogatory attitude toward the others, his supposed friends, soon changes. Ideology cannot tolerate an intimacy based on contestation and interrorgation, and it thus annihilates all modes of oppositional intimacy and friendship by assimilating them into the notion of intimacy as a supportive friendship. Nick suddenly changes after being at Harold and Sarah's house for a day and after his close, quasi-sexual contacts with Chloe. On Sunday, the day before everyone's departure, he is seen in a distant shot talking to Harold under an archway. He and Harold are framed in the image of two persons engaged in fairly intense negotiations. At breakfast on Monday, it is Harold who, in response to Meg "collecting addresses," casually reveals that Nick is going to stay with Harold and Sarah for a while, working on and living in the same farmhouse that Alex loved. It is implied that he will also inherit Alex's girlfriend Chloe although Chloe knows he is sexually maimed. In fact this sexual inactivity adds to the notion of intimacy advocated by the film. Nick's connection with Chloe is now depicted as the most intimate and supportive way of relating in that it is not a collective friendship based on any social cause and moreover it is not even sexual. It is a dematerialized relationship based on pure spirituality that is an instance of transparency, presence, and plenitude: the moment that two persons appear to each other without the opacity of difference in mind or body. This relation with Chloe is thus more private than Alex's connection with her because it goes beyond the intimacy of sexuality (the closest mode of personal discourse) and becomes completely transdiscursive. Through a "spiritual" relationship that is totally dematerialized, the contradictions that plague ideology are erased and an instant of translucency and harmony is created. By such harmony between individuals, the film suggests, a harmony in culture in general will be achieved, but such a move renounces the sociality of change, relationships, and life itself.

The move Nick makes from interrogation to accomodation is completed in the film when on Monday morning after Harold's announcement he moves toward Sam. Standing behind him, he places both hands on Sam's shoulders; Sam returns the gesture by covering Nick's hands with his own—not a word is exchanged. "Speech" (like "sexuality"), which is normally the highest mark of presence, is transcended for an even more exalted level of knowing. In the silence of speechlessness "true" intimacy emerges and the discourse of confrontation, contestation, and interrogation maintained by Nick is assimilated into the discourse of a supportive, nonquestioning closeness. A truce is accomplished; the conflicts are resolved; and an "imaginary" relation is established. Intimacy is once more affirmed as an asocial, private, and personal matter between two persons; and its quality is defined as one of emotional support rather than intellectual contestation.

It is in the absence of any interrogation and self-reflexivity that the film manages to present the weekend as a sweet and warm moment of communication. The personal warmth is so sustained in fact that it melts away all such "social" characteristics as jealousy. When Sarah learns that Meg desires to become pregnant, she kindly arranges for her own husband, Harold, to impregnate Meg. The act signals a sexual transcendence in Harold and Sarah's relationship: they have now, symbolically, arrived at a moment in their life in which intimacy has moved from the social to the sexual and from the sexual to the transdiscursivity of pure spirituality. Their mode of connection echoes Nick and Chloe's relationship and marks this form of extrasocial, extramaterial relating as the authentic mode of connecting. Because of its asexuality, this way of relating is, of course, a unisexual model of intimacy put forth as a subject position for both men and women in the film. It is, in other words, an absolute mode of intimacy that transcends social, sexual, gender, and other "material" barriers in order to arrive at pure spirituality.

The Big Chill represents intimacy in friendship as essentially an internal mode of knowing, a private and personal connection with another person. In this light the pastor, Alex's mother, and especially Richard, Karen's husband, are represented as alien to the notion of intimacy because they are distanced from the private. However, in the actual presentation of those that the film regards as having an ("inside") intimacy—instances of transparency and presence—the film discovers that there is no such

thing as nondistanced relationships. Absence, gaps, and difference are inscribed in all relationships engendered by a culture
that is itself fraught with contradictions and absences.

All the friends in the film are looking for intimacy as a
mode of internal knowing but are apart from each other because
of interference from the opacity of life and the times. Harold and
Sarah are separated by her affair with Alex; Alex and Chloe are
separated by a sense of crisis resulting in suicide. Karen and
Richard are separated by different values, while Sam and Karen
are separated by Sam's desire for independence. Michael and
Meg have little in common anymore, and, of course, Nick is different and distanced from everyone else. Intimacy in friendship
consists of an emotional coming together of two persons with the
understanding that there will always be a respect for each other's
separateness. This sense of separateness, the idea of a sovereign
self, is a necessary social requirement: as was pointed out before,
intimacy follows the contours of the dominant social theory of
relationships. To solve these distances, absences and contradictions, the film postulates the idea of supportive friendships: relationships that are not interrogative. Such friendships perceive
their "gaps" as the problems of life as such and conceal the way
they are engendered by the social contradictions of a particular
historical moment. Moreover, these problems are accepted without question because they have no solution. Thus through the
institution of private intimacy, the dominant ideology produces
subjects who consent to social contradictions and naturalize
them as the eternal difficulties of life.

In presenting intimacy as supportive emotionality, *The Big
Chill* is responding symbolically to a complex cultural contradiction contemporary American society cannot solve in reality. The
culture of late capitalism defines intimacy as, paradoxically, the
moment of absolute closeness and thus an instance of transparency, presence, and fullness, but at the same time, it postulates that in this boundaryless moment the domain of the
sovereign self (the privacy of the individuals involved) should be
respected and not transgressed. In respecting the boundaries of
the individual, a distance is always inscribed in that which is presented as boundaryless. Such boundaries are necessary because
through them identity is established, and by virtue of identity the

social visibility of the person is produced. Contemporary American society, like all postindustrial societies of the West, is based on the notion of individual competence, competition, and the responsibility that goes with them. In an interrogative intimacy the intimates deconstruct the idea of friendship formulated by the demands of the contemporary social order; and in demystifying their own relationship, they end up dismantling that which is presented to them as the universal and natural mode of relating to others.

The Big Chill recirculates the notion dominant in postmodern American culture that social and political affiliations are too fragile to be the solid foundations for a fulfilling friendship or intimacy. A permanent relationship cannot be based on temporary social affairs but must be built on lasting friendships rooted in a private intimacy as instances of plenitude and transparency engendered, far away from the call of society, by a supportive affiliation. In doing so it participates in the dominant ideological project designed to suppress collective and "fused groups" and celebrate the isolate individual as a sovereign self willing to compete in and contest the economic terrain. The material prosperity enjoyed by most of the friends gathered at Harold and Sarah's estate and the overall "sweetness" that the film exudes are the rewards for such compliance. These are also the rewards to the spectator who accepts the viewing position offered here: to consent to ideology and produce a "tale" in which the real is constituted as an originary, authentic privateness, on the one hand, and a derivative, false sociality, on the other.

3

The opposite of intimacy in postmodern culture is, of course, "loneliness." The anxiety of loneliness that pervades contemporary American life and determines its emotional and social boundaries is ultimately the anxiety of exclusion: the uneasy feeling that one has become redundant in the social group(s) to which one desires to belong. It is through the representation of social life as a mosaic of various competing groups rather than as a collectivity of persons that the existing social order reproduces its dominant cultural values. A group's main cultural function is the validation of the identity of its members; it is a congregation of separate sovereign individuals who have competed with others to get into the group and once in the group continue their rivalry with other persons in order to stay in it. As a group they also vie with other groups to increase their power (desirability) as a social organization. The value of a group in contemporary culture is in fact directly determined by the amount of competition it takes for one to be accepted by it—the more exclusive a group is the more appealing it is to join it. The worth of membership in a group then depends on its scarcity, which is in fact a mode of commodification of human relationships and a reproduction of the logic of capitalism in daily practices.

In postmodern culture, groups reproduce two foundational concepts of the capitalist social order: first, the notion that people are free-standing, sovereign, moral, and rational agents who not only form the social sphere but whose individuality constitute the uncontested grounds for all human and social values; and, second, the belief in competition as the only valid determining force in social life. This is partly the reason why the prevailing ethics of American life repudiates the idea of social collectivity (as opposed to social groupings that preserve the individual as a free, unbounded entity) as human collectives are transindividual and inclusive thus negating restrictive selection and competition. Collectives are instead founded on the idea of constructing subjectivity and agency through joint participation in the social domain and its discourses. The dominant bourgeois view of human relationships considers a collectivity of people to be a state of entropic anonymity because such a social organization rejects individual competition and is the effect of cooperation. Thus collectives unlike groups are seen as the denial of individuality.

It is the mark of the successful socialization of people in this society that they have learned to equate their inclusion in desired groups with their accomplishments in life and the denial of membership as their own failure. It is also a sign of this triumph of socialization that people have become conditioned to privatizing their failures; if they are rejected by a group, the rebuff is an indication of their own moral insufficiency and not the politics of inclusion-exclusion. Moreover, this rejection is exclusion that creates the condition of loneliness—a circumstance, it is emphasized, brought about by the individual's worthlessness. In an ideological move, this prevailing ethics represents rejection or loneliness as a private matter that has nothing to do with the social situation of the lonely. Loneliness, however, is neither private nor personal, rather it is, in the last analysis, a social condition and so, too, are the means by which it can be overcome. It is nonetheless part of the social pathology of contemporary culture that instead of attempting to abolish loneliness by forming human sociability and collectivity through cooperation, it resorts to emotional coercion and manipulation of others to form exclusive groups that are expected to provide people with the assurance that they will always be protected from loneliness. The more fragmented the social becomes the more desperately people seek selective groups that can accommodate them.

James L. Brook's *Terms of Endearment* is a film constituted out of the tissues of groups: groups composed of mother and daughter; husband and wife; mother, daughter, and father; mother, sons, father, and lovers. Each group attempts to encompass a few and banish all others. The members of each group, to keep their relationship intact and free from alliances with others, manipulate each other and turn their groups into closed spaces. The film reproduces the logic of exclusion-inclusion in these interactions and represents it, with tremendous charm and humor, as the inevitable mode of relating to others. The film depicts human community as a set of exclusive competing groups: from the opening scene of the film, in which the voice of Emma's father (representative of the symbolic order) intervenes between mother and daughter in an attempt to reappropriate the mother back within the boundaries of the wife-lover subject position, thereby excluding the baby, to the final scene, in which Garrett and Tommy move toward Garrett's swimming pool thus distancing themselves (as male subjectivities) from the others at the reception and inaugurating a new restricted group. Through such representations, the film naturalizes the individuality and separateness of members of various groups and denies human collectivity. Futhermore, it offers exclusion-inclusion as the universal underlying logic of all human relationships.

Of the three major clusters of relationships (evolving around Aurora, Emma, and Flap), the most energetic centers on Aurora. This aspect of the film is quite significant in its politics of gender: the subject positions offered to women in patriarchy are always at the boundaries of exclusions. The spectator is positioned in a site of intelligibility from which Aurora's attempts to be "included" are seen *naturally* and not *politically*—in terms of the instincts of a mother rather than in terms of the social subjectivity of a female who is so constructed as to become intelligible to herself and others only as part of an (intensely emotional) group (mother, wife, daughter). Aurora's main concern in life is to prevent her own loneliness by keeping the exclusivity of her relationship with her daughter, Emma: she has to keep "their group" intact from the desires of Emma's father as in the opening scene in which she climbs into Emma's crib instead of returning to her husband; from Emma's closest friend, Patsy; and above all from Emma's husband, Flap. After Emma's father dies and thus leaves Aurora and Emma alone together, Aurora has to fight off Patsy's invasion of her emotional terrain. Emma and Patsy are close friends, so close in fact that their relationship sometimes borders on sexual infatuation. Emma kisses Patsy on the lips, for example, while her mother, who is furious over her decision to marry Flap, is standing in the hallway shouting and banging on her bedroom door. The kiss is, of course, a gesture to reassure Patsy that Emma's impending marriage to Flap will not interfere with their friendship.

All the relationships depicted in the film are more or less like the one between Emma and Patsy in the sense that they are anchored in the exclusivity of the group. If for whatever reason a new person has to be included, the group experiences a sense of crisis that will have to be managed by emotional pacification or blackmail. The model of relationships that lies behind all these interactions, in other words, is the notion of connection as a closed space that is protected from competition but is, like all ideological constructions, the outcome of a paradox. The fact that the relationship is "beyond" competition is the effect of a successful competition; thus the relationship is an unstable entity as it is always already part of a new series of competitions. In this claustrophobic closed space the persons involved in the relationship feel safe and celebrate their insulated connection as an instance of intimacy.

When Patsy grows up and moves into a new space, both geographically and emotionally, Aurora declares a truce with her since she is no longer a rival and in fact recruits her into a new exclusive group fighting Flap for Emma's closeness. The rivalry over Emma between Aurora and Flap dominates the film and overshadows all other contestations for inclusion shaping the pattern of relationships in *Terms of Endearment.* Aurora naturalizes her jealousy of Flap in socially acceptable or at least familiar terms. He is, as far as she is concerned, an incompetent, unintelligent, and very ordinary person who will not be able to take care of Emma. Her objections to Emma's marriage to Flap therefore have a rather traditional appeal; they are the expressions of a mother's concern for her daughter's future. In actual terms, however, Aurora is deeply resentful of the success with which Flap has been able to shatter the exclusive relationship that she has had with her daughter. No longer restricted, it has had to accept Flap and through Flap it will also expand to encompass others, the children, Tommy, Teddy, and Melanie.

This sense of lost exclusivity and Aurora's attempt to somehow regain her privileged relationship with Emma in its original purity and singleness manifests itself throughout the film most notably through the phone calls that she makes to Emma. The first phone call comes early the morning after Emma and Flap's wedding, which Aurora had refused to attend. The phone call interrupts and thus subverts the moment of intimacy between the couple and inserts Aurora into the uniqueness of their relationship. Aurora attempts to seduce her daughter by offering to tell her the latest gossip, but Emma resists the seduction and insists that Aurora apologize to her husband—compelling Aurora in other words to open the closed space of their relationship to include him. But what Flap wants is in fact not an opening up of the Aurora-Emma relationship to encompass him, thus enabling an emotional cooperation between the three of them to develop, but a restricted relationship of his own with Emma. He assures Aurora that no apology is needed but asks Aurora to remember that he and Emma are married now (i.e., have their own closed space) and therefore not to call so early in the morning. One should, of course, note that the telephone as medium of communication is itself a one-to-one mode of talking that normally excludes others.

Not all Aurora's phone calls, however, are directly addressed to Emma. From time to time she talks with Flap (intentionally or because he happens to be the one who picks up the phone). Her conversations with him are always aimed at undermining his masculinity and have a castrating force in them. The spectator is led, by the framing ideology, to produce a tale in which she deserves to be excluded because she is "hostile" and thus not worthy of intimacy. The spectator perceives Aurora's loneliness—against which she fights so persistently—from the subject position that represents woman-mother as "by nature" emotionally regressive. She has to suffer loneliness as a "punishment" because she is destructive, hostile, and unyielding. The mother's regression, however, is culturally acceptable because it lends support to the ideology of intimacy; moreover, such emotional regression is the constitutive element of the contradictory subject positions offered to women in patriarchy. Aurora's phone calls are thus seen by the spectator as her attempt to reduce Flap to a nothingness or even remove him completely from the scene. Aurora calls Flap, for instance, while Emma is in the hospital, interrupts his backyard barbecue with his children, and tells him that he is not competent to take care of his children "while chasing women." In doing so she laterally introduces the idea of taking custody of the children when Emma is dead and thereby subverting his exclusive relationship with his sons and daughter.

The ideology of the film naturalizes the restrictiveness of relationships and the notion of competition as the inevitable dynamics of all human connections and thus justifies Aurora's desire as a mother to monopolize Emma's affection. The film represents Aurora as a dedicated mother whose "jealousy" is culturally acceptable because her possessiveness is aimed at the welfare of Emma and her children. The scene in the hospital in which Aurora becomes hysterical over the nurse's delay in giving Emma her painkiller is a further explication of this culturally acceptable, castrating-regressive motherly love because it further naturalizes the effect of the dominant ideology in positing private intimacy as constitutive of individuality at its most authentic. In a raging temper, Aurora admonishes the nurses for neglecting her daughter. Her anger is naturalized as the fury of a loving mother over her daughter's suffering, while in actuality it is the outcome of her realization that she no longer can control or restrict her relationship with her daughter now that nurses, doctors, and other hospital staff have driven a wedge between them. The closed space of intimacy between herself and Emma has vanished forever, and without intimacy, according to the spectator's tale of intelligibility, she is nothing.

It is part of the (ideo)logic of the narrative that Aurora comes out in the end as a "winner" and Flap is depicted as a loser. His failure is represented as inevitable because he is morally inept; he is a man who not only is an adulterer but, more important, willingly gives up the custody of his children. Thus by implication, he accepts the collectivity and role of a nonpossessive, nonindividualistic parent. Even Flap himself is apologetic about his act and at Emma's bedside tells her that he never thought of himself as a man who would give up his children; this apology acts to contain his dangerous implicit acceptance of the collectivity of parenting. The ideology of the film further suppresses it by stressing that he is a "bad father." Throughout the film, he is the absent father, always more attentive to his professional life (and we later learn his mistress, Janice) than his children. His failure is the denial of exclusivity: refusing to confine himself to the closed spaces of family intimacy, he is thus literally excommunicated and at the same time produced as a singular person. In spite of disconfirming him as a "father," he is confirmed as a free individual: the mark of his freedom is the "oddness" of his role as father.

It is clear from the contradictory subject positions offered to Aurora and Flap that ideology ceaselessly hails the subject (spectator) and makes the world senseful only through its own discourses. The only possibility of refusing the interpellation of ideology is through an interrogatory "reading" of its discourses—a "critique" in other words that displays its contradictions and thus opens up the folds and creases along which the heterogeneous, self-dismanteling discourses of ideology are sutured and represented as unified and contradiction-free. The oppositional subject position for the spectator is thus constructed in the intersections of the framing ideology's contradictions.

The same exculsivity Aurora requires from her affiliation with Emma she also demands from her relationship with Garrett. At first she assures Garrett that she does not mind his various affairs with other women, but after a short while she discovers "relatively late in life" that sex is "fantastic" and grows more and more monopolistic in her relationship with him. The demand that he restrict his attentions to her in fact shows up as early as their first date. In the restaurant where they are having lunch, Garrett, in his usual manner, ogles a young woman who is sitting at the next table only to be put on notice by Aurora who tells him that she thinks it is very rude to stare at another woman when "you are with *me*."

It is characteristic of exclusive relationships and their competitiveness that all who are involved in them are always uncertain of their duration and fearful of losing them. There is always the very real threat that the closed space of intimacy may be violated by the entry of new people and the individual may lose her privileged position in the relationship. Such a constant fear eventually develops into a feeling of mistrust for others since all people are seen as potential emotional rivals, and individuals with whom one has an exclusive relationship suddenly come to be regarded as betrayers. This view of one's intimates as potentially unfaithful and of others in general as emotional competitors forms an emotional matrix of cultural paranoia and leads people involved in these noncollective relationships to finally view themselves as the only reliable and trusted partner in affection. Out of fear of being betrayed by others, they become the object of their own desire for intimacy and affection. This form of exclusive relationship with oneself is a mode of narcissism that, like other human emotions, is socially produced: it is individuality in its extreme form.

Garrett's mode of relating to others is a clear instance of this (defensive) narcissism. He, like Aurora, is seeking a restricted relationship, but his relationship does not have another person as its object of desire, only himself in his role as hero (astronaut). Intent on himself, he is unable to embrace others and thus ends up with passing affairs with a variety of women including Aurora. In the scene in Aurora's summer house when he sees her for the last time as her lover (he reappears two or three times after this meeting but largely as a friend), he tells her that he must break off their relationship because he is beginning to feel an "obligation" to Aurora and he is not prepared to make a commitment. Garrett's closest companion is the water in which he continually swims, and its liquidity embraces him without any resistance. It is significant that when Aurora criticizes him for decorating his room with memorabilia of his days as an astronaut and tells him that such use of his profession to impress and seduce women is a trivialization of the most significant part of his life, Garrett responds by saying, "You have to use all that you have." All that he has are "images" of himself as an astronaut which he worships and relies on for emotional self-sustenance.

Although Garrett is represented as self-indulgent, self-wor-shipful, and separate, a free-floating individual who is extremely unself-aware, his emotional contact with the world is not all that different from the other characters in the film. Almost all of them are, in one form or another and in varying degrees, as nar-cissistic as Garrett. Narcissism is inscribed in any exclusivist rela-tionship privileged in contemporary American culture because one seeks this mode of relating primarily for one's own emotion-al security. All the characters, like Garrett, make some gesture toward reaching out and showing love and involvement in the lives of others, but at the roots of these gestures are self-protec-tion and self-intimacy. Garrett, for instance, in the airport in Lin-coln, tells Aurora that he loves her and in the reception after Emma's death attempts to show affection to Emma's children. In another case, although Aurora's possessiveness for Emma is nat-uralized in the film as a "mother's love," it is clear that beneath the "mother's love" is in fact Aurora's deep narcissism. When Emma marries Flap, Aurora feels so displaced that she is not capable, as a sign of her "love" for Emma, of attending her wed-ding. She is so self-preoccupied that even making an appearance at the simple ceremony, thereby recognizing the primacy of Emma's connection to Flap, would dislodge her privileging of herself and disrupt her emotional life. This is the same emotional disorientation that Garrett has felt ever since his glorious days as an astronaut came to an end: he does not know how to live in a world in which he is not the sole focus of attention. He, like Aurora, lives in an emotional blankness. He fills this blank space by changing women, by getting drunk, and by such antics as steering his Corvette with his feet while Aurora presses the gas pedal. All these activities are moments of regression into what Jacques Lacan calls "the imaginary": a desire to retrieve the unmediated, unique affiliation with the mother. For Aurora the blank space is filled mostly with her emotional exploitation, blackmail, and bribery of Emma and her intimidation of Flap.

Emma's relationship with Flap is an escape from Aurora's emotional exploitation, but Emma herself is as exclusive in her relationships as is Aurora. In the scene where Emma presents Flap with a tie, the symbolic resonance of this gift in the Emma-Flap group is especially telling. Flap is surprised and then mildly upset because he sees in the gift more of Aurora's presence than Emma's love (her assurance of exclusivity) for *himself.* He thinks Emma is giving him the tie because she is embarrassed by the way he might appear, without a tie, in Aurora's house. Emma, however, objects to this interpretation declaring that she bought the tie because the act of buying it made her "happy." She then accuses Flap of being insensitive to her happiness and unaware of the desires and needs of any person other than himself. This is a paradigmatic scene in the sense that husband and wife are each interrogating the motives of the other and pointing out the narcissistic relationship each is seeking with himself or herself by excluding the other. In other words, Emma's final point is that Flap is so restrictive in his love of himself that there is no room for her: he cannot but spoil all her moments of happiness because for him to become aware of her happiness means to be distracted from himself. Flap, on the other hand, makes it clear to Emma that everything she does is in fact aimed at making herself the sole object of uncontested desire: she intends her feelings of happiness to be the focus of attention.

Even sex is not so much a sharing of intimacy in these groups as a further means of narcissistic assertion and control. When Flap avoids making love with Emma for several weeks she demands sex as a sign of her emotional hegemony over him and the primacy of her own pleasures. In an extension of this emotional dominance, Emma allows herself to have an affair with Sam, the Iowa banker, while denying Flap the emotional satisfaction of being in love with Janice. Both Emma's affair with Sam and Flap's relationship with Janice are marks of the ultimate loneliness that besets the exclusive relationship they seek by using each other. If one adds Aurora's affair with Garrett to these two, one sees that all the major characters in the film, to attain some degree of emotional fulfillment, have to develop short-lived sexual liaisons with others and, while the affair lasts, deceive themselves into the illusion of a moment of emotional lucidity and warmth.

Flap's self-interested pursuit of his own pleasure, particularly his affair with Janice, completely breaks up his connection to Emma. As Flap's colleague and mistress, Janice not only intrudes into Emma's special group but also represents that side of Flap's life which is most alien and removed from Emma's control. Flap is a college teacher, and in a sense he uses his profession to disrupt those groups preventing him from forming even more exclusive associations for himself. First, to separate Emma from Aurora, he moves to Iowa to teach, taking Emma with him and thus literally placing a huge distance between her and Aurora. Then, to establish an entirely exclusive relation of his own with Janice, he moves his family even further to Nebraska where Janice has a new teaching position. On discovering the affair and the reason for the dislocating move, Emma confronts Janice who responds by saying that she can "validate" Emma's emotions. The term *validate,* which Emma angrily repeats over and over again to Flap, does not conform to the commonsense language of emotions used in her relationships, rather it marks the "professional" code in which Janice and Flap participate and signals Emma's exclusion from this professional-lover group. Emma reacts to this violation of her special relation to Flap by later preventing him from having custody of the children when she dies. Not only does she reject Flap and bar him from any exclusive connection to his children, but she also ensures that Janice will never be able to establish any relation to her children after her death. By dictating that the children are to be raised by her mother, Emma perpetuates her control over a newly exclusive relationship—this time with her children and mother—even after her death.

The relationships between Emma and her two sons are emblematic of her modes of contact with the world. The younger son, Teddy, loves her exclusively—he attends to all her wishes and obeys her commands. The only way Teddy can feel secure is by making sure that he is loved even if such love is attained at the cost of his relinquishing his own childhood freedom. Tommy, on the other hand, as the first son, is jealous of Emma's acceptance of Teddy; and, to show his resentment of this intrusion into the special relation he had with his mother before Teddy's arrival, he becomes more and more silent, withdrawn, and outright critical of Emma. From his viewpoint Emma has even broken up his intimate group with his father. Emma's strategy for normalizing Tommy's feelings of resentment and his demands for exclusivity is to tell him (in her last goodbye from her death bed) that she knows he loves her. The affirmation she desires from Tommy, but which he denies her, she articulates for him, imposing in the end exclusive intimacy on him. Tommy had begun to find her intimacy constraining and criticized her for being too lazy—that is, narcissistically self-preoccupied and self-involved—to look into the possibilities of his joining another exclusive group, the Boy Scouts. In the same manner that the ideology of the film justifies Aurora's exploitation of Emma by appealing to the commonsense logic that such treatment is the logic of a mother's love, Emma's exploitation and emotional intimidation is justified by her love for them. When Emma dies and thus excludes Aurora from their relationship forever, Aurora takes the three children as a substitute for Emma. Now the group which, in its originary form, consisted of Emma-Aurora-Emma's father and was then reduced to Emma-Aurora is now expanded to include the three children and Aurora. But all indications are that soon this group will again be reduced to Aurora and Emma's daughter, Melanie—but only after Aurora successfully contests Patsy for her. Melanie is a substitute for Emma and the person through whom Aurora's desire for emotional exclusivity will be perpetuated.

Aurora's relentless attempts to form exclusive groups in which she can feel secure and accommodated are in fact attempts to forestall what she regards to be her inevitable loneliness. By representing her efforts in the name of a mother's love (as far as Emma is concerned) or a lover's desire (in respect to Garrett), the film normalizes her refusal to cooperate with others, to form collective, sharing relations capable of embracing others. The spectator is placed in an ideological frame from which he constructs a tale justifying her actions implies that even if she wanted a cooperative, inclusive group she could not attain it because "it is the nature of things" that everyone else is seeking the same degree of exclusivity with others as is Aurora. Garrett, Emma, Flap, and all the other characters in the film, like Aurora, are each attempting to escape or prevent loneliness by forming exclusive groups that they hope will provide them with the warmth of uncontested connection.

The world of *Terms of Endearment* is, beneath its surface of easy charm and humor, a world of competition and fierce individuality. "Love" (in its various forms) is used to construct intimacies that further this individuality and thus hail the spectator to take up subjectivities necessary for the existing social arrangements. Humor is used in the film to deal with the intolerable pressure that competition and the pursuit of "groups" entails, and thus, in the last instance, humor becomes an ideological strategy for containing collectivity. The film, despite itself, depicts the networks of (non)relationships constituting contemporary bourgeois society: relationships in which atomistic individualism—in the name of freedom of the individual—prevents any sustaining collectivity of people and the institutionalization of competitive groups engenders a deep bleakness. The film, however, naturalizes this bleakness, presenting it as an amusing set of quarrels between various people and thus not only masking the deep isolation of people in such a society but in fact putting forth competition as the inevitable, inherent logic of all modes of relating to others. Competition, in other words, is represented as the natural outcome of free individuality—those who do not compete are not fully viable members of the culture. In presenting competition as the basis of human connection, the film manifests the ideological aim of making competition as such the sole arbiter of social life and thus offering the logic of capitalism as the universal logic of human societies in general.

4

The historical functions of many of the institutions of contemporary life such as family, friendship, marriage, and parenting (in other words, the various modes of intimacy) are put in question by the cultural contradictions of postmodern society. However the prevailing ideologies of contemporary culture that support and legitimate the dominant social order are produced and circulated through these institutions. It is therefore politically necessary for the continuation of the existing socioeconomic relations to preserve and prolong these institutions and the values they foster. One of the most ideologically effective moves to prolong the life of these institutions of intimacy has been to deny that they have been historically formed in response to certain socioeconomic demands that, judging by the crisis these institutions are now facing, may no longer obtain.

By denying the historicity of intimacy, these institutions are represented as "natural," universal phenomena beyond the constraints of any particular historical moment and thus "eternal." Presenting "family" or "marriage," for instance, as "natural" provides the commonsense logic of culture with a way of explaining away the crisis that faces these institutions at the present moment. If the institutions of intimacy can be proven to be natural and thus universal and transdiscursive, then the ills that have befallen them in postmodern culture are easily demonstrated to be matters of "accident" and not of the "essence" of the institutions themselves. By naturalizing social organizations such as family and separating their "essence" from the circumstantial "accidents" (namely history) affecting them, the dominant ideology privatizes the problems of intimacy represented in marriage, family, and parenthood as the failures of individuals. In doing so it demonstrates that these institutions of middle-class life are in good shape and far from breaking down, saving them from the pressures of a sustained interrogation and enabling the continued mystification of their practices in contemporary thought.

Wim Wenders's film *Paris, Texas* is an exemplary instance of such mystification of the postmodern bourgeois family. The film's ideological purpose is to provide a post of intelligibility from which the spectator produces a tale in which the seeming crisis that has affected the family and problematized all kinship ties is narrated as being engendered by individuals and their private problems, whereas the family as an institution is seen as not only remaining intact but continuing to provide the ultimate grounds for living. Wenders's project is carried out in terms of a close study of the families of two brothers (Walt and Travis) whose five members are portrayed in a home movie within the film. The home movie is shown at a strategic point when the first "quest" of the film—retrieving Travis from the wilderness—is completed and before, as Wenders himself puts it, "the movie turns and starts walking on a new territory" (Dieckmann, 1984–85, 4). The "new territory" is, of course, the film's second "quest," in which Travis's wife Jane is retrieved from the Keyhole Club, a peepshow palace in Houston. It is true that the home movie within *Paris, Texas* echoes Wenders interest in metafilm and in the question of filmic reflexivity in general, but the home movie (the film within the film), like all modes of postmodern reflexivity, has a specific political function beyond its aesthetic specularity. Its function is to record in an honest and truthful manner the life of the two families together before crisis hits one of them. As a "home movie" it is honest in that it is unmade, unadorned, and above all silent, which is to say it is, like Travis, "mute" and, in Wenders's vocabulary, signals "authenticity" and the "veracity" of experience. As a film within a film, it has the authority of truth that a reflexive text obtains by turning itself into its own subject of inquiry, thus acquiring a solid, incontestable basis for its terms of intelligibility. Its veracity results from its awareness of itself as a filmic production—by admitting that it is a film it puts its "honesty" above question. The home movie is a "document" of connection, human togetherness, and above all family happiness. This sense of family happiness as recorded in the home movie becomes the implicit standard of human happiness and self-reflexive presence against which all human experiences in the film are measured.

The home movie portrays Walt and his wife, Anne, who is French, and Travis and his wife, Jane, and their son, Hunter. It is shot during a vacation and is the only vivid sign that Hunter has of his mother, who has since abandoned him. The happiness recorded in the home movie ended when Travis suddenly disappeared and Jane left Hunter with Walt and Anne who have raised him as their own child. Tavis's mysterious disappearance is the ostensible cause of the breakdown of his family, but later in the film, it is explained in terms of his own private emotional problems. He is unable to deal with the complexities of life, including living with another person, Jane. For him Jane is the site of otherness: he neither understands her nor is able to accept his lack of understanding of her utter difference as part of the problematics of human communication. To feel related to Jane he must turn her otherness into his own sameness and to achieve this goal he resorts to emotional and physical violence. The spectator inscribed in the dominant ideology makes sense of the disintegration of their marriage by regarding it as the effect of Travis's pathological desires and not as the outcome of marriage itself—marriage as a private mode of intimacy. All Travis does is to take the idea of private intimacy to its logical conclusion and unknowingly reveal the contradictions of the ideology of intimacy as a private mode of connecting: love as owning the other and thus a naturalization of the code of private property.

During the early stages of his marriage to Jane he is happy. But he becomes more and more dependent on her, and although he describes this dependency as the sign of their utmost happiness together—they cannot leave each other even for a short period of time—the film constructs his dependency as a mark of his deep-rooted troubles. He becomes so in need of Jane for his emotional sustenance that he gives up his job so that he can stay at home with her all day. After a while, to support her, he has to go back to work again, but this time while he is at work all day his mind is on Jane wondering whether she is spending her day with another man. Coming home he is angry and unleashes his violence on her. Travis lives with the constant fear that Jane may run away; it is this fear that makes him tie a bell around her ankle so that if she tries to leave in the night, he will hear the bell. The entire sequence of Travis' actions involving Jane has echoes of psychopathologic behavior, and his account of this period of his life with Jane ends with an engulfing fire that almost kills him. One night he gets up to find Jane, who always dreamed of running away, has left with Hunter and flames of fire are consuming his clothes. He manages to escape the fire, but once outside his house, he does not stop to look back. He continues to walk for several days, and this unbroken walk begins his journey that ends, after four years, in the parched Texas desert—the opening scene of the film. The breakup of his family is thus directly linked to Travis's emotional problems and mental state. He is produced in the film as jealous, sexually insecure, and intellectually incapable of dealing with such complexities as the opacity of another human being. He is possessive (the other side of his sexual insecurity and jealousy), sentimental (the underside of what he calls his love for Jane), and lacks the rigor and toughness of a grown man—which allows the film to represent him largely as a "child," a child who for most of the film has to rely on his own child to orient himself in the world of adults. Thus Travis—and not the marriage-as-private-intimacy—is responsible for the disaster that befalls them.

The psychomythical dimension of childhood and its effects on the adult (a loosely Freudian model of the "family romance") is elaborated in the film; in fact it forms one of the ideological strategies of the film for asserting the personal causes of family crisis. It claims that the person involved precipitates the crisis because of his or her own childhood traumas. Travis, the film implies, has had a childhood of unsettled emotions. His father and his part-Spanish mother (another marker of otherness in the film) were never really visible to each other. The problems in Travis's family, in other words, are referred-deferred to his father's family and thus protected from a political and social understanding. His mother was a "plain" woman but his father (who like Travis was a complex of troubled dreams and visions) refused to see her as such. He saw her as a fancy woman from Paris, which turns out to be Paris, Texas, but his father, in introducing her or talking about her always drops his voice and eliminates Texas so that it is often misconstrued as Paris, France. Travis has heard from his father that his parents conceived him in Paris, Texas, and as a way of finding a connection with his origins and holding on to a tangible link with his parents, Travis purchases a vacant lot in Paris, Texas, which is little more than sand and tumbleweed. The ideological position in which the spectator is located foregrounds Travis's attachment to his past, making his troubles intelligible only in terms of the dark, inaccessible recesses of his unconscious. History here means "going back"; it is a mere chronology and not the social, economic, and ideological practices of culture that interpellate the individual as the subject of private intimacy. By such emphasis on his private troubles, the film undermines the social side of the family crisis that Travis-Jane-Hunter are facing and accents Travis's own role as the troubled source of the crisis.

The film stresses this personalization of difficulties by, among other things, representing them in Travis's physique: from the opening shot of *Paris, Texas*, he is seen as "different." Wandering in the Texas desert he wears a white shirt and tie, a faded double-breasted jacket, a baseball cap, and shoes so worn out nothing is left of them. It is not only the confused ensemble of his garments that places him in a different space from the norm. His face has the vacancy of the mentally lost: the lines of his face reflect the agonies of sleepless nights, and his eyes are those of someone intimate with alien realities.

Travis is not only responsible for the breakup of his family, but also for the plight of Jane. After he left, Jane also disappeared, ending up in a peepshow palace called the Keyhole Club in Houston, where lonely men talk to the women of their desires for a fee. The connection between the club's male patrons (one of whom is Travis) and the women is through a one-way mirror and a telephone, that is by means of words: a narcissistic relationship that was, the film implies, all Travis had with Jane at the beginning of their marriage and is now all he has with her at the end of his contact with her. Narcissism is inscribed in bourgeois intimacy but is concealed in the folds of its contradictory discourses. Although Jane, like Travis, has left her son (Hunter), unlike Travis, she has not forsaken him; every month out of her meager income she has sent some money for Hunter. Whereas the neurotic Travis is self-mesmerized and can think only in terms of himself, Jane is constantly worried about their child. Although she finds any knowledge of him too painful to bear, there is an unbreakable *blood relationship* between her and Hunter.

It is exactly this lack of blood relationship that marks the otherwise completely comfortable and almost luxurious life Hunter is living with Anne and Walt. Not only do they love him, but, as a mark of their love, they provide him with the entire range of contemporary "kid culture" so that he is part of the contemporary languages of his culture. He owns not only an impressive array of electronic gadgets, but, most important, he is fully immersed in the discourses of his culture. He speaks a language that is a tissue of references to space technology, astronomy, and science fiction. Although Travis is a complete alien to this culture, Walt is quite comfortable with it. In fact Walt owns a company that erects billboards all over Los Angeles to make the discourse of consumer culture available to everyone. Hunter has no visible problem communicating with Walt, and Anne is the embodiment of an unconditional love for Hunter. She is so close to Hunter and so attuned to his emotions that she cannot imagine a life without him. When Travis is found in the Texas desert and brought home by Walt, Anne senses that the end of her "motherhood" is close at hand and realizes that the arrival of Travis signals the termination of her own "family." First she tries to discourage Walt from the "business" of pushing Hunter and Travis together. When Walt violently objects, reminding her that they *are* already together by virtue of their blood relationship, Anne resorts to the last device left to her. She reveals to Travis that Jane sends a nominal sum of money for Hunter every month and that she had the money traced to a bank in Houston. She hopes Travis will go in search of Jane and leave Hunter alone. Travis does leave to find Jane but takes Hunter with him.

After his arrival, Travis attempts to open direct communication with his son but fails at first. There is a sharp conflict of discourses here. For instance, he does not own a car ("nobody walks anymore," Hunter tells Anne in response to her urging him to walk home from school with Travis); he is not dressed "properly" (that is in the attire of a successful professional); and he does not speak the contemporary language of a consumer culture. In fact the first day that Travis appears at the school to walk home with Hunter, Hunter is so embarrassed that he hides and rides home in a neighbor's car. Later that evening Walt finds Hunter in the garage sitting behind the wheel of his car "driving"—thus signaling his utter discursive difference from his "natural" father. The second time—after Travis has familiarized himself with the discourse of fatherhood by wearing a three-piece suit picked out with the help of Walt and Anne's Spanish maid, who symbolically becomes his "nanny," helping him to grow up into the codes of culture—Hunter walks home with him, but allegorically for two-thirds of the way home, they walk on opposite sides of the street. The third time Travis appears at the school, he is more at home with the discourses of paternity and the culture; he is even driving an old battered pickup truck. Thus, when he informs Hunter that he is about to leave in search of Jane, Hunter decides to go with him. The three meetings between father and son show the decreasing emotional distance between them, but the discursive gap remains more or less the same. They rarely talk to each other directly, and it is interesting to note that, when they are driving in the pickup truck, we often see Hunter sitting in the open back talking through a walkie-talkie to his father who remains inside the cab.

Hunter's decision to leave his life with Anne and Walt and go with Travis, with whom he cannot communicate most of the time, is "explained" in the (ideo)logic of the film as a mark of his instinctual pull toward his "real" (i.e., biological) parents. Although Hunter has grown up with Walt and Anne and has spent four out of eight years of his life with them and despite the fact that the discourses of the culture he is familiar with are utterly alien to his father, the spectator (from the viewing place offered by the framing ideology) produces a tale in which Hunter is seen as "knowing" that he should be with him. This assertion of the priority of blood relationships over discursive relationships in the film is of primary significance and offers a set of subjectivities that have profound social and political implications for naturalizing the dominant social arrangements. The film sets up two kinds of families: the natural family based on blood ties; and what might be called a *discursive family*, whose members do not have biological ties but share in the common codes of culture. The film privileges the biological family and thus reifies the traditional bourgeois family as the very grounds of a person's existence. Through such privileging *Paris, Texas* reconfirms the "values" that bourgeois culture derives from the family: the idea of the "individual" as a unitary person whose wholeness and totality is provided through the cohesion created by uncontested connections with the family. The most significant idea extracted from the reification of the traditional family is the notion of authority. The biological family implies that it is "natural" for the father to be the dominant figure and for the mother and children, in varying degrees, to be subjects (of his desire and command): within the (patriarchal) family, the father acts as what Althusser called the "unique and central other *Subject*," in whose name members of the family are interpellated as subjects. In other words, the "natural" authority of the father authorizes the subjectivities of the family members—those subjectivities required for continuing the relations of social exchange, which in turn confirm and legitimate the organization of the patriarchal family. In the same way that one cannot break a (natural) family tie, one cannot avoid its dictates, which are all based on the notion of the authority of the father. The natural family then is an ideological space in which the underlying abstract hierarchy of a patriarchal society is translated into everyday practices. It is a closed entity placed outside history and in the realm of nature. The "discursive family," on the other hand, is not "eternally" bound, and as such it is a free congregation of people who are joined together by a set of codes; if those codes change their relationship will change. Such an open space is inherently unstable and threatening because it constantly reorganizes itself through its codes; and codes, unlike genes, are transformable and changing.

Paris, Texas then has Hunter leave his discursive family as emotionally unsatisfactory—as somehow lacking the natural qualities of a family—and join his natural father. By doing so it reinstates the codes of patriarchy that were bracketed for Hunter while Travis was away. In rejecting the "artificial" discursive family, here represented by Walt and Anne, the film implicitly rejects all family organization based on shared social codes rather than genes (natural codes), and Wenders's target of attack is ultimately the socialist idea of family. The socialist model of the family, which like Anne-Walt-Hunter is based on a set of shared (and thus changeable) social codes and political practices, is the most frightening challenge to the bourgeois sense of self-hood, parenthood, authority, and of course private property, which is transmitted through true natural heirs. To emphasize the alienness of such a concept of parenthood, the film represents the "mother" of the discursive family in the film (Anne) as an "alien," a Frenchwoman who cannot even speak English without an accent. The fact that Hunter confesses that he has no clear and vivid image of Jane except the one seen in the home movie, however, reveals, despite the film's purpose, that "distance," "otherness," and "alienness" are conditions of possibility of the natural family as much as they are, supposedly, the enabling conditions of the discursive and artificial family.

Enroute to Texas in search of Jane, father and son have a grand time together: they are engaged in an incessant set of games, and the trip becomes a timeless blot in which the two recapture the innocence of childhood. Hunter is away from the "surveillance" (unnatural suppression) of Anne, the school, and other social agencies and Travis in his truck has a domain of his own. Father and son (members of the biological family) are immediately available to each other—the two know each other although they do not fully understand each other, and the notion of "parenthood" as a mode of plenitude, presence, and transcendental knowing is strongly developed by the film.

After locating Jane in the peepshow palace, Travis cannot talk to her at first. Looking at her through a one-way mirror, he breaks down and leaves his booth abruptly. In his second visit to the place, Travis manages to tell Jane, again through the telephone and one-way mirror, the allegory of his life: the loving but self-destructive husband whose emotional knots break up his family. Travis's project in finding Jane is, of course, to bring Hunter and Jane together because the relationship between mother and child—natural intimacy—according to him is the most authentic form of connection. The subject position enabling the spectator to make this intelligible is based on the ideological assumption that such a bond is so "obvious" that even someone so pathologically narcissistic as Travis cannot avoid acknowledging it. The spectator, in other words, is reassured of the founding notion of the natural family. The child comes from the body of the mother and as such the connection between the two is the most "natural" and unconstrained by the codes of affection that culture imposes upon other modes of relating. Through privileging the body-blood relationship between mother and child, Travis justifies his own action in taking Hunter from his discursive mother and reuniting him with his biological mother. It is also his belief in the body connection that finally explains not just the title of the film but also Travis's almost mystical act of purchasing a piece of land in Paris, Texas. It is to own the place of his conception, to go beyond the ritual of parenting to the locus of the act of begetting himself that

Travis buys the land. There is, obviously, a close connection between Travis's view of the body (the site of genuine affection) and the land itself because the land—especially the wide open desert spaces of Texas not yet tamed by culture—like the body is truthful; it lies beyond and under all the surface changes (of culture) and remains literally the final ground of all modes of living. The conjuncture between body and land in *Paris, Texas,* is what gives meaning to the obscure picture of the vacant lot he always carries with him. The significance of the picture is not clear to others: Walt almost ridicules him for buying a vacant lot, and Hunter teases Travis about his dream place because going to Paris, Texas, can only mean "living on dirt" to the sophisticated boy raised by Anne and Walt.

Travis's act of reuniting Jane and Hunter is a symbolic reinscription of patriarchy in culture—the natural family is back together, and the values of family life are reaffirmed. Fullness is returned to family life in the same manner that Travis achieves wholeness of self by purchasing the lot in Paris, Texas. This completeness of self is "expressed" through the language of silence—silence being the mark of the authentic subject in the film. Thus, when leaving Hunter, Travis says his farewells in a tape-recorded message since he cannot use the language of direct communication between father and son. The taped message is once more a sign of his cultural inability; it is a form of muteness and thus conveys the veracity of his emotions. His "muteness" in this section of the film draws upon the ideological investments made in the sign of "muteness" in the first part of the film. In a sense the entire film is framed by these two moments of "nontalking": between his waking up, after a heat stroke, in a clinic in the Texas desert and his leaving the hotel after having made a taped message for Hunter. The "talking" that takes place between these two moments of muteness and silence is nothing more than cultural bubble—talk of the mundane and the quotidian.

Critics, who have regarded the film as a split between a "hugely portentous opening" of mythic dimensions with "desert, vultures, dogged muteness and an attempt to flee back to the desert," and a rather disappointing and empty second part that is hardly more than a "tiny domestic drama" that no television producer would accept, miss the typological nature of the film's structure. Elements of the second part of the film assume their significance only by reference to points established in the first part: the first part of the film is not a literal "exposition" and "preparation" for the second part but a matrix of signifiers that are the enabling conditions of the "meanings" of the signifieds of the second part. The taped message that Travis leaves for Hunter is clear enough on its own terms only if one is interested in the "informational" content of the message. But without locating the taping of the message in the general set of signifiers of "muteness" that are elaborated and developed in the first part, the ideological investments of the film remain unclear. The film is a statement about the "natural" status of the family and represents the "natural" as a state of existence that is understandable without any mediation of language, culture, or other forms of textuality. It is as available, real, concrete, and obvious as the desert in which Travis was found wandering. "Muteness" is part of the transgression of cultural boundaries and their linguistic codes, and it is seminal to the reinscription of the natural in the general ideological climate of the film.

In fact the entire film is made, according to Wim Wenders, as an act of asserting the "natural" and the uncontested real that lies beyond all modes of cultural textualities and political mediation. In the *Film Quarterly* interview, he elaborates his views on the subject of the "real" as it relates to the act of film making, and since what he says about the art of film making is directly related to the ideological pressures in *Paris, Texas,* it is necessary to quote him at some length:

> I've made quite a number of films that were more concerned with reflecting themselves than reflecting anything that exists apart from movies. And you can call that life, or truth, or whatever. Reality. Doesn't matter. I mean, all those forbidden words. And I see lots of movies and was getting frustrated not only by my own work and the reflexiveness of it but with other movies, too, because it seemed there was no more way out. Whatever film you went to see, it had its nourishment or its life or its food, its roots, in other movies. In movies. I didn't see anything anymore that was really trying to redefine a relation between life and images made

from life. Whatever you go to see these days, you sit there and after some time you realize that you're involved again in something that was born and has been recapitulating an experience that comes from other movies. And I think that's a really serious dead end for something that I love very much, which is movies. And I did my share of that. *Paris, Texas* was—I wouldn't say desperate, because I wasn't so desperate while I was making it—but at the end of *The State of Things,* there was no other choice than to redefine, or find again, or rediscover what this is: to film something that exists, and film something that exists quite apart from movies. (Dieckmann, 6)

"Muteness" in Wenders's new cinematography is the sign of this possibility of breaking through the intervening systems of signification—stopping the language whose signifiers constantly refer to other signifiers rather than a "real" located uncontestably beyond them—and reaching the state of the real, the natural. Talk is unnatural; it is the work of culture. Muteness is natural; it is an antilanguage that blankets the bubble of culture and attains the purity of plenitude and self-presence.

In fact, in absolute "muteness" Jane and Hunter first encounter each other in the hotel. Their natural intimacy finds expression only in the natural language of nontalk, silence, and muteness—the ultimate mode of forceful "presence." There is nothing *said* between them except the caresses and spinning embrace Jane gives Hunter. While the bodily relationship (mother and son) is resurrected, Travis, who is looking up at the hotel room from the parking lot, leaves once again to disappear into the muteness of the lands that lie beyond the skyscrapers of Houston.

Travis's self-effacement in bringing mother and son together, like his muteness, is typologically anticipated in the first part of the film. In that section of the film, Walt selflessly goes to Texas to bring his brother back in spite of all the difficulties he encounters (Travis's silence, his refusal to leave the ground and fly to L.A., his attempts to return to the desert). Walt's devotion to the idea of family—recovering his "natural" brother and reuniting him with his "natural" son, Hunter—as the basis of human connection is reasserted in the ending. The film's ideological move to "prove" that family is the uncontested "natural" ground of community and living comes to a rest with Travis's bringing together mother and son—something that, the film implies, he himself never had and whose lack is behind his failure as a father. His leaving the scene eliminates the element of crisis that the family has been facing, and his absence thus assures the continuation of the natural course of living in the family. Travis along with Flap and Emma are all individuals who have failed in establishing private intimacy; thus they disappear so that the sphere of the family as the site of free subjectivities cultivated through the call of intimacy remains intact.

CHAPTER 5

CHANGE, HISTORY, NOSTALGIA

The relationship between contemporary American culture and the past is fraught with contradictions engendered by incoherencies in American society's view of social "change." America, like other consumer societies, regards change as the sign of vitality and negation of inertia, which it associates with the past, with history, and thus sees change as opening up the future, which is understood as limitless possibilities. Although admiring change, American society nevertheless is fearful of it because change in ushering in the "new" also produces discontinuity and disorientation. Change, therefore, is conceived of, in a contradictory fashion, as the condition of breakthroughs (upon which the entrepreneurial imagination is based) and also a thinly disguised chaos (which undermines the principles of an orderly society protective of the rights and properties of the individual). The American romance with change and history has placed a tremendous pressure on its thinkers, artists, and civil leaders to find a resolution to this contradiction: to make change safe and not dislocating; to make sure, in other words, that "change" always serves the purposes of the dominant interests in constantly moving things without transforming them so that the existing relations of production can be perpetually reproduced without seeming to be so. Controlling change is necessary because the logic of late capitalism requires change to be equated with progress and civilization itself, as only a philosophy of the "good life" based on change will lead to further and further consumption (consumption being the hallmark of moving into the future and discarding the past).

To make change as harmless and nondisorientating as possible, American culture has had to fall back on history itself and recuperate the past that in the name of change it had discarded. However for the past-history to be made usable for the present, it has to be first turned into "tradition." Through the invention of tradition change (the present-future) is made part of an ongoing continuity without breaks and jarring discontinuities.

Tradition, as the frame of stability, is a collectivity of familiar and dominant ways of making sense of the world organized according to an ideological agenda. The role of ideology in the invention and construction of tradition, however, is systematically suppressed so the view of reality offered by tradition will seem inevitable, natural, and universal. This transformation of history into tradition removes the opacity and alterity of the past, rendering it as a moment of lucidity, transparency, and sameness in which the interests of the present (i.e., the dominant economic order) are visible. The concerns of the present, therefore, are represented as not merely the interests of the moment but as everlasting urgencies: important in the past as well as the present with the strong implication that they will also be of significance in the future. Tradition, in other words, dehistoricizes history and produces a timeless instance in which things change without ever becoming different—the past is made to seem always inscribed in the present as well as the future; thus, change is always a move toward the past not away from it. This ambiguous view of the relationship between alterity and sameness, present-future and past is clearly captured in such films of the 1980s as *Back to the Future* in which the needs of the present reinvent the past, thereby preparing for change which is always beneficent and never dislocating. *Back to the Future,* however, is not the only film attempting to resolve this cultural contradiction; the question dominates almost all contemporary films. A more indirect attempt to deal with the problematic relation of past and present, change and stability is Albert Brooks's *Lost in America,* which deals with the problem by traditionalizing the past and homogenizing history.

As a result of such homogenization of the past, a synthetic history is produced that, like all ideological versions of history, is in an odd way ahistorical if not outright antihistorical. Such history is a free-floating moment that is not the effect of economic, political, legal, and philosophical practices of a society but a moral fable—an interpretation of the past as is required by the ideological needs of the present. In this fable the specificity of history as the site of the struggle of contesting class relations is removed, and instead a generalized, vague, and evolutionary march of events (what Althusser calls *historicism*) is substituted. This generalized history is then commodified as "nostalgia" and circulated for the consumption of people who need the assurance of stability while facing change. In nostalgia they have a retreat from the restlessness of the changeful present but, paradoxically, the more they become immersed in it the more they find that in spite of its seeming remoteness the past in nostalgia is in an uncanny way like the present. The changeful present loses its alien face and merges with the equally "charming" traditionalized past in a panhistorical moment whose ideological function is to make change (consumption) palatable without disrupting the existing relations of production. Nostalgia, the product of a dehistoricized past, is then an ideological apparatus that constructs the subjectivities needed for the dominant social order and its underlying economic practices—it is the discourse that distances individuals from the past thereby preparing them for the demands of the most important side of late capitalist practices: to stabilize change.

Albert Brooks's film *Lost in America* is a somewhat parodic and amused exploration of the fantasy of freedom in postmodern America and an ideological maneuver to reinscribe, albeit humorously, the existing economic order by "showing" the impracticality of an oppositional relation to it. However, the film becomes, in spite of itself, more a discourse on history, revealing the need for a homogenized "tradition" in a consumer society, than a treatment of self-origination, which is its professed goal. It thus demonstrates that the fate of individuals cannot possibly be scrutinized outside a larger inquiry into history itself and its related elements such as change, including, of course, the problem of no change—the starting point of the narrative.

The film's opening scene shows David and Linda Howard, the ultimate "yuppies," having late night anxieties about David's forthcoming promotion in an advertising agency in which he has worked for eight years and second thoughts about some of the details of their new $440,000 home. Both have lost their ability to grow personally and socially: their upward mobility and personal development are inextricably intertwined. They hope that by unblocking one through a new promotion the other will also be stimulated. Linda is quite straightforward about their predicament when talking later with a coworker, "Nothing is changing anymore, we've just stopped." She is also quite aware that the promotion may not be able to inaugurate the badly hoped for change, and she may have to resort to divorce or other violent acts to separate them from their past (history) in order to start moving in new directions. To sever from the past, in other words, is the condition of entering the future. The immobility that has paralyzed their life, however, is concealed from the ordinary eye by the profusion of signs of consumption: their combined salary is over $100,000; they have an expensive new house, and at the office David spends most of his time on the phone discussing the color and material of the upholstery for the Mercedes-Benz he intends to buy when his expected promotion to senior vice-president is made. They have all the signs of being well-placed members of a consumer society. David's job as the "creative director" of the West Coast division of an ad agency is an index of his relationship with that society; he is not a simple consumer but the custodian of consumerism.

The noncorrespondence between the signifiers of their upward mobility and the signified of their inward stasis become part of the theory of meaning that informs the nonsaid of the film: it draws attention to other such instances of noncorrespondence between the signs of the real and the reality itself. When David is told, contrary to the signs given him by his boss as well as all his friends, that not only is he not getting the desired promotion but is being transferred to New York, the relationship between the signifier and the signified, sign and its referred reality, become absolutely confused for him. His angry protestations against this discrepancy and its disruption of his expectations end up getting him fired. The ensuing stretch of incoherencies force David to look for a new reality; a reality that is supposedly more reliable (i.e., corresponds to the signifiers) and does not evaporate as quickly as the reality of his life and values in the ad agency. David and Linda sell their belongings and with a "nestegg" of about $200,000 begin a journey across America—a journey whose purpose is to renew them and restart the process of "change" in their lives. However, they realize that as long as they hold onto their private past, such change is not possible. So, although the ostensible dimension of the journey is that of the present-future, their actual goal is to join the collective past and the history of people they believe have achieved change, spirituality, and thus happiness in their lives. The destination is the past because, as their own life testifies, the present (and by implication the future) is sterile. They use the present to arrive at an authentic mode of being that they believe is to be found only in the past: a past they intend to be an instance of otherness, one that cannot possibly be integrated into the sterile present and its appendage, the future. The past they choose is the past represented by those who have "dropped out" of society as a gesture of protest to the present. They, too, will leave society, "touch Indians," and, as part of this collectivity of the dissenting margin, hopefully be renewed. "Linda, this is just like *Easy Rider*," David declares at the outset of their journey, "Only now its our turn." The comic treatment of *Easy Rider* situates the spectator culturally so that she "reads" the film as a tale in which all alterities are trivialized as not serious, as a mode of social regression.

They leave Los Angeles to the tune of "Born to Be Wild" in their brand new Winnebago headed for Las Vegas, a place where they intend to get remarried as a symbolic gesture towards their life of renewal and affectivity. Remarrying is a mark of the intense emotions they would like to bring to their stagnant life and the need to get away from the logical functionality of their present mode of living and understanding. The road to the past, the film amusingly implies, is filled with traps and full of hardship. In Las Vegas they lose all their money (the "nestegg" is broken), and this loss is the final break with their own past and the first sign of the beginning of their new life. The sharp difference between the new and the old is made clear when David, using skills acquired in his past life in advertising, fails to persuade the casino manager to return their money as part of a publicity campaign. When the manager rationally explains that a casino does not need the image of big-hearted generosity he wants to create for it, David is once more confronted with the noncorrespondence between the signs he knows and the reality they are supposed to refer to; he cannot comprehend a business, even a casino, not desiring a benevolent image.

It is a feature of David and Linda's deep involvement with bourgeois values and therefore their limited familiarity with non-middle class sign systems that they, like all "yuppies" of the 1980s, are narcissistic "bad readers"—that is to say, readers for whom only familiar signs have a reliable meaning and the unfamiliar is not regarded as a different kind of meaning but as non-meaning, confusion. When Linda loses all their money gambling, thus placing David and herself in a completely new situation, they both have great difficulty "reading" the event, interpreting it and understanding it. David takes the signs (Linda's losing money) to be basically moral in nature: Linda, according to him, is "irresponsible." Linda's own self-reading is essentially psychoanalytical: she thinks she "blew" all their money because of her pent up emotions caused by years of working in an office that did not even have a window. Neither can go beyond the "moral" or "psychological"; that is to say, beyond the reading of signs on any basis other than an individualizing one. The fact that wanting to win, to "beat the house," to accumulate more money, and to provoke the admiration of others at the gambling table might have "caused" the *loss* does not occur to them because they are blind to the bourgeois ideology that has produced them and has instilled "competition" in them as the only mode of relating to the world. They are also bad readers of the signs in their own relationship, especially during its post-Las Vegas phase. They privatize their difficulty in coping with the casino episode. Only after Linda has temporarily left David and hitched a ride with a fugitive does David begin to slightly reorient his reading of her act. But the materiality of signs—the persistence of reality in its opacity—dawns on them only after they start looking for jobs to support their new life; that is, after they openly reenter the economic sphere (which, of course, they had never left).

From the very beginning of the film, David and Linda are very conscious of the relationship between history, change, and the present. When they are still trying to get some sleep in the very first scene of the film, Linda tries to explain their reasons for buying a new house in the same neighborhood in terms of more "space," whereas David vehemently objects to that mode of understanding. He believes a house is more than so much space, because if it was just a question of space they could have simply rented a few lockers. A house, he implies, is nothing less than the history that one develops with it; through such a history the house, evidently, is transformed into a home. David also emphasizes his personal "history" with the ad agency. Working eight years for the agency entitles him, he feels, to the position of senior vice-president. In other words, his past should enable his move into the future (the senior vice-presidency). Yet he is not only denied the future his past-history has earned for him but his transfer to New York, to a new account and a new director, also denies his history. He responds to the agency's negation of his past and betrayal of his future by running through the halls shouting at his coworkers, warning them that "I have seen the future, and it is a bald-headed man from New York." The failed promotion leads him to reject his past; while his college classmates were spending their time finding themselves, he was, he now knows, wrongly devoting himself to business management studies. He feels betrayed by the business ethics he obeyed so loyally. He finds that his version of history was wrong: the future does not follow the route he had anticipated. Now he wants to rewrite his history by setting out on a journey of renewal into the collective past of the nation's dissidents. For Linda the only way to move into the future should David's expected promotion fail to bring the desired changes is to cut off from the past (get a divorce). In going along with David on the journey and selling their house and property, she joins him in the attempt to resituate themselves in history.

In their new life, the present, the forces of change and the future are represented by two frightening images and experiences: Las Vegas—the site of "action"—and Hoover Dam—the emblem of change and technology. Hoover Dam is simultaneously fascinating and frightening; it is fascinating in its taming power but frightening in that it conceals inside itself the tremendous destructive energy that could be unleashed at any moment. The change the dam symbolizes is thus both fascinating and frightening. Linda's succumbing to Las Vegas "action" (gambling) is, of course, another instance of the disturbing unleashing of the forces of change and transformation (from well-paid slavery in a windowless office to the impoverished freedom and open spaces of the Nevada desert).

In their search for new grounds for their life, David and Linda want to get as far away from the temporal (the present) and geographical (Los Angeles) coordinates of their current life as possible. The outer limits of their journey, however, are already determined by the film *Easy Rider* (Dennis Hopper, 1969). The film in fact becomes a measure of their new life and more than a mere personal point of reference. *Easy Rider* acquires a symbolic dimension on at least two levels: thematically it provides a cognitive frame for David and Linda, and aesthetically it gives *Lost in America* as a film a dimension of self-reflexivity. *Lost in America* absorbs *Easy Rider* within its own filmic discourse and thus situates itself as a film with a history. In other words, by foregrounding *Easy Rider* and reinterpreting some of its themes, *Lost in America* emphasizes the question of change and transformability.

As the visual and thematic point of reference for *Lost in America*, *Easy Rider* is used as the standard against which most of the characters of the film and their experiences are tested and either found wanting, and thus rejected as inauthentic, or considered to be sympathetic to the social act of "dropping out" undertaken by Linda and David. The manager of the casino, who refuses to give their money back and is fond of Wayne Newton, has not seen the film nor has the employment agent who likes to make fun of David for leaving his $100,000 a year job to find himself. He has, however, seen *Easy Money,* a rather vulgar film starring Rodney Dangerfield. In contrast to these two older people, the middle-aged highway patrolman who stops them for speeding in Arizona has seen the film many times. Linda then suggests that since they are all members of the same community—those who have seen *Easy Rider* and for whom the film constitutes a major interpretive and reading experience—the patrolman should let them go without a fine to which he agrees. The old therefore have not seen the film nor have the young such as Skippy, the adolescent manager of the hamburger joint in which Linda finally gets a job. But Linda, David, and the policeman have each seen the film over and over again. *Easy Rider* is the only common cultural experience that binds these people together in their middle life. These people, one should add, are all caught in dead-end work whether that of a $100,000 a year ad executive, a policeman handing out speeding tickets, or a personnel manager in a windowless office in a posh department store. The constituents of their shared experiential heritage and its significance for the exploration of history and change in *Lost in America* is revealed when one examines more closely the themes and what Raymond Williams calls the *structures of feeling* of *Easy Rider.*

Easy Rider is about the discontinuity of feelings and understanding in America. As the lawyer who accompanies the two hippie protagonists of the film puts it, "You know, this used to be a helluva good country. I can't understand what's going on in it." The past as remembered is "good"; the present as experienced is "bad"; and this is "natural." The ideological effect of such representations interpellates the spectator to put up with the daily contradictions of living in a capitalist culture, even though they have become intolerable, because "this is the way things are." Nothing can be done about the "natural" order of things without harming the one who undertakes an oppositional intervention—as in the tragic fate of the lawyer in *Easy Rider.*

The epistemic break that the two hippies imply in their behavior and (non)speech is between the established American commonsensical mode of knowing—represented in its most narrow concerns and forms by the rednecks they encounter on the road who harass them, eventually shooting them—and the anti-commonsensical modes of making sense of the real represented by themselves. For the most part, they act out this anticommonsensical approach—high on drugs, traveling on odd-looking motorcycles to the beat of the music of Steppenwolff, Jimi Hendrix, Electric Prunes, and the like, and above all by making a point of not talking. It is mostly through this silence (called *self-righteous taciturnity* by one infuriated critic) that they take their stand: they want to drop out of the discourses of a consumer society and Western modes of knowing in general. They have responded to the call of ideology by participating in a more subtle conformity: they want to be intimate with the mysterious and unarticulable. However, they, too, in the end, are free subjects and in their freedom freely accept the limits of bourgeois ideology. One of the opening songs of the film, "I Smoke a Lot of

Grass," for example, indicates their disgust with the "logic" of a bourgeois society and their desire for a transcendental form of immediate, unmediated understanding through breaking down the barriers of rationality. They are retreating from the existing "present" and are reluctant to enter the "future" in the customary, commonsensical, and conformist manner. Yet their claim to dropping out remains just that—a claim. Such "transcendental" arationalism is, of course, the ideological ideal of nondiscursivity—the space in which free individuals derive the authority of their freedom from "themselves." Both they and Linda-David are looking, above all, for "freedom" and as such are interpellated by dominant ideology.

Their entire journey of stepping beyond the discourses of Western life and knowledge has been made possible by selling heroin (which they have smuggled from Mexico) to satisfy the very appetites of a consumer society that they now designate as being unacceptable. The question here is not the discovery of a mere contradiction between their claim and their living, but the very possibility of personally dropping out of culture (in contrast to collective political opposition) and, in the absence of such a possibility, the viability of personal forms of resistance to postmodern capitalism. The two hippies decide to privatize the contestation of values and, by supposedly "dropping out," make their separate peace with the world. But this private peace is not only not a substitute for a political critique, it in fact reproduces, in its logic, the very conditions from which they claim to want to escape; namely, the bourgeois ethics and politics of free individuality and taking care of one's own interests and desires. In a manner not dissimilar to the ethics of rebellion assumed by Wren and Susan (in Seidelman's *Smithereens* and *Desperately Seeking Susan*) but on a different level, the two hippies are in a sense not really critical of the specificity of their own political situation. Instead of seeking a concrete history of oppositional citizens contesting the practices of a capitalist regime, they have traditionalized the conventional life-style of the "bohemian" margin. They emulate mere "dissent" and even then traditionalize (dehistoricize) it. One gets a glimpse of their prototype when they visit a hippie commune on their way—a site of self-deception if not "cut rate spirituality" as one critic has put it. They do what they fantasize a bohemian on the margin should do to distance himself from the mainstream. In their traditionalization of the (bohemian) past, they are as much involved in nostalgia as their ostensible opponents, the rednecks, or their lawyer friend, all of whom also traditionalize the past and fantasize about an America that never existed. By authority of that fantastic America the rednecks seek to contain the forces of change and the break with history represented by the two bikers. In the bikers they see that side of "change" and "future" which is a barely veiled chaos and anarchy—an anarchy that must be eliminated.

Although David and Linda think of themselves as belonging to the party of the two hippies represented as uncompromising "rebels," they belong just as much to the company of the rednecks. Like the rednecks David and Linda traditionalize the past that is left for them, but this past left by the hippies is itself a homogenized past of bohemian life. Thus they become involved more in a nostalgia about the bikers than in the historical legacy of opposition in America—they, like the bikers, lack a political critique of the institutions they presumably desire to change. The bikers, in other words, homogenize the history of dissent in America and by traditionalizing bohemian modes of thinking attempt to reach some transcendental moment that is as antihistorical and apolitical as the American history that the bourgeoisie invents. The rednecks homogenize a pastoral view of America that is a nostalgia for the ethics of a small town. David and Linda end up homogenizing the already homogenized modes of dissent left to them and their generation by the bikers of *Easy Rider* and other representations of hippies. It is in the light of such observations about *Easy Rider* that the description of the film in its advertisements acquires a rather ironic side today. *Easy Rider* has been described as a film about two persons who are "in search of America," but, in the words of the publicity materials, "They couldn't find it anywhere." They failed because their America belongs to the domain of nostalgia and not history.

Lost in America both refers textually to *Easy Rider,* thus creating a self-reflexive dimension for itself as an instance of intertextuality, and also comments structurally on *Easy Rider* by reproducing some of the major components of the thematic patterns and motifs. The results of such references, however, are not one-sided: *Lost in America* in commenting on *Easy Rider,* in other words, comments on its own underlying ideology and theory of reality. As David says, "Linda this is just like *Easy Rider;* only now it's our turn." Their "turn" as suggested earlier takes them over the terrain of nostalgia, a rehearsal of that which was in a sense rehearsed by the hippies in *Easy Rider* through their nostalgia for a bohemian mode of thought and life-style. David and Linda's journey in *Lost in America* is even patterned on the trip taken by the two hippies in *Easy Rider* from California to Florida. The biker's journey starts by having scored a big drug deal; they are literally loaded with money when they embark on their trip. The Howards are similarly loaded with money from selling their assets. The source of money in the two cases may, on first glance, seem very different, but in actuality they are almost the same: both come from pandering to the appetites of a consumer society. One couple sells heroin; the other couple by creating advertisements and managing sales personnel are involved in selling goods and services whose consumption in turn is also often addictive. The two couples are in a supplementary relationship with each other. And, obviously, for both money is the enabling condition of freedom! The bikers immerse themselves in a joyful, depressurizing indulgence at the New Orleans Mardi Gras; David and Linda go to Las Vegas to get remarried. The bikers visit a very expensive brothel while in New Orleans; David and Linda pay a $100 bribe to the desk clerk to get the best honeymoon suite in the casino hotel and (parodically) end up in a junior honeymoon suite with heart shaped beds and a gaudy brothel atmosphere. ("If Liberace had children," David comments in bitterness, "this is where they'd live.") The bikers go on an acid trip in a cemetery; Linda goes on a gambling binge. Both couples encounter killers; in *Easy Rider* the couple are actually shot, but in *Lost in America* the ex-convict merely bloodies David's nose and threatens to come back and make David "history."

    Lost in America not only makes fun of David and Linda but also ridicules *Easy Rider* in its comic reproduction of that film's structure and themes. Its implied juxtapositions of hippies and David-Linda suggests "history" is a cycle: David and Linda are the latest form of dissent, and similar to the previous modes, they are doomed to fail. The satire directed at David and Linda is quite overt and is in fact signaled in an open fashion at the very beginning of their trip. David in his brand new Winnebago (his bike!) passes a motorcyclist (who is involved in his own fashion in the nostalgia about bikers of the 1960s) and as a mark of camaraderie gives him a thumbs-up sign to which the biker in return gives David the finger. The anonymous biker obviously thinks of himself as the authentic rebel and views with contempt David and Linda's huge middle-class vehicle and its contents. But there are no original bikers, only competing versions of nostalgia. However, each nostalgist has a truth claim to her version of history. By displaying these various contesting views of the authentic mode of "dropping out" and rebeling against the deadliness of contemporary consumer society, *Lost in America* trivializes the whole oppositional position toward the institutions of postmodern capitalism. By showing David and the biker in an exchange of gestures and by referring the genealogy of both back to *Easy Rider* (which is in turn a subject of ridicule in *Lost in America*), Albert Brooks is implying that there is no possibility for any real opposition because all modes of opposition are merely an imitation of an imitation and dropping out is a mere dream, a private fantasy. Therefore, why not acquiesce to the existing order of things? *Lost in America,* in other words, is situated in an ideological space in which any form of dissent is merely a source of endless amusement for those who do not get involved in dissent but remain noncommittal observers of it. People may "dissent," but dissent, it is implied, is really a form of adolescent political tantrums: one grows up and recovers from it or one regresses into life-long infantalism and is thus banished from the society of adults. Brooks, like Seidelman in her *Smithereens* and *Desperately Seeking Susan,* considers "dissent" to be ineffective but his logic is that of a liberal reformist. "Dissent" is indeed ineffective but not for the reasons Brooks and Seidelman offer. It is ineffective because it is an idealistic distancing from the existing institutions of capitalism and not a materialist critique of its operation nor an intervention in its economic order and class organization of culture.

In ridiculing *Easy Rider* by revealing the comic underside of its overly serious themes and episodes, *Lost in America* not only denies the possibility of a political critique in the past but also expresses doubts about its possibility at the present time or in the future. *Lost in America* never inquires into the political desire of oppositional subjects; the film merely trivializes it by making fun of its inadequacies. The implicit logic seems to be that all modes of opposition are as ridiculous as the life we are now living so why bother to change, to take a position? This logic is, obviously, based on the comfortable equation that *Lost in America* makes between *Easy Rider* (David and Linda) and an oppositional politics. Such an equation, more than anything else in the film, unmasks its own ideology, which is hidden in the nonsaid of the film. An interrogation of the film reveals that, in the last instance, it is undertaking such an equation to reproduce the idea of nondisruptive change and a traditionalized past as guarantor of a civilized life. Opposition, it implies, is a transient action undertaken by the immature; the adult life is lived in the traditionalized space of an uninterrupted history relating the past without displacement to the present and the future.

In fact the film offers a frightening view of a disrupted, mutant future that has not gradually evolved from the present and the past. In the first image, the future is represented by the "bald-headed man from New York"—the ad executive, for whom David would have to work. New York is the site of remoteness and urban decay for David and such a move leads to disruption and chaos. Another image of the future is even more calamitous and displacing. When the highway patrolman lets David and Linda go without ticketing them, they try to return the friendly gesture by asking him if he has seen a film called *The Terminator* (James Cameron, 1984). When the patrolman answers, "no, but I've heard about it," David tells him he should see the film and that he looks like the terminator. *The Terminator* is a nightmare about what the future will do to the human race. It is a film focused on the action of a robot terminator (played by Arnold Schwarzenegger) clad in jackboots and fingerless gloves made of studded leather. He is sent back from the year 2029 to the present to kill a waitress whose crime is that her as yet unconceived son will lead humankind to victory in World War IV. The view of the future represented in the figure of the automaton Schwarzenegger is one of uncontained brutality and the annihilation of anything that stands in its way; the future is part man, part metal. It is mutant—a chaotic change that has anarchically gotten out of control. Again in *The Terminator* there is no future—the reason the film is quoted in *Lost in America*. Change is always frightening.

For David then the future, the negation of the past, is either a bald-headed man from the site of urban decay and decadence or a computerized automaton bent on assassinating human beings. *Lost in America* by its references to *Easy Rider*, on the one hand, and *The Terminator*, on the other, situates itself in a place with only two options: escape into a pastoral past or living in a mutant future; the trees or the jungle of metal. There is nothing else that a person can do as the option of living in the present state of society has already been rejected by David and Linda who sell their house and uproot themselves because life in its present state is not worth living. By framing the human options available as a choice between a nonexisting past and an equally unclear future, the political critique of the present is reduced to an extended satire that can at best (if it is successful) amuse and provide some distance from the harrowing life in a postmodern capitalist state. In *Lost in America* this leads to the reinscription of the present rather than its interrogation.

In fact *Lost in America,* having taught David and Linda a lesson by displacing them and showing them the hardship of unemployment and homelessness, quite overtly resituates them in the present and forecloses the possibility of any oppositional stance toward it. After serving as an assistant manager to an adolescent boy in a hot dog joint Linda is ready to go back anywhere, and David whose stint as a crossing guard is nothing but an extended humiliation by children is more than ready to go even to New York. They accept their position but with a slight difference: now they don't seem to take themselves so seriously. David upon arriving in New York spots Brad, and although he is clad in a business suite and seems quite serious outwardly, he chases Brad in a rather playful manner. The film ends with the two seeming to be engaged in an adult version of hide-and-seek. This seems to be all David can do: to start playing after a fairly long period of seriousness. The question of "dropping out" of society, which is his way of expressing his desire for an oppositional position, is thus erased. David and Linda's desire for change is "shown" to be a misplaced desire: an adult person cannot step out of the dominant practices of culture. And yes, this is absurd, but life has absurd moments; all one has to do at such times is to keep one's skeptical sense of distance and sense of humor. Skepticism and a sense of humor are, of course, two powerful ideology strategies of the bourgeois used to trivialize the urgencies of history and change. Within such an ideological context, change, especially a violent one such as that undertaken by David and Linda, will lead nowhere: the only change that the film allows David and Linda is a change of scenery, from Los Angeles to New York!

CHAPTER 6

THE CENTER AND THE MARGIN

1

The question of the relation between the center and the margin haunts almost all contemporary films. This preoccupation with the center (as the ensemble of established and thus "obvious" discourses of culture that underwrite the accepted patterns of understanding the world) and the margin (as the discourses that have an adversarial and critical relation with the dominant modes of knowing and behaving) is itself a symptom of the crisis of postmodernity and uncertainty about the norms that might "justify" and "explain" the acts one undertakes. The margin, and its oppositional relation to the center, pressures the settled norms of culture, which have become an integral part of its common sense and "second nature" to members of that culture. The margin's intensive interrogative pressure reveals the naturalness and "givenness" of cultural norms to be mere ideological constructs of the dominant class, gender, and ethnic groups, whose values—necessary for maintaining the subjectivities required by the prevailing social relations—are presented as universal and representing the interests of all groups. The margin, in short, in its adversarial relation to the center—its nonconformist behavior, its nonmimetic art, its noncoalitionist politics, and its historical understanding of the social—points up the arbitrariness of the center's values. It demonstrates their historicity, their materiality, and thus their rootedness in the specific class, gender, and race relations of culture. In undertaking such a political project, the oppositional margin becomes the dangerous supplement of the center, and as such it is the target of all the discourses of the center: its arts, films, sciences, literatures, and, of course, its laws. The relation of center and margin is finally one of exclusion and inclusion and thus ultimately a political one because the exclusions and inclusions are, in the last instance, about power in culture and the relations of exploitation that having or not having power set up among people. To investigate the connections between a culture's center and margin then is to inquire into the politics of values.

In most Holywood films (for instance, *Terms of Endearment*), the relations between center and margin are always represented in such a manner that, by the end of the film, the threat from the adversarial discourses of the margin are contained and the center emerges, reasserting its cultural authority. The Hollywood film, like all other centered discourses of culture, deals with the margin through various strategies of containment. These films attempt to recuperate the radical margin as a "reformist" discourse. The margin and its discourses, in a gesture of open-mindedness, are seen as having a "positive" effect on the center. By critiquing the center, they are viewed as "cleansing" the center and freeing it from nonfunctional and dead elements. In *Terms of Endearment*, for example, the crippling relation of a conventional marriage is subjected to the pressures of the marginal discourse of "having an affair," which threatens the unity of the family. The marginal discourse of "an affair" reveals the problems in the marriage (difficulties that Aurora, as the voice of the center, had anticipated from the beginning). But rather than represent these problems as those of institutionalized marriage itself, the film localizes the margin's critique as merely an indication that this particular marriage has failed because of the incompatibility of the persons involved—a move that is repeated almost identically in *Paris, Texas*. Once the margin's critique is briefly represented and the difficulties of the marriage are aired, the film proceeds to eliminate that discourse and reassert the center that, having benefited from the margin's critique, is now even stronger. Thus in *Terms of Endearment*, the side-discourse of the affair is quickly dismissed, and the "family" as an ethical unit is restored in the end through a reconfiguration of its members. The mother dies from cancer (she is punished for her infidelity) and her unfaithful husband, who jeopardized the family unity, agrees to give up his children and move away (he is penalized for his transgressions) so that the loving grandmother (the matriarch of the center) can take over the traditional role of "parent" and reunify the family. The center's gesture toward the margin is thus a recuperative one: it seizes the adversarial discourses of the margin and turns them into reformist moves that only strengthen the center.

The center's containment of the margin, however, takes many forms, and one of the most effective and subtle ways is the center's recuperation of the margin from within the margin itself through discourses that disguise themselves as marginal—as in films that self-consciously represent themselves as nonmainstream, non-Hollywood, and "independent." My focus in this chapter is on these films that deal with the margin from inside the margin itself. The containment of the margin in these films is elaborate and complex: it does not occur through a crude reestablishment of the center but rather by a subversion of the adversarial margin itself. As a result of this subversion, the center acquires a new legitimacy as the only site of mature, adult values, ideas, and behaviors. The subversion of the margin is often accomplished by trivializing it—by ridiculing opposition and thus rendering that which seems to be different as merely a degraded variant of the same. The margin in these films becomes the place of posturing and the discourse of the fraudulent. In the 1980s the most articulate of the "independent" film makers who have successfully addressed large audiences is Susan Seidelman, and her first two films, *Smithereens* and *Desperately Seeking Susan,* are devoted to an exploration of the center and the oppositional margin. In both films the nonconformist margins of society are depicted as the site of cultural regression and hoaxes.

2

Seidelman's first film, *Smithereens,* became a postmodern classic, winning prizes not only at such film festivals as Cannes and Telluride but also turning into a hit at the box offices of alternative movie theatres in Greenwich Village as well as outside New York. Commenting on her film, Seidelman told an interviewer, "I wanted to people the film with characters who were products of the mass culture of the 1970s and 80s, kids who grew up on rock and roll" (*The New York Times,* 26 Dec. 1982). The film, however, is not, as Seidelman seems to imply, a disin-

terested study of the contemporary scene, although she does her
best, by using a rather humorous and at times even affectionate
idiom in her presentation of events and people, not to sound
didactic and ideological. *Smithereens* ostensible object is a por-
trayal of punk rock music and its subculture, but its actual subject matter, as she admits in the same interview, is the view of
reality and moral vision lying behind the postmodern arts and
held by their practitioners in the oppositional margin of postmodern culture. "When people's values get perverted," she
observes, "the products they create reflect perverted values."
Her goal is thus to expose the prevailing perversions and, by
doing so, help to restore a sense of moral health to the arts and
community. Her project, in other words, is a reaffirmation of the
center and its view of social reality. The outcome is a frightened
film that conceals its insecurities in jokes and ironic statements
and projects a nostalgic moral universe rooted in the political
conservatism that swept Europe and the United States in the late
1970s and 1980s.

The realistic cinematography of the film is itself in a sense
an aesthetic dramatization of its moral and political conservatism
and its hankering after domesticity, common sense, and other
middle-class proprieties. This realism, however, like its political
conservatism, is a rather sophisticated one that is not only aware
of the experimentation and innovations of such directors as
Godard, Truffaut, and Fassbinder but is also quite knowledge-
able about the narratological economies of such modes as car-
toons. *Smithereens* realism is, in other words, a postexperiemen-
tal mimesis—a realism that acknowledges innovative and
nonmimetic cinematography but, boldly and humorously, rejects
it in favor of a no-nonsense, and seemingly straightforward presentation of the narrative subject. Seidelman's film, in many
respects, resembles the writings of such neo-realist American fic-
tionists as Ann Beattie, Raymond Carver, Jayne Anne Phillips,
Amy Hempel, and Jay McInerney. The narratives of these writ-
ers introduce a new form of realism in contemporary American
fiction by demonstrating a high degree of awareness about the
innovative works of such radical contemporaries as John Barth,
Donald Barthelme, Thomas Pynchon, and Kathy Acker but
moving toward a reappropriation of traditional realism, especial-

ly its view of reality as ultimately experiential and nonlinguistic in nature. Beattie's fiction, Seidelman's films, and the neorealistic paintings of William Bailey and Philip Peralstein all point to a new development in contemporary American arts: a desire to restore mimesis. Such an aesthetic move is motivated by the political climate of the 1970s and 1980s and its overriding imperative to bring back the order of the familiar and expel all modes of otherness as represented by the margin. The desired order is a moral one based on the traditional Western humanistic values of common sense, pragmatism, and a deep suspicion of alterity. Otherness is in fact equated in the film with frivolity, which is another term, in the idiom of the film, for immorality and a disregard for the fundamental categories of a communal and centered reality, a disregard that eventually leads to disguised chaos and substitutes for the authentic reality a faked, pretended, and thus illegitimate one. The political purpose of the dominant "moral" order in the film, however, is in the last instance, as will be shown later, the relegitimation of a particular economic order that is threatened by the unproductive margin.

The notion of faked reality—the margin—is thematized rather powerfully in *Smithereens* and is in fact violently introduced into the film at the very beginning of the narrative. The film opens with the camera focusing on a huge pair of black-and-white op-art sunglasses dangling from the hands of a woman who is evidently absorbed in observing the scene in a New York subway. The screen is, for a few moments, almost totally occupied by these glasses, which through close-ups overwhelm the spectator and forcefully pose the question of the perception and interpretation (i.e., "seeing") of reality in the film. The dangling sunglasses are suddenly "ripped off" by a young woman, a would be punk groupie, who, having taken them, runs through the maze of the subway and on entering the world aboveground wears them. Her face is thus marked as a site of falsehood, covered up by the illegitmately obtained screen of dark glasses. This illegitimacy, which is the illegitimacy of disorder represented in the act of theft that violates the birthright of the bourgeois to hold private property, is equated by the end of the film with the mode of reality proposed by the contemporary margin represented by punk rock and, by extension, other forms of unconventionality and otherness.

The phony and inauthentic life lived by the sunglasses's thief, the heroine of the film, Wren, is futher dramatized by her seemingly absurd act of pasting pictures of herself inscribed with the enigmatic question: WHO IS THIS GIRL? all over lower Manhattan. It is a Warholian gesture echoed in her job: she works in a photocopy center and her life, it is suggested, like her job is characterized by reproduction instead of production; it is a copy, a nonoriginal and secondary effect that depends on a primary term. The photocopy center is a place for the reproduction of images, and Wren's only preoccupation in her life is with images and surfaces. She is a talentless woman (she wants to join a group of punk rock musicians but does not know how to sing or play any musical instrument) who is driven by a set of signs of media celebrities and hype—swimming pools, fans, and autographs.

Wren's narcissism, however, goes far beyond an innocent and harmless pasting of photocopies of herself all over the city; she is—as Paul, the centered figure in the film, tells her—morally deficient: she is so absorbed in herself that she cannot respond to other people and have any genuine concern for them. People matter to her only in so far as they can be useful to her and feed her ego. She is, in short, dehumanized by "hype," the collective falsehood of postmodern culture, which is itself seen as an illegitimate usurper of the self-cohering and totalizing culture of modernism. Her mind is so numbed by the postmodern synthetic reality produced by media and popular culture that it is a mere unassorted jumble of opinions, dreams, impressions, and fantasies without the maturity to recognize the adult boundaries between the real and the dreamed up. What is even more frightening about her is that not only does she lack the sophistication to see the shallowness of her beliefs and recognize that she is living in fantasies pathologically severed from communal reality but she pursues them with absurd single-mindedness. Her only grounds for justifying her conduct is her "self." Her indifference to the actual human predicament and her inability to appreciate the subtle negotiation of the real in any complex human situation gives her thoughts and acts a raw quality and brutal tone that the film expands and associates with contemporary punk rock and the margin of culture, which is impatient with a nuanced "argument" about the foundations of beliefs and the acts they justify. The crude, narcissistic, and relentless pursuit of power, which marks punk rock music in this film, is seen as the underlying order in the night clubs and bars that Wren and the others frequent and shapes their relationships. This barbarous search for power is, in the moral idiom of the film, a mode of fascism characterizing the contemporary music scene and, by extension, other forms of nonmainstream and avant-garde art. Punk music is viewed, in other words, ultimately as a form of fascism that appeals only to powerless youths who are feeble-minded enough to take its claims seriously and who hope that by submitting themselves to it to gain some sort of (self-)visibility. Like other modes of fascism, it is embedded in violence. Although Wren's language, body movements, and gestures as well as her contacts with the people around her all hint at this violence, the person who is its perfect embodiment is Wren's object of adulation, Eric.

Eric is first seen in the film getting out of a cab in front of a bar in which Wren and Paul, the quiet painter, end up spending their first date. Stepping out onto the curb, Eric grabs the purse of a young blonde woman who is in the taxi and orders the driver to take her away. As the cab pulls out the woman leans out the window screaming, "I hate your guts!" at Eric. Later in the film, in a desolate moment when Wren is knocking on Eric's empty apartment door, we learn that the blonde (who remains nameless in the film) is Eric's wife. To Wren, Eric represents freedom and creativity—he has cut an album called "Smithereens" a year or so ago—but the film presents him as just another phony artist who is unable to create anything of artistic value and all his waking hours are spent swindling admiring women (including Wren) and engaging in what he calls "business deals." Brutality and emotional violence are the only terms by which Eric relates to the world. His cruelty is imagistically summed up in one of the most expressive scenes of the film, in which he leaves the cafe where Wren and one of his other women friends have started fighting over him. While they are rolling on the floor pulling each other's hair, Eric, his mouth full of food paid for by the woman now being attacked by Wren, walks away. His handsome face, seen through the cafe window in a close-up shot from inside, is lean, evil, snickering, and amused by the fight: its sensual beauty void of any moral understanding. Wren confuses Eric's violence with artistic power, and this in the film is testimony to her moral and imaginative naivete. Her desire to become a groupie is in fact a sign of her inner insecurity as, like other followers of fascism, she adores power because she is herself so powerless.

The ultimate passivity of Wren's mind—the underside of the power seeking fascistic personality—and her inability to analyze ideas and sort out competing views in her mind is visually portrayed in a rather amusing but very effective series of shots of her pad—a room full of scattered clothes, empty food boxes, an unmade bed, and a small portable television set that follows her throughout the film like a pet animal. The TV set repeats her total saturation with "image" and "hype" and at the same time her complete separation from any sustaining human contact. She soon is denied even this confused and confusing space when her landlady locks her out of the apartment for nonpayment of rent. In a scene in the hallway, we see the old, decent, hardworking landlady sweeping the floor and Wren trying to presuade her to let her into the apartment since she "will be paid tomorrow by 10 o'clock." In a matter of two or three minutes the audience sees Wren using a range of verbal tricks from sweet-talking to threatening to abusing the landlady (strategies that will be repeated several times in the film against her brother-in-law and even Eric). Throughout the landlady remains firm and reminds Wren of all her previous broken promises—another indication to the spectator of Wren's moral deficiencies. The spectator's sympathy is with the landlady to such a degree that when, at the end of the scene, she tosses Wren's clothes onto the street and ends the ritual of throwing her out by pouring a bucket of water on her head, there is nothing but laughter from the audience. The water symbolically acts as the pissing of the bourgeois audience on the riffraff of the earth. At the same time it signals Wren's drowning in a world of homelessness and absolute loneliness that eventually leads to prostitution (the ultimate symbol for the bourgeoisie of the degradation and punishment of the disobedient dissident daughter who is thus overtly placed in an exchange situation).

Between her eviction and the last freeze frame hinting at her future life as a whore, Wren is subjected to an unending series of humiliations and ridicule. For instance, while calling on her sister and brother-in-law in an effort to borrow some money, Wren at first gets rather angry, but soon her anger disappears and she becomes a rather compliant woman who tries very had to be pleasant and even starts smalltalk with her brother-in-law. The spectator gets the point: Wren is a hypocrite who, to get what she wants, does not stop at anything. Her seeming desire for independence and an unconventional life is just a convenient pose. The same point is brought up again in Eric's pad. Getting up after a night spent with an indifferent Eric, Wren, like a sweet housewife, tries to get his attention by offering to make him breakfast. Eric, like her brother-in-law, rudely reminds her that her verbal tricks won't work. The audience meanwhile is reassured of its own subject position, that its moral stand and its antipathy to Wren is "right."

Although the film, through its ironic tone, various devices of humor, and visual anecdotes, tries to present itself as nondidactic, the underlying moral anger of the film toward marginal and unconventional life-styles breaks through the facade of humor. The impatience that the film expresses toward punk rock music and other forms of experimental art is grounded in its vision of an authentic mode of living and a viable form of art, which is presented in the film in the figure of a quiet, soft-spoken (genuine) artist whose "psychedelic" painted van (reminiscent of the 1960s), around which Wren and other characters circulate, is the only redeeming feature of the urban wasteland. Paul's 1960s is by now so incorporated into the centered discourses of culture that they have become harmless moments of nostalgia rather than radical arguments for changing the bourgeois order of truth.

The artist, Paul, is introduced in the film almost simultaneously with Wren as if to suggest from the very beginning a familiar and thus acceptable alternative to the strange otherness of Wren. Paul is presented as a man of contemplation and depth who penetrates the surface of reality and reaches behind facades. The figure of the seemingly different man of the margin is fascinating to Seidelman. She attempts in her films to indicate that the radical, oppositional margin is fraudulent whereas the familiar, "authentic" other (and this is the main function of her "alternative man") is merely another way of ending up at the mores and manners of the center. The center's "other," in Seidelman's moral and political idiom, does not have to be an adversarial margin. It could and should be a cooperative margin that can form a moral coalition with the center. In her second film, *Desperately Seeking Susan,* Seidelman represents this coalitionist margin in the character of Dez. Paul and Dez legitimate, in Seidelman's filmic universe, the politics of reformism through which the center sheds its dead practices after they become historically unviable.

Contrary to Wren, Paul is aware of the complexities of the human situation, but unlike her and her friends, this knowledge does not lead to moral and intellectual helplessness—the blankness of the rock musician. Paul is a "real"-ist artist: a portrait painter who archetypically represents the artist to the middle class. But for the bourgeoisie the portrait painter is not merely an artist, a person with enviable skills in depicting the marvels of human features; he is also a man of perception and vision, a sage who inscribes an interpretation within the reflection of reality his art creates. His paintings are thus an informed mode of interpretive mimesis, and the audience is to understand that this is the same (self-reflexive) aesthetic mode in which the film itself is conceived.

Although Paul is located in the (post)industrial world (his van is parked at a symbolic site in the "wasteland" of a junk strewn abandoned lot), he is not situated in it: his vision of reality is pastoral as he stops over in New York on his way from Montana to New Hampshire. A detached observer of the busyness and hustle of the contemporary world, he is able to see through it and express its futility. When he is with Wren in the bar, for example, his body contracts in reaction to the phoniness of those around him, and his recurring request to Wren is "Let's get out of here," "Can we get out of here?" This knowledge of the unauthentic and futile makes him a real threat to those who come into contact with him—all are worried that they may be "found out" by him and "discovered" to be wanting. As the film progresses, the knowing innocence that surrounds Paul increases and becomes charged with religious overtones, so much so that the local pimp finds (Saint) Paul's presence in the neighborhood a menacing sign and several times tries to drive him out by offering to buy his van. The van is, of course, to be purchased ostensibly as a mobile headquarters and lounge for his "girls," but actually it is to get rid of Paul. Paul is the symbol of clarity, harmony, and understanding and his van represents a sanctuary of comfort and succor that the film demonstrates by showing one of the prostitutes taking refuge in his van from the bitter cold night while Paul talks with her about her mother, home, and homemade food.

However, for Wren, Paul's van is merely a negative space, a site of survival and nothing more. When she arrives at the van tired, depressed, and exhausted after having been thrown out of her apartment and denied help and shelter by all whom she thought would accommodate her, Paul provides her with shelter, tries to comfort her, and make her aware of the larger contexts of life. But she is, as might be expected within the representational ideology of the film, ungrateful, insensitive, and, of course, selfish. She is, in the idiom of the film, using Paul, a fact that is made even more evident by the erratic pattern of her nightly visits: she comes "home" late or some nights does not return at all. Paul's van is only a last resort to fall back on when she cannot find more "desirable" companions. Paul, too, as might be expected, is understanding, kind, and above all patient-looking and puts up with Wren's obnoxious behavior and disparaging comments about his previous girlfriend or his ideal living space; that is, New Hampshire.

The symbolic opposition of Wren (the thief) and Paul (the sage) thus provides the ground for the perception of reality in *Smithereens:* Paul is the insightful artist in touch with himself and the elemental power of nature and informed by deep human emotions, whereas Wren is full of TV artifice, attracted and constructed by trivia and media hype. Paul is the spiritual man who is not corrupted by carnal knowledge (like an innocent boy, in one of the scenes that take place in his van, he peeks at Wren's breasts while she sleeps); Wren, on the other hand, is the urban materialist, promiscuous and exploitative. The world is seen as a site of contrasting binary terms; namely, the spiritual and physical and their various manifestations in such pairs as moral-immoral; innocent-promiscuous; sensitive-insensitive; giving-taking–selfless-selfish. Such binarism is an ideological construct based on the ultimate privileging of the first term (spiritual) and suppression of the other (physical). This hierarchical opposition, which provides the grounds for the film's view of reality, is actually not as secure as the film assumes, and on closer examination, one can see how the warring forces, which are projected as separate from each other, are indeed inscribed within one another. Paul is, in the end, quite similar to Wren; and what is presented as "spiritual" in the film is already itself constructed by the "physical." The two opposing terms that provide the film's ontological ground, in other words, are not as clearly and "naturally" distinguishable as the film pretends; their difference is more ideological than given. In the absence of distinct separate terms, the system of reality upon which the polarized moral universe of the narrative is built falls apart, revealing the ultimate economic and political metaphysics of the film, which in fact requires these ideological binaries for its own justification and consequently represents them as natural contraries. The film thus does its best to conceal this ideology and to present its terms, in the figures of Wren and Paul, as morally antagonistic.

Paul's relationship with the world around him, like that of Wren, Eric, and the others, is basically one of give and take; in other words, a situation of "exchange." But it is part of the political metaphysics of the film that his relationship with the world and people around him is dissimulated by situating him outside the sphere of exchange. Consequently, we never see Paul in anyway related or adjacent to financial matters. We don't ever learn how he actually earns his living. All we are given to understand is that he *has* money. He is a painter, but, unlike Wren, Eric, and the others, who are engaged in menial work or resort to thievery or the constant search for someone to fund their projects and provide them with some form of financial support, Paul never works, steals, or talks about "business deals." Again unlike Wren and Eric who are stuck in New York because the lack of money prevents them from going to their utopia, L.A., Paul is "free" (has the means) to go to his ideal state, New Hampshire, whenever he wants. It is for him a matter of desire not monetary consideration.

In spite of such powerful acts of diverting and concealing, Paul, on a closer look, is fully and completely involved in the same rules of exchange. In fact it is Wren who has placed herself outside the situation of bourgeois exchange and is thus "punished" for it by the film. Quite contrary to the overt text of the film and because of the limits of the ideological and cultural contradictions in which it is inscribed, its terms are unstable and the ground upon which the film's theory of reality is based is revealed to be not a moral one (spiritual-material) but an economic one. Paul is presented as providing shelter and friendship for Wren without any ulterior motive or any expectations, just out of the "natural" goodness of his heart. His apparent lack of purely sexual interest in Wren emphasizes this idealistic and moral relationship. However the "unsaid" of the film articulates that Paul needs Wren as much as she needs him. His dependence on Wren and his expectations of her are undeniable. He provides a shelter, as did the landlady, and like the landlady expects to be "paid back" although not in exactly the same terms. He does not expect "money" from Wren (he, the film has made clear, does not need money) but rather a monopoly on her "love" and "emotions." It is part of the morality of the bourgeoisie that "money" is different from "love"—the former is vulgar and the latter spiritual—so the landlady who expects money in exchange for shelter is never placed by the spectator on the same level as Paul, the pure artist. The politics of this relation is that "love" is outside the system of exhange; it is, in other words, nonmaterial and beyond cultural constraints, it is given not constructed. But both "money" and "love" are material and participate in the economics of exchange. Paul expects Wren to observe these terms and respond in a responsible and "adult" fashion (i.e., adhering to the laws of the bourgeois exchange system). When she refuses to do so and continues her night life free of any obligations to (Saint) Paul, the provider, he gets angry and confronts her. He accuses her of being morally selfish. It is, nonetheless Paul who is selfish and not Wren; it is Paul who wants (to appropriate) Wren for himself alone, and he is, in fact, as power-seeking as Eric, Wren, and all the others who are part of the punk rock scene in the film. It is precisely when his power (over Wren) is challenged by her erratic behavior, that his facade of rationality and reasonableness breaks down and his own violent nature surfaces. In one scene he is standing in front of his van in the vacant lot, Wren is sitting on a broken couch, and Paul starts lecturing her on her selfishness. As he gets more and more angry, his body loses its poise and composure and his tone its normal calmness, while the violence that overcomes him manifests itself in his forcefully breaking pieces of wood and feeding the fire. The fire in an instant becomes the symbol of Paul's inner turbulance: he, after all, turns out not to be the calm man of reason but a very agitated person of unresolved emotions. The soft-spoken artist is transformed into an evangelical preacher with wrath as his source of authority.

Paul's expectations of Wren are frustrated because she does not follow the rule of middle-class behavior: reciprocity. This violation of a pattern of behavior is ultimately a negation of the laws of exchange that dominate the relationshp among individuals and between individuals and groups in capitalist society. By ignoring Paul, Wren in a sense symbolically transgresses those laws. It is for this violation that she is "punished" in the film. And the whole punk rock group, which similarly places itself outside the circle of exchange, is also condemned. It turns out that Eric, Wren, and the other punk followers are all in one way or the other transgressing the laws of exchange—they are takers but not givers: the margin in the political economy of the film is thus represented as "parasitic." Wren's brother-in-law, her friend, Cecile, and almost all the other "responsible" characters with whom Wren comes into contact make this clear to her. She does not reciprocate, and for this she is thrown out of houses, pads, and apartments. As if this were not clear enough, the film opens with Wren stealing (a pair of sunglasses); and toward the end she again *steals* (when she and Eric "roll" a tourist, leaving him penniless and pantless). Eric in turn *steals* from her (when he runs off to L.A. with the money they took from the tourist). The "margin" is nothing more than the set of such lies, betrayals, and thefts. This underlying notion of exchange as the regulator of all human relations is even more tellingly revealed in the next to last scene of the film. After Eric has left Wren penniless, her last resort is to again seek out Paul. Unaware that Paul too has left and his van has been purchased by the local pimp for his prostitutes, Wren opens the door of the van and unexpectedly sees the "girls" sitting around eating, chatting, and relaxing. Since this is the symbolic site in which she and Paul had made love, the sequence of acts occupying that space—Paul and Wren followed by the paid prostitutes—places them all on the same level, exposing them as instances of exchange.

Syntactically this scene is used to lead to the final act of exchange in the film. In the last scene, Wren, the rebel who has so far violated the rules of exchange by not submitting to them, is forced to acknowledge their reality and in a self-humilating gesture accept them. The act takes place while Wren, having lost everything she had, is walking back to New Jersey, a place to which she had promised herself never to return. On the bridge she is accosted by a driver who wants to pick her up. At first she ignores him, but as soon as he reminds her that she really does not have a place to go to that night, she stops and stepping back, moves toward the car. The closing freeze frame (catching her move toward the car) suggests the life waiting for her: the exchange of sex for money. The answer to the initial question, WHO IS THIS GIRL? is now provided: SHE IS ONLY A CHEAP TRICKSTER. The answer, of course, points beyond Wren's individual predicament and becomes the film's statement about contemporary punk rock, and by extension, all other modes of alterity and nonconventionality—the oppositional margin. Following a rather traditional conservative pattern of social diagnosis, *Smithereens* mystifies the actual economic and political conditions of contemporary history as "moral" issues and then singles out a particular group whose "immoral" practices are seen as the real threat to Western civilization and its values. This interpretation of contemporary history is not only entertaining but also very reassuring for the middle-class spectator, whose values and goals are reaffirmed in the way that the "tale" of the film makes contemporary reality intelligible to the spectator. The bourgeois viewer becomes a self-cohering subject to herself and thus acquires cultural certitude and moral authority by also making sense of the world in terms of a binary reality of good (center) and evil (margin): a center whose morality of "love" is beyond the give-and-take of exchange and a margin that is parasitic and feeds upon this moral generosity of the center. What is reaffirmed, however, is not a set of moral codes but the political economy of bourgeois life that, in the "unsaid" of the film, is in fact founded on reciprocity and exchange of the most material form.

3

In fact Seidelman's artistic ambitions seem to be evolving around such dissimulations. In her interview with *The New York Times* mentioned earlier, Seidelman declared her goals as a director in unequivocal terms, "My dream is to take the best of both worlds (i.e. Hollywood and NonHollywood film making)." Such eclecticism, itself a reflection of bourgeois ethics, finds its more overt expression in Seidelman's second film, *Desperately Seeking Susan,* which, like *Smithereens,* is a study of the moral grounds of conduct in postmodern culture and a condemnation of all the heterodoxies of the margin. *Desperately Seeking Susan* continues Seidelman's teasing, voyeuristic gestures toward inquiring into the relationship between the center and the margin in contemporary culture.

The ideology of the film represents the center (the status quo) as the site for the mature negotiations of communal values, whereas its constructs the margin (the locus of oppositional politics and culture) as an instance of libidinal self-indulgence, transgression, and extremity. Seidelman's fascination with the (dis)connections between the center and the margin and the dynamics of these two modes of cultural understanding is interesting in that it enacts what might be called the "politics of reluctance" of her class and generation. Hers is the fairly successful upper-middle-class who in their youth (during the 1960s) learned a political language and a set of social and intellectual attitudes and behavior that has been put under pressure by the political "realities" of the 1980s and the social and family demands of a new cycle in their own lives as they have entered their middle years. They have discovered that their desired political stance, which might be loosely defined as neoliberal, is fraught with contradictions and does not have the resourcefulness and energy to interpret (and thus guide them through) the paradoxes of a bourgeois life in postmodern capitalism. Their professed political position has located them on the cultural margin, a zone of inquiry into the constitution and genealogy of morals and values in contemporary society and politics. Their own actual daily undertakings and engagements, however, have committed them in a rather perturbing way to the very cultural center whose grounds they desired to interrogate. They have been, in short, continually finding themselves returning to and participating in the very political and social practices that they thought they had examined and found wanting. The majority of these upper-middle-class professionals have been reluctant to follow the lead of the more articulate minority of their former friends and allies, who have clearly denounced the margin and embraced the center (which, in its reincarnation in the late 1970s and 1980s, has been known as social democratic reformism in Europe and as neoconservatism in the United States). But their actual political stance and social acts have all supported and provided a justification for the center, the status quo. This disquieting relationship with the center and its reformism has, for the most part, led to their becoming politically ill at ease and defensive because, in their earlier days, they had regarded the margin to be the most authentic space for an oppositional politics and the interrogation of the political common sense of culture, but now they find that they have been subsumed by the center and have become part of the conservative power network of culture and its exploitative social relations.

In his famous analysis of myths ("The Structural Study of Myth"), Levi-Strauss has suggested that myths are symbolic acts through which a given society attempts to solve the political and cultural contradictions that it faces but cannot in reality deal with (1963, 206–231). By extending the implications of his theories to the analysis of other forms of what Fredric Jameson in *The Political Unconscious* (1980) terms *narrative* (socially symbolic acts), one can clearly see *Desperately Seeking Susan* as a narrative through which the real political and social contradictions that confront a particular community of values and beliefs (the liberal upper bourgeoisie) in the era of postmodern American capitalism are "resolved" in formal and aesthetic terms. In other words, contradictions, which remain unresolvable in the "real" world of economics and politics, engender a filmic resolution in *Desperately Seeking Susan* that provides a frame of cognition and interpretation through which members of this particular cultural community can "solve" (historically determined) problems.

The film resolves these contradictions in large part by universalizing them. It presents the historically specific contradictions in the life of upper-middle-class professionals as the inevitable, general, and almost "natural" problems of living: a complex and mature life, it is assumed, is inextricably involved in incongruities. The incoherences of the middle class are thus encoded as what is "nuanced" and put forth as the general condition of "complex and mature" living as such rather than the result of class and history. On the other hand, it points up the contradictory moments in those contemporary modes of thought and living that openly take an oppositional stance toward the central values of culture in the domains of politics, sexuality, and norms in general. The more the instances of incongruity and incoherence in other social groups are foregrounded, the more the political and social contradictions that have riddled the life of upper-middle-class professionals are seen as "natural" and their historicity is suppressed.

In her first film, *Smithereens*, Seidelman depicted the bohemian life in the East Village as the site of immense contradictions and went so far as to suggest that in the character of Wren the margin of culture, at least in its manifestation in bohemian life, was parasitic, "fake," essentially void of serious, enduring values, and therefore not worth the attention of mature persons whose daily life is negotiated in the cultural space of the center. In *Desperately Seeking Susan,* Seidelman's political project is once again to resolve—that is, to universalize—the contradictions of her class by unveiling the inconsistencies of another marginal life-style, that of an oppositional woman who has distanced herself so far from the center that if she is not isolated and revealed as inauthentic and "fake" her appeal to the community may indeed raise fundamental questions about the legitimacy of the center. Wren and Susan both are, of course, far from being outside the dominant ideology inscribed in the central discourses. In their pursuit of freedom they are both responding to the hailing of ideology that recruits the individual into the existing social order as a free subject. In seeking "freedom" as individualized subjects, Wren and Susan are thus largely the same as the "yuppies" they condemn. But this is not the point Seidelman tries to make; rather she criticizes Wren and Susan's search as not conducive to genuine individuality. In other words, Seidelman does not reject the ruling ideology that interpellates individuals as free subjects, instead she criticizes Wren and Susan's ways as inadequate routes to free subjectivity. Wren and Susan, it should be made clear, are only "dissenters" from liberal ideology and without a sustained critique of it. Their acts are ad hoc improvisations aimed at displaying their nonconformity rather than an interrogation of oppressive practices. What is missing in their understanding of their own situation is a theoretical analysis that can provide them with a materialist view of resistance and oppositionality: a view of a political margin that can intervene in the economic, political, and ideological conditions of cultural subjectivities and subjection.

Seidelman's vision, which is intensely moral and sternly didactic in spite of her easy sense of humor in the film, maintains that an oppositional distance from the center is in principle unachievable and that Susan (the independent character in the film) is merely pretending to be outside the center. She is actually a self-indulgent "phony" who has no sense of the "complexities" of a mature life. It is significant that the first shot of Susan in the film is one of self-adoration. She is seen lying on the floor of a luxurious hotel room taking pictures of herself. In the following shots we see her playing with the camera (like a child) taking pictures of others: life is play for her; it is not serious. Having exposed Susan as childish and narcissistic, the next scene shows her "moral" character. She is seen stealing a pair of beautiful earrings from the man with whom it seems she has spent the night (as well as taking various other items such a silverware from the hotel room). She then leaves him while he sleeps, and the unsuspecting man is subsequently murdered by a hit man who is looking for the priceless earrings. Susan (like Wren) is thus represented as both a thief and a selfish woman who lives off people then discards them once she is through with them. The significance of this theft, however, exceeds the "meaning" assigned to it by the film. Susan "steals" the earrings not because they are priceless (she is unaware that they are missing museum treasures said to have belonged to Nefertiti), but because they are highly ornate additions to the rest of her junk jewelry. Her theft of the earrings symbolizes her values, which differ not only from the norms of the center but also from the pecuniary interests of the hit man with whom the film attempts to associate her.

In *Desperately Seeking Susan* as in *Smithereens,* Seidelman is enthusiastic, energetic, humorous and thoughtful. Thoughtful, one must add, in the manner of a person who is deeply insecure and cautious and has to "think" in order to "master" uncertainties and thus avoid costly "mistakes"; thinking, in other words, for Seidelman is a protective measure. Consequently, in its explorations of the center and margin, *Desperately Seeking Susan* shows a cognitive anxiety that propels the narrative forward at the same time that it inhibits discoveries out of a fear of unexpected surprises, a dread of being taken off-guard by the permutations of events that one is curious about but does not want to get out of control.

The ostensible narrative of the film evolves around a cultural cliche: the wife of a hot-tub salesman, who is more interested in making television commercials than in talking with his wife, becomes bored with her comfortable suburban life and to escape her terrible loneliness starts fantasizing about an exciting romantic world. The young, bored housewife, Roberta, seeks the passion and freedom symbolized by Susan, a nonparticipant in the practices of the dominant culture and one whose life is thus marked by its marginal stance. Unlike Roberta, who is tied down to her house in Fort Lee, New Jersey, Susan has no home; and this leads to the dangerous assumption that she therefore is the owner of all homes whose use she demands at will. She thus threatens the very principle of private property. All the people who let her use their homes beg her not to abuse their possessions, steal from them, or otherwise damage their residences. This concern with the violation of private property also informs *Smithereens* as indicated in by Wren's stealing the pair of sunglasses in the opening scene. Seidelman's preoccupation with property is in fact the matrix of her theory of reality. When not taking over her friend's apartments, Susan spends her nights in hotels freeloading off the men she stays with until they get "serious"; that is to say, until the relationship begins to lose its freedom and marginality and starts to be constrained by the restrictions of a centered life. Unlike Roberta who is presented as an emblem of trust and innocence, Susan is distrusted even by her friends, who regard her as irresponsible and dangerously impractical. Repeatedly they implore her not to do something embarrassing and wild ("no dramatics") that might interfere with the routines of their lives. Whereas Roberta is shown at home in such feminine places as a beauty salon, Susan is a habitue of the Port Authority Bus Terminal, living out of a suitcase and bus locker. Susan's life and her attitude toward friends, strangers, and the dominant values around her contest the norms of the center (for instance, the privileged position of "love" in bourgeois life). All her acts undermine the center and take an oppositional stance toward central modes of thinking and living. It is this contestational position and, consequently, her indifference to the most cherished notions of mainstream culture that the film attempts to put in question, unveiling them as "immature," "irresponsible," and finally "amusing." In revealing Susan as morally incoherent and socially "phony," *Desperately Seeking Susan* tries to legitimize the politics and values of the center; politics is disguised in the film as "moral" norms such as "irresponsibility," "selfishness," and financial parasitism. Underneath this seemingly "moral" debate in the film lies of course the social and class antagonism that eventually isolates Susan in the film and discredits her modes of living.

At the same time, Susan's oppositional approach to life and her manner of enunciating that opposition in her behavior, clothes, and relationships has a certain attraction for the center. She is defiant and unaccepting of the "normal" practices of culture, refusing to treat them as "natural" or "inevitable." Although Susan's nonconformity is expressed in the film almost entirely in terms of behavior, manners, and clothing and consists more of ad hoc acts of rebellion than a sustained interrogation, it can function, nonetheless, as a partial critique of culture and as such have great political implications. It is in fact in response to such implications that Roberta becomes attracted to her: Susan defies the master code of love in bourgeois life and treats it with irreverence and playful casualness. Such casualness unsettles the code of domesticity and the politics of the relationship between Roberta and her husband, Gary, propelling Roberta to search for Susan. The film's main project is to neutralize the larger political implications of the defiant marginal life. To contain Susan's positions, the film, in a typical liberal move, simultaneously acknowledges their "attraction" (thus acquitting Roberta for her unthoughtful fascination with Susan) and trivializes them as merely "interesting" and "intriguing"—qualities that are, in the end, distracting and not serious.

To achieve this end, namely, to depict Susan's stance as "attractive" but ultimately frivolous, the film constructs her as an instance of the exotic. She is made an embodiment of otherness living in a world strange and remote from the reality of normal adult life as lived by thoughtful people. In Susan's world, as one commentator has said about the world inhabited by Madonna, the rock star who plays Susan in the film, "Yuppie women ... need not apply, though they may ... press their noses at the window and consider their option." Roberta does indeed press her nose at the window; and it is to steer her away from Susan as a seductive option that the film transforms her into the inaccessible exotic who can be watched from afar but never approached or used as a model. To widen the gap between Susan and Roberta (the binary terms upon which the valuational hierarchy of the film is constructed) and to keep these two terms as distant from each other as possible, the film turns Susan into the signifier of the "weird." In the hierarchical separation of the "normal" and "weird" the film reproduces the ideological frames within which the practices of the dominant class are legitimated. If the "weird" and the "normal" were to be exposed as not so much different *from* each other but different *in* themselves and thus unstable, contigent, and historical constructs, the entire set of practices and ensemble of values founded upon their absolute polarities would collapse upon itself. It is therefore necessary to keep the two mutually exclusive. All signs of "strangeness," "foreignness," and "difference" are associated with Susan. Among these signs her clothing is the most visible. She dresses in a manner that no conventional woman would dream of emulating: stretch-lace tights and tops; bare midriff; exposed underwear; micro-mini skirts, and layers of junk jewelry. But above all, she wears a sequined jacket emblazoned on its back with the "alien" erotic symbol of a pyramid. She is, however, not the kind of person who fetishizes items of clothing, and as soon as she is attracted to a pair of gold-lame boots, she trades the jacket for the boots. She is a woman who celebrates the process of experience not one who embalms it in objects.

The ideological frame of the film, however, demands that

the excess and proliferation of meanings of such a sign as Susan be contained. In response to this ideological imperative, the film makes Susan so exotic that she is equated with the outlandish, and her attraction is naturalized by the code of patriarchy as merely harmlessly "crazy" and therefore "charming." The spectator is allowed to enjoy this "charm" of the exotic, but at the same time the film places the "charming" in the sphere of the nonserious while attributing seriousness to the nonexotic, familiar values of the center. Such strategies separate the terms *margin* and *center*, preventing alterity from mixing with the same and ordinary in this film as well as in *Smithereens*. As a result the unfamiliar is denied its freeing, historicizing, defamiliarizing effect on the familiar. Such defamiliarization of the familiar would, obviously, put the grounds of bourgeois life into question, whereas the film's project is the preservation and restoration of the grounds for the center.

The film, however, does not necessarily locate the values of the center it seeks to preserve in the most conventional places such as Fort Lee, New Jersey, where Roberta and her husband live. Rather it discovers them in such "odd" places as a back alley, Chinatown loft, and among such seemingly marginal figures as Dez, Roberta's new lover. The politics of such a representation is that the "center" does not have a specific place. It is a set of universal values and as such it is "everywhere." In its "everywhereness" the operation of the center becomes more clear: as a set of values, the center is the effect of ideological binarisms that place various cultural phenomena in a relation of mutual exclusivity to each other. By valorizing the first term over the second in such oppositions as male-female, speech-writing, experience-knowledge, center-margin, a system of values is maintained. It is, of course, part of bourgeois common sense that the two terms of an opposition are ultimately naturalized as moral categories; namely, good-evil. In Seidelman's work, binarism serves as the form of understanding within which the center is valorized for the purpose of suppressing the margin—representing it here as exotic in order to render it inessential.

The film exoticizes and thus trivializes Susan in an immediately understandable way by displaying her love life and opposing it to Roberta's more conventional one. The significance of this duality is readily accessible to the audience because "love" is perhaps the most privileged signifier of bourgeois life. In this emotional space Roberta's initial dissatisfaction with her life is articulated; and in this same space she starts her examination of an alternative to the emotional life offered by her busy husband. Susan, on the other hand, is constructed in the film as utterly casual about love—not only does she sleep around but her steadiest love relationship is conducted in a terrifyingly playful manner that undermines the seriousness with which the subject is treated by middle-class viewers. Susan and her boyfriend have no stable and stablizing meeting place nor do they have a regular time for meeting. Whenever he wants to find her, he places an ad in "The Personals" announcing "Desperately Seeking Susan" to which Susan responds: the ultimate romantic rendezvous. This is an intriguing, playful, but as Roberta soon discovers, very irresponsible and dangerous way to treat "love."

The fragmentary spaces of "The Personals" form an exemplary urban collage of loneliness and the pursuit of romance. Roberta's voyeuristic imagination turns these ads into gateways to a world of fantasy, fulfillment, and freedom as she reads them with the same avidity that other female readers plunge into Harlequin Romances. Roberta and Susan are "connected" in the interstices of these personal notices, and it is among the fragments of the ads and the sites they specify for the rendezvous in the streets of lower Manhattan that Roberta first glimpses Susan. She follows Susan through these streets, while making sure that she is not seen, fascinated by Susan's otherness, difference, and "exoticism." Roberta's quiet chasing after Susan from afar, in a sense, acts out the intepretive arc of the film: the desire that Roberta's class has for the moving margin, but its inability to situate itself there. The closest that Roberta comes to Susan in this early stage of their "relationship" is in the clothes shop where Susan exchanges her seductive jacket with the pyramid on the back for the gold-lame boots. As soon as Susan leaves, Roberta "buys" (privately owns) Susan's discarded jacket and thus metonymically possesses Susan. She wears the jacket and takes it home where Gary finds it unfathomable that a woman of Roberta's class and wealth would think of buying used clothes, obviously oblivious to the symbolic value of the jacket.

Seidelman uses the various street scenes of lower Manhattan and shots of life in Battery Park where Roberta first sees Susan and subsequently roams to emphasize the difference between the shabby and shadowy life on the margins of the city and the centered reality of Fort Lee. On finding a Port Authority bus-locker key in Susan's jacket, Roberta uses "The Personals" to arrange a meeting with Susan in Battery Park, where she witnessed Susan's original rendezvous with her lover. Seidelman presents the park and streets, like Susan, as charming but dangerous. The audience is given enough clues to be intrigued by these images of life in the postmodern metropolis but clearly discouraged from desiring to reside there. The constant danger of city life is brought home to the audience by the mob hit-man's attempt to run down Roberta whom he mistakes for Susan because she is wearing the pyramid jacket. The hit-man is seeking the wearer of the pyramid jacket—Susan, whom he saw leaving an Atlantic City hotel room just before he threw her latest lover out the window—to retrieve the "hot" Nefertiti earrings Susan took. In attacking Roberta, however, he merely causes her to hit her head and suffer amnesia.

The idea of "amnesia as a plot crux in 1985!" has outraged film critics who naturalized *Desperately Seeking Susan* as a realistic film. The uses of such plot devices, however, is of great ideological significance: the device points up the middle-class presuppositions of the narrative that one cannot be conscious and at the same time live a life of imaginative energy and vitality. "Adult life" does not allow Roberta such a combination, so for her to be able to experience the "other," she has to literally forget the "same." The realistically implausible plot device, therefore, reveals the political incongruities in the life of the uppermiddle class—forgetfulness as the enabling condition of a relaxed self-knowing. This theme is repeated in Roberta's house when Gary, her husband, smokes a joint with Susan and, in a rambling dialogue with her, forgets Roberta. The scene is obviously offered as a joke and perhaps also as an ironic visual reference to such films on the margin as *Easy Rider*, but it is nonetheless ideologically quite telling. Both Roberta and her husband, have to experience a form of amnesia. The other side of such a statement made by the ideology of the plot device is, of course, that Susan as well as her personals-writing boyfriend, who is always on the road, are themselves in a constant state of amnesia. Their "freedom" is nothing but forgetting adult responsibilities, and, by extension, the margin is construed as an escape from the center, not as an oppositional space with terms of its own. The film refuses to accept the possibility of being fully "awake" and yet free in life. Life is a dreary mode of enslavement. Of course, the film maneuvers to conceal the fact that the dreariness of life for a particular class is universalized.

The amnesia Roberta experiences opens up an entirely new space for her. This is the space of freedom from her former self—essentially a negative moment as it is acquired through escape and forgetfulness. It is, as she is soon to discover, a rather harrowing and confusing realm: the domain of fantasy in which she is allowed to become that incongruous combination Susan-Roberta, a blurring of lines between the center and margin that the film tries to demonstrate is, in reality, impossible because it threatens the underlying binarism of the film's ideology. In this middle part of the film the margin and center are mixed up in such a way that the effect is either farcical or immensely painful. The confusion gradually becomes so unbearable that a clear unbinding of the two and a restoration of the purity of the polarity becomes almost inevitable. In the meantime this fantastic space allows Seidelman to poke fun at the ideas and life-styles of the margin and teach Roberta a lesson. It also enables her to give ideological support to the audience to become intelligible to itself as coherent subjects by providing them with the humorous "evidence" to reject the Roberta-Susan figure and yearn for its decomposition (with some "reforms") into a clear-cut Susan or Roberta.

Roberta's adventures underground are more or less a rehearsal of Wren's wanderings in *Smithereens,* where Wren is kicked out of her own apartment, the homes of relatives, and the flats of her bohemian friends. At the end of this series of displacements, in a rather cliched freeze-frame, Wren is shown heading towards New Jersey (home), but instead she realizes she cannot go back and gets into a car to spend the night with a "john" and presumably start her new life as a prostitute. The underside of the middle-class valorization of love is that prostitution awaits all women who transgress the bourgeois codes. The equation of prostitution with any risk taking in the life of a woman is evidently something that haunts the director's imagination because the same motif is repeated in *Desperately Seeking Susan*. When searching for Roberta does not yield immediate results, Leslie, Roberta's sister-in-law, speculates that perhaps Roberta is a prostitute, maybe even a lesbian prostitute. Again the ideological weight of this speculation (which is offered to the audience in a semifacetious manner) is enormous and indicates the power of patriarchal thinking that dominates the values of the film. Leslie's speculations are in fact materialized in the film by a scene in which Roberta, dressed like a "floozy" for her semiburlesque role as a magician's assistant, gets mugged by the same hit man, who is still following Roberta-Susan for the earrings, and then is arrested for prostitution by the police, who also later refer to her lover, Dez, as her "pimp." In the police car (under the surveillance of the law, which is represented as protection, and moreover under the supreme power of patriarchy), the shock she has received from being knocked down sets Roberta-Susan's mind back in order, and Roberta remembers her own real name thus accepting her previous identity. This image reveals the metonymic relation between the police as a repressive state apparatus and identity as a socially enforced "legal fiction." Any efforts by women to violate the norms of middle-class morals and ethics will be punished: the notion underlying the film is "obedience."

The ethics of compliance that dominates the narrative itself is evidently also at work in the production and direction of the film. In an interview the "star" of the film, Rosanna Arquette, is quoted as saying that "She [Seidelman] was scared if she didn't get results right away, and she had so many people breathing down her neck that she couldn't loosen up" (*The Village Voice*, 3 April 1985). Seidelman's "dream" to "take the best of both worlds," that is, the codes of both Hollywood and independent film making (*The New York Times*, 26 Dec. 1982), is also an expression of the desire for success with the inevitable yielding to the dominant ideology and the power of patriarchy "breathing down her neck." The fact that she has played the role of a compliant woman director to get her film done is clear from several remarks made about the influence of studio executives in dictating several scenes in the film (*The Village Voice,* 2 April 1986). The dilemma Seidelman has here is the dilemma of her class: to be successful one has to comply with the very values that one has intellectually and politically rejected. This pressing problem makes it even more urgent for Seidelman to put in their place Susan and other figures on the margin, who insist on living "differently": they are presented as "thieves," "prostitutes," "lesbians," and "pimps." Such embodiments of moral degradation and sexual deviation are also part of the exotic. The desire to populate the margin with such figures and to equate this region of culture with the most feared elements is, of course, part of the ideology of the film that resecures the "obvious" of the culture. If the film makes it possible for the spectator to "see" and produce a "tale" (from the subject position postulated by the narrative) in which the center is subverted by a margin consisting of thieves, prostitutes, lesbians, and pimps, then it will be able to recruit the audience in support of its own ideology—the reaffirmation of the center as the uncontested space of moral and ethical values (morality being a way of concealing the politics of the issues involved).

Roberta's adventures underground are devised so as to amuse the audience and thus prevent any sustained inquiry into the chain of events that befall her. The life on the margin is shown to be violent, dishonest, selfish, and an unceasing series of utter silliness. The audience is intimidated by the unfamiliar and is allowed to release that tension only through laughter so that it will not entertain the idea of examining the unfamiliar. However, in the film the most tame part of the margin is recuperated by the center, and in such recuperation, the audience's curiosity about the margin and its attraction to it is satisfied in a self-congratulatory moment of seeming openness to otherness. This recuperation of the harmless part of the margin and its incorporation into the center also takes place in the domain of the master code of love.

Roberta-Susan's most significant discovery underground is, of course, her encounter with Dez, in whose problematic figure the film deals with another aspect of the relationship between the center and margin. Dez's job as a projectionist in a rundown

movie house that exhibits B movies almost automatically designates him (for the general viewer) as a figure of the margin; perhaps even as a nascent artist or film director, waiting for his big
"break." The first time the audience sees Dez he is behind a pro-
jector trying to fix a torn film when he gets a call from his friend
Jim, who is also Susan's boyfriend, asking him to go to Battery
Park to make sure that Susan is all right since a "stranger"
(Roberta) has also placed an ad "Desperately Seeking Susan."
Dez responds that he can't go because "he has a job." The
response is reassuring to the audience since it affirms from the
very first moment that Dez, despite the impression made by his
marginal job, is a "responsible" man—he is not going to aban-
don his post without first at least finding somebody to cover for
him. There is, nonetheless, one point here that might make the
audience uncomfortable and that is Dez's refusal to take care of
his friend's girl. But that "doubt" about Dez's adherence to the
code of loyalty is immediately dispelled by his decision to go to
the park anyway, even if it means "borrowing" the scooter of a
friend who will become angry with him. Jim in the same call is
"revealed" as a "jealous" lover and thus really not all that "liber-
ated" from the code of love valued by the center—he is, in short,
a phony, hypocrite liberationist. Dez arrives at Battery Park at
the symbolic moment that Roberta (mistaken for Susan) loses
consciousness. Becoming "unconscious," as I have already suggested, signals the opening of a desired space for Roberta. What
follows is a kind of dream dreamed in waking hours: she is
awake but separated from the identity that has made her life so
undesirable, so boring.

Since Roberta-Susan is also helpless, Dez, in another act of
responsibility, takes her to his loft. The moment of their arrival
at his loft also reveals the construction of Dez as a reliable man
even though he lives on the margins in a back-alley Chinatown
loft. They arrive just as Dez's girlfriend, Victoria, is removing
everything from the loft as she leaves him for a "creepy,"
"effeminate" man who is "obviously" Dez's inferior. Victoria
herself is depicted as a "bitch." She is the kind of woman who
has no sensitivity to the emotional side of a relationship; she
offers to send Dez a check for the sentimental objects she is taking, a gesture that only infuriates Dez and once more confirms

the "obvious" of the culture that "money" and "love" have nothing to do with each other. Victoria is pictured as so domineering, mean, and petty that she takes not only many of Dez's personal belongings (his past history) but also his full refrigerator (his food and sustenance for the present). His entire life is changed; his "home" has been destroyed and will have to be reconstructed from the foundation up. In this context Roberta's first utterance upon arriving in the bare loft—the very domestic observation that it has such good lighting and real possibilities to make a nice home—acquires its ideological resonance in the film. No matter where she is, no matter how much she has seen and suffered, a woman will always be a caring, sensitive homemaker. It is also significant that the first night Roberta and Dez are in the same place they don't sleep together. Dez believes in chastity and loyalty, and his moral character is demonstrated in several shots showing him tossing and turning and pressing himself against the hard floor while resisting his desire for Roberta-Susan. He is a trustable person and in many ways resembles people that the audience identifies with; at the same time he is also a detached person who has the added attraction of being a marginal figure—and artist-filmmaker.

Although Roberta-Susan is suffering from the confusion of her life on the margin, Susan is portrayed as an opportunist manipulating Gary, who is somewhat belatedly worried about Roberta's well-being and anxiously searching for her. Susan is once again free loading: eating and having a good time in Gary's home. Roberta, the constructive nurturer, is shown cooking and caring for Dez, in other words, trying to build a new home for the abandoned male, while Susan, the destructive consumer, is wrecking Gary's home, endlessly eating junk food and scattering leftovers and garbage around the house. The purpose of this comparative rendering of events is of course to produce a "tale" in which the margin is a deviation from the center and show its inhabitants as parasitic.

For the film to achieve moral believability for its "tale," it presents itself as equally critical of Gary's life. He is shown as superficial, insensitive, and living a spiritually "empty" life. The presentation of his emptiness is, however, done through so many cultural cliches (he is always running to work, has little time for anything but business, and so on) that it flatters the audience by making it possible for them to feel superior to Gary while at the same time adhering to the values of the center. This ideological maneuver leads the audience to the conclusion that Gary is living an empty life because "he" is at fault, not the values he is subscribing to: he is a jerk, but I (the spectator) am not; the spiritual emptiness is presented as coming from "personal" problems not from the codes of the center. And this emptiness can take place at any site in culture: Gary's life is as empty as Susan's (when hers is stripped of the extra trappings of freedom and carefreeness). Emptiness, in other words, is presented as a more or less universal condition. Susan tries to escape from it; thus she is immature and idealistic in thinking that there is a nonempty mode of living. But Gary submits to it because he (like any businessman) is a pragmatist immersed in the ethics of consumption and acquisition.

It is part of the ideology of the film to represent both Gary and Susan as sovereign selves: the moments of actualization of absolute free subjectivity. Gary is what he is because he wants to be that way, and similarly Susan is what she is because she has chosen to be so. The audience is never allowed to interrogate such self-sustaining individualities. If Susan enjoys being "homeless," for instance, what is the politics of her pleasure? Analogously what accounts for Gary's insensitivity? What does that reveal about contemporary living? What do the qualities of the characters' lives indicate about life, intimacy, and work in a late capitalist state? Yet the film merely presents these as part of the way "things are"—the obvious of culture.

For the film to make its ideological moves in the most nonideological and "natural" fashion, it therefore denounces not only Susan but also Gary. But the rejection of the two takes place for radically different reasons: Gary is an ineffectual member of the center whereas Susan is a dangerous part of the margin. The film then proceeds to reappropriate and renew the center by assimilating the margin's fringe that is least dangerous, represented by Dez. Dez stands for those archetypal marginal figures through whom the center historically has regenerated itself by recruiting them for the reaffirmation of the values of the center. This absorption of the margin's fringe for the center takes place in the domain of love, which is, as was suggested earlier, the master code of bourgeois domestic life and the guarantor of all family and (capitalist) state values.

In the end of the film, Roberta, now disentangled from the shadow of Susan, leaves Gary and moves in with Dez. This is a cue to the spectator to read the center as nondoctrinaire, liberating, and always open to newness and otherness. But the otherness presented, namely Dez, is in fact "sameness" disguised as the "other." Dez is a handsome family man, calm under pressure, self-confident, generous, and loyal. He stands for (benevolent) patriarchy whereas Gary, who has the signs of the traditional aggressive, selfish male, is shown to actually be effeminate and ineffectual; he not only loses his control under pressure, becoming emotional and eating like a woman to calm his nervousness, but he is also dominated by his sister Leslie who has to tell him what to do and guide him through the crisis. He is unable to take care of himself let alone a family; he cannot be trusted as the guardian of central values. By denouncing Gary the film preserves the ideals of the center and in replacing him with Dez expands its range of domination. Dez is the sensitive "new man": caring, vulnerable, and egalitarian, whose friendship with Susan and Jim is more a result of his sense of democratic pluralism than his sense of belonging to an interrogative cultural margin. In other words, he allows equal truth to different life-styles, thus enabling their coexistence, but without questioning the politics of their difference.

The differences between Roberta-Dez and Susan-Jim are made clear in the last scene of the film. This finale is significant because it has almost the force of the traditional "moral" of conventional narratives: it aims at providing the spectator with a post of intelligibility from which Roberta's desertion of Fort Lee and Gary is not taken to mean that she identifies with the values Susan represents. The final scene depicts the two couples in entirely different spaces. Roberta-Dez are seen in action (producing) in the projection room with Dez running the film and Roberta approaching to kiss him. Susan-Jim, on the other hand, are sitting passive in the audience (consuming), eating popcorn, and watching the images projected on the screen. The image of Susan sitting, eating, gazing, and giggling reemphasizes her moral emptiness, which the film suggests is concealed in her overactive life-style and childishness. The parasiticism and hedonism that this last image projects on Susan is the concluding ideological move of the film through which the contestation of ideas and values in culture between the center and margin are moralized as occurring between the forces of "good" and "bad" and therefore rendered, in the last analysis, transcendental and nonpolitical. The margin is thus strategically framed and the hegemony of the center is reaffirmed. The two terms of the binarism are thus kept apart and the political hierarchy founded upon them is reassuringly preserved.

CHAPTER 7

IDEOLOGY, DESIRE, AND GENDER

1

As postmodern discourses are restructured in response to an increasingly complex system of commerce and exchanges in contemporary society, certain modes of thinking, talking, and desiring along with the spaces of power that they inhabit are publicly inhibited and repressed in the mainstream of middle-class life. These repressed powers and desires, however, return to the communal life through various strategies of cultural transference (the displacement of unconscious desires from one site to another) that enable them to be attached to new, unexpected ideas, signs, objects, and activities and thus pass through the censor of public inhibition. The repressed returns again and again and each time in the guise of a new set of signs and activities. In other words, when a sentiment, feeling, idea, or wish becomes "taboo" in mainstream culture because of new historical conditions, it acquires a new life in (acceptable) disguise through transference. This disguised life, more often than not, is a life that is conducted on the margins of culture. If, for instance, the desire to dominate women is (for ideological reasons) no longer acceptable to the liberal consciousness of the middle class, the deep desire of a patriarchal order to control women finds its expression in the symbolic enactment of this desire in the space of a margin where the liberal imagination enacts its cultural fantasies through the mediation and agency of others. The symbolic site for the enactment of consciously repressed desires is usually removed enough from the main culture to allow an individual to flatter himself that he is morally superior, tolerant, and open-minded and has a sophisticated ethical consciousness but close enough to provide him with a viewpoint from which he can vicariously participate in the acting out of his deep desires and repressed wishes. An individual, confronted by historical social developments that inhibit him from freely expressing his desire for domination, becomes in short a voyeur by using various strategies of transference.

If we agree with Louis Althusser ("Ideology and Ideological State Apparatuses," *Lenin and Philosophy,* 1971, 127–186) that ideology is "a representation of the imaginary relationship of individuals to their real conditions of existence," we can regard these transferential strategies and similar devices to be the effects of ideological apparatuses for the interpellation and recruitment of subjects. They produce a set of representations through which people (mis)recognize the real conditions of their situation and "make sense" of those conditions in such a way that their intelligibility "explains" and "justifies" the existing relations of production in which gender plays a significant economic as well as political and ideological part. John Huston's *Prizzi's Honor* is one of the most powerful instances of this ideological operation of cultural transference. The film acts out the repressed desires for domination and subjugation of women that for various historical reasons are no longer overtly permitted in mainstream culture. In the symbolic space of a Mafia family, the film provides a set of mediating agents through whom the repressed political desires of patriarchy and the structure of its power and exploitation are articulated.

To understand the operation of the film's ideology, one has to bear in mind the contradictory position of women in contemporary capitalist societies. In its attempt to recruit women for its cheap labor force, the capitalist "free" market, which is desperately in competition with the Third World labor force, has had to produce new subjectivities for women so that it can recruit a self-sustaining and efficient work force. To construct these new subjectivities, the contemporary exchange system has placed a great deal of pressure on the relations of production to develop a new mode of public negotiations and discourses about women—the aim of which is to give women the psychological and social skills they need to perform confidently in the work place. Women in postmodern discourses are represented as equal to men, and the order of patriarchy is "officially" rejected. The need to have women in the work force, however, runs counter to the ideological need of men at the center of culture and society's power network to be in control. Thus, under capitalist-patriarchy, the construction of women is fundamentally fraught by contradictions: she is, on the one hand, represented as authoritative, efficient, and highly intelligent; but, at the same time, she is expected to honor the old code of allurement, submissiveness, and "dumbness." This political contradiction (the conflicting subject position(s) of efficient but helpless, authoritative but submissive, intelligent but "dumb") is resolved in such cultural texts as John Huston's *Prizzi's Honor.*

The film, in spite of its overt subject (life in a Mafia family), is about the contradictory situation of women in postmodern culture and operates as an ideological device to build a set of imaginary representations to enable men to (mis)recognize their relation with the actualities of the contemporary economy. The film tames the new woman, bringing her back into the old order; and, when resistance to such taming is encountered, it annihilates her. The spectator is made intelligible to himself by consenting to construct a "tale" of the film in which men and women are situated in relation to the power structure in such a way that men are always in unquestionable control.

The symbolic space of a Mafia family is the filmic site for reinstating women in the patriarchal order and resecuring the subjectivities required to reproduce the dominant social arrangements. This space is far enough removed from the mainline of middle-class life to allow the strategies of transference to operate without being immediately identified with the ethics of the bourgeoisie but close enough to enable the repressed desires of the postmodern bourgeoisie to be "realistically" articulated. The middle class has always had a double-sided and highly charged relation with the Mafia. Morally it declares the Mafia reprehensible, and politically it opposes it because of its disregard for legitimate private property. At the same time, the middle class is almost erotically fascinated with the Mafia because it holds illicit power that places it beyond the reach of the laws of the state while allowing it to be ruled by the laws of a desireous subject whose very identity is based on transgressive acts. The Mafia, in short, is the space in which the culturally repressed fantasies of the bourgeoisie find their most forceful articulation.

The opening scene of *Prizzi's Honor*—a wedding—is a celebration of the traditional woman: woman as a family person both
in the sense of a homemaker and a loyal member of a group (in
this case the Prizzi Family). The wedding is an elaborate and
rather gaudy affair in which the values of the traditional family
served by a woman and dominated by a man are consecrated
and sanctioned by religion. As "Ave Maria" is sung, the ceremony extols woman's virginity and monogamy in the relationship,
values that are highlighted by the contrast between Don Corrado Prizzi's two granddaughters: Theresa, the bride, and her sister, Maerose. The bride, named for the celibate saint, is dressed
in the traditional virginal white wedding gown while her sister,
whose name is reminiscent of the femme-fatale Mae West, wears
a strapless black gown with a dazzling hot-pink sash over one
shoulder. When the family matriarch attempts to reconcile
Maerose and her father, Dominic Prizzi, her father points to
Maerose's dress and asks why she is dressed like a "whore." The
two modes of womanhood, "the Virgin" and "the Whore," are
thus established in the very beginning of the film and constitute
the two modalities of subjectivity: the film situates the viewer in
such a relation to the events that he will produce a tale in which
the subject position of woman as virgin is resecured in opposition to the denigration of woman as whore. The virgin and the
whore are in fact the only frames of intelligibility that the men in
the film seem to have for their relationships with women. If a
woman does not fall into either category, the men experience a
cognitive and emotional confusion; they become paralyzed and
do not know how to relate to her. Charley Partanna's reaction to
Irene Walker is an exemplary instance of such confusion and
paralysis. When Charley discovers Irene's professional life and
becomes familiar with her background, the information he
obtains about her is so unsettling that it puts Irene beyond the
virgin-whore binarism. Charley, in a moment of incoherence and
disorientation loudly asks, "Do I ice her? Do I marry her?" Such
a dilemma is a sign of the crisis of binarism in patriarchy, which
can only divide women into the virgin and the whore, under
pressure of postmodern discourses that produce subject positions for women that seem to exceed the patriarchal signifying
system. The desire of patriarchy to continue with the old taxono-

my of virgin-whore nonetheless continues, and the result of the conflict between the repressed binarism and postmodern subject positions for women (which reproduce in gender relations the contradictions of political, ideological, and economic practices) is the kind of disorientation that Charley confronts. However, he must come to terms with this confusion, and the film eventually resolves his (culture's) dilemma by returning to the binarism and reinserting women back into patriarchy.

The motif of monogamy announced in the opening scene is rearticulated later when Charley allows it to be known that Maerose—in response to his philandering—ran away with another man only to be brought back in disgrace by her father. As a result Maerose is now a nonperson in her family which has exiled her from Brooklyn (the fiefdom of the Prizzi family) to Manhattan where she earns her living as an interior decorator while Charley is an honorary son of the family. She is held responsible for breaking the code of monogamy and is quite aware of her position as the family outcast when she ironically comments on her strapless gown: "I gotta reputation to keep up."

The limits of the "new" womanhood, however are primarily tested in Irene. She is first seen in the film sitting in the balcony of the church looking, in a rather distracted way, at the ceremony. When Charley notices her, she seems not only to enjoy the attention but in an uncanny way to have expected it. The "tale" of the film constructs her as such a scheming woman that the spectator, retrospectively, should be inclined to think Irene planned this "chance" meeting. As soon as Charley spots her, he tries to find out who she is; he hires a photographer to take pictures of her and even calls Maerose (for the first time since the broken engagement four years earlier) to see if she knows anything about Irene. The call sets in motion Maerose's "jealousy" of Irene, suggesting that the film produces a post of intelligibility for the spectator to regard the rivalry between women as inevitable, as somehow "natural" to the very "essence" of womanhood. No matter what kind of woman is involved—the homebound Theresa or the free, sophisticated, Manhattanite Maerose—a woman is a woman in certain "essentialized" characteristics such as jealousy that are pancultural and transhistorical.

Irene is a woman of stunning beauty. Outwardly, therefore,

she fits the traditional feminine code of alluring sexuality, and in fact her physique is the only reason Charley is attracted to her since he does not know anything about her at the time. Through this convention of love at first sight of a beautiful woman, the film once more asserts its underlying ideology about woman: she is reduced to that in her which is openly visible; woman is a surface. Her surface, moreover, determines all her connections, social relationships, and entire life. Thus Irene is attending the wedding ceremony and reception, apparently like a member of the "family," but this is only an appearance. It later turns out there is quite a different reason for her presence at the wedding. This duplicity of appearance and reality in Irene is repeated throughout the film and is one of the significant features of her "character": she is other than what she seems to be. She is scheming and fraudulent. This motif of fakeness and counterfeit is captured most clearly in the image of her purse. When she is dancing with Charley, she does not let go of her purse, a rather odd gesture given the nature and place of the ceremony. It soon becomes clear that even her purse is other than what it seems: it hides a gun, the mark of violence that is the antithesis of femininity in the dominant codes. The purse is in fact a case for holding the tool of her trade: a pistol for murdering a member of a rival mob family. She, unlike other guests at the wedding, has been flown in from Los Angeles as a hired gun. She is, in other words, not what she seems to be. She is a woman recruited into the work force to "supplement" male labor and to shield men from the law. If she kills an enemy of the Prizzi family while everyone is attending the wedding then each one will have a perfect alibi. The working woman enters the labor force only to provide relief for the working man. Thus Irene is neither a family friend nor a traditional woman. She is socially, in Derrida's words, a "dangerous supplement." Angelo Partanna, Charley's father, burns a photograph showing him standing next to her as evidence of an unwanted connection. Although she "supplements" the male work force, as a woman she is herself made intelligible in the tale of the film as an instance of lack: she is the opposite of (feminine) plenitude and presence. She is not a complete woman, not a complete hit-*man,* nor can she be a complete wife, a complete member of the Family, nor a complete mother (the only child she holds in her arms is a doll).

Before being called away to perform her professional duty and eliminate the Prizzi family opponent, Irene agrees to dance with Charley. Charley, however, is oblivious to most of the revealing signs emitting from Irene, because, like a real man, he is in love; and love (at first sight) makes him blind. A slightly bored, no-nonsense, super hit-man for the Prizzi family and a special favorite of Don Corrado himself, Charley is a very traditional man, unattached and without any particular direction, goal, or ambition in life. His attempts to find out more about Irene, through both the photographer and Maerose, all remain fruitless until Irene herself calls later that night ostensibly to apologize for leaving Charley in the middle of their dance. The spectator later discovers that her phone call not only conceals her homicide (the reason she left the reception) but also is a ruse to entice Charley as part of a larger scheme that Irene has invented to neutralize Charley as a hit-man, who as the emissary from the Prizzi family, will, she knows, eventually be sent to eliminate her. On the phone she is charming, coquettish, and, after informing Charley that she is in California, quickly agrees to have lunch with him the following day in Los Angeles. The effect of the telephone call is to further enhance, from a traditional point of view, the impression of Irene as an aggressive, fast woman. An impression that is reinforced at lunch. She is too "active" and "assertive" for a woman, so active and assertive in fact that she makes Charley look like a helpless boy. She orders their drinks, in Spanish; she takes Charley to an outdoor restaurant for lunch; she drives him in her (very expensive) car; and she does most of the real talking— Charley, the mobster hit-man, is reduced to near silence and incoherence; his conversation is limited to informational questions such as the name of the drink, the name of the language in which she ordered them, the name of the song the band is playing. In a sense the traditional roles are reversed: Charley is the passive one following Irene's active lead. This reversal, in the cultural context of the film, is seen as a transgression of the established code and resulting in the construction of Irene as a nonwoman, a quasimale, in other words, a "lack." According to the film's ideological markers, the spectator "knows" that this is not a normal state and will have to be transformed. The elimination of the nonwoman is therefore foreshadowed.

During lunch Charley confesses to Irene that he is in love with her. Irene's repsonse (her obvious insincerity manifested in her cliched gestures and oversentimentality) arouses the spectator's suspicions about her motives. Later in the film the viewer discovers that his suspicions are well-grounded: she has schemed and planned the whole affair from the very beginning. Not only is she a devious, scheming woman, she is also an adulterous one since her affair with Charley takes place while she is still married. Moreover, the spectator's tale is supposed to foreground as Irene's reason for making Charley fall in love with her is that she has stolen over half-a-million dollars from a Prizzi casino and she knows the Family will send its super hit-man after her and her husband, Marxie Heller. Charley and the Family, however, are unaware of Irene's involvement with Marxie or the scam. After murdering Marxie in his wife's California home, Charley is shocked to discover Irene enter and cheerfully shout, "Honey, I'm home." Learning that Irene is Marxie's wife, Charley refuses to believe her pleas that she was about to get a divorce from Marxie and instead mocks her "Honey, I'm home," asking her if this is the way an estranged wife addresses her husband. By having Charley interrogate Irene's endearment, the film requires the spectator to construct Irene as duplicitous, immoral, and a scheming, adulterous con artist. Irene's credibility erodes as the film progresses. No matter how grave Irene's crimes against the Prizzi family and against Charley, he cannot, as Irene very well knows, kill the woman he loves. Irene, it must be added, is also quite aware that in a world dominated by men she is alone, and in her aloneness she must take care of herself. She therefore further deceives Charley, returning only half of the stolen money and feigning ignorance of the half she keeps for herself.

Charley returns to Brooklyn but is unable to forget Irene. Irene is the most seductive, feminine woman he has ever met, yet she is a hit-*man*, just like Charley himself. She is a "foreigner," a Polish woman who has "changed" her name (like the untrustworthy Italian Finlay, the embezzling head of a bank in which the Prizzi family holds 25 percent interest); and she is blonde, unlike the women of the family. The code of patriarchy that Charley abides by is neither clear nor helpful in dealing with such a high degree of complexity, thus causing Charley's deep

polarization and complete incoherence ("Do I ice her? Do I
marry her?"). He eventually decides to marry her, and the couple settles in Brooklyn despite the warnings of Charley's father
that whenever Irene walks into a roomful of Prizzi women all
talk will stop. Irene will be an extraterritorial person, a woman
in exile, a transgressor of the hierarchized binaries of patriarchy,
and finally an object of female jealousy. Maerose's comment
about Irene that "Just because she's a thief and a hitter doesn't
mean she ain't a good woman in all other departments" is a
many-sided statement aimed partially at making Charley aware
of the fact that Irene is indeed a thief and a hitter and thus to
denigrate her, but in a rather ironic way it is also a statement that
comes closer than any of the comments by the men in the film to
capturing Irene's immense complexity as a modern woman: a
complexity that the common sense of patriarchal ideology, in
terms of which the film makes sense, naturalizes as "deviousness" and "scheming."

Irene is a highly intelligent, self-sufficient, professional
woman who is tough and unsentimental. She is deeply aware of
her aloneness in the world of men and the necessity of taking
care of herself all by herself. She has a political pragmatism that
derives from her awareness of the predominance of the code of
patriarchy and her maginality in it. She is, for example, the
woman behind the kidnapping of Finlay, the crooked bank executive. She not only plans the whole affair to the absolute amaze-
ment of Charley and his father but is crucial to its successful exe-
cution. She is, next to Charley, the "second hit-man." During the
kidnapping when the police captain's wife accidently walks into
the middle of it, it is Irene who quickly responds to the situation
and shoots her. The shooting sends the city police department
into a frenzy of violence against the Mafia. Irene know that as a
woman she is expendable and that sooner or later the Prizzis will
turn her over to the police so that the rampage against the Mafia
will stop and they can return to business as usual. This deep
awareness of her marginality, the need to take care of herself, is
represented in Irene's desire to have as much money in the bank
as possible—she know the ruthless operation of a capitalist
mode of exchange and does not want to be beaten by it. She
therefore insists that the Prizzi family return to her the money

that she had originally stolen from their casino since the insurance company has already compensated them for the loss. Regaining the money is a matter of principle and self-sufficiency for Irene even though she knows that insisting on her principles and "rights" diminishes her chances for survival within the Prizzi family patriarchy. Thus she pressures Charley to put her case before Don Corrado.

It is a mark of her intelligence, political pragmatism, and professional skills that when Charley calls her from Don Corrado's house to tell her that everything is "100 percent O.K." and that her money will be returned, she realizes Charley is lying and that she is doomed. Charley in his meeting with Don Corrado is given the bleak choice of either killing Irene or being abandoned by the family. His appeal that Irene is his "family" does not get him very far with the logic of the Prizzi family. His father, to persuade him, argues that the marriage tie does not mean very much as he has known Irene for only a few weeks; he then reminds Charley that he had told him not to marry a woman who is in the business—a warning, in other words, to stay away from the new working woman.

To save herself Irene flees Charley and the Family, but Charley follows her to Los Angeles. With his knife hidden in his jacket, Charley arrives at Irene's home to kill her on the eve of her departure for Hong Kong. Irene, of course, knows that he is there to kill her and prepares to defend herself. However, in representing the murder scene, the film reverses the situation. The ideology of patriarchal gender relations places the spectator in a post of seeing from which he obtains a view of the murder scene that justifies Charley's action. Although Charley has premeditated Irene's murder and has arrived with a knife at the ready to terminate her life, the camera dwells lavishly on Irene's bedroom in which she is seen loading her gun, attaching the silencer and getting ready to kill Charley. Irene, not Charley, is presented as the murderer. The film's ostensible justification in depicting Irene as the murderer is that she fires on Charley before he throws his knife at her; the history is completely ignored: Irene pulls a gun on Charley only because she knows his mission is to kill her. Irene's self-defense is thus turned into another example of her murderous nature. When Charley pins Irene to the wall with his knife, the film reaches a climax: the moment in which the new woman is punished for all her acts of transgression against the code of patriarchy. Through the agency of a Mafia family and the figure of a transgressive woman, postmodern capitalism dreams its deepest dream of domination. Resistance against domination is eliminated, and the regime of patriarchy is restored in the relationship between men and women. Irene is removed from the scene because she resists the "hailing" of ideology to accept the subject position of compliant "feminine" woman and to submit to the dominant practices of patriarchy. In the political economy of "love" there is no room for her as an oppositional subject who intervenes, through her actions, in ideology's efforts to recruit and install her as the "object" of desire without acknowledging her own "different" desires.

The other strong woman in the film, Maerose, Charley's former fiancee and Dominic Prizzi's daughter also resists the interpellation of patriarchy at first. She has been disowned by her family because of her violation of the code of monogamy. However, she is not murdered like Irene but rather is tamed back into the code of patriarchy. She is allowed to live because her transgressions are not as disruptive and dislodging of the codes and practices of patriarchy as Irene's and because she consents to take up the "modified" subject positions offered to her. She is a reformist not a revolutionary, a dissident like Susan in Seidelman's *Desperately Seeking Susan*. The ending of the film is quite significant in this respect. After killing Irene, Charley returns to Brooklyn where he feels lonely and needs a companion to help him forget his trip to Los Angeles. He thus calls Maerose and invites her to dinner. Maerose's answer, which is strategically placed at the very end of the film, is a revealing one: "Holy cow, Charley! Just tell me where you want to meet!" "Holy cow!" is an outdated verbal expression, and although it is thus "ironic," it also signals the historical regression in which Charley's codes of patriarchy have clear "meanings." She is ready to be recruited as a feminine woman, and her response to Charley is a declaration of her readiness and acceptance of the code. The film represents Maerose's "consent" as her redemption and offers as her redeeming trait her unquestioning adherence to the code of romance. She loves Charley and is prepared to do anything for him and to commit any act to get him. She, like Irene, has a goal and knows how to achieve it, but unlike Irene, she is never self-interrogative and critically aware of her goal and its political dimensions. She is, in other words, not a politically self-questioning person and, to a very large extent, treats her "love" for Charley as "natural"—inevitable. She does not inquire into the ideology of "romance" and her love for him. She is casually unaware of the workings of the dominant ideology of patriarchy that interpellate her as a "lover." She never "asks" herself why she loves him. The spectator is to understand her love as the effect of the "natural" attraction of a man and a woman, especially two who grew up together. "Love," in other words, is self-evident; it is a plenitude that explains itself outside the politics of patriarchy. Consequently she suspects that she is socialized to love a man beyond and above everything else and that such unquestioning love is far from being "natural" and is indeed an instance of the operation of the ideology of patriarchy in interpellating her as a woman and placing her in the relations of production.

She is represented in the film as an artist, a woman sensitive to the aesthetic side of life. Whereas Irene has a political pragmatism that enables her to see through the operation of the code of patriarchy, Maerose becomes fascinated by the texture of life, not seeing beyond appearances, thus aestheticizing her experiences as a woman in the political economy of reality constructed by men. In the language of common sense, she is typically feminine: attentive to details and responsive to the "beauty" of life; in other words, an artist. She also has a "philosophy" of life but her philosophy is entirely aimed at the aestheticization of experience: "Everyone sees shapes differently, but color is forever." "Shapes," masses that occupy space differently and give different impressions to different people, are merely relative (historical); "color" is unvarying (absolute). She is in search of an absolute ground for her life: "color" provides this for her in her professional life as an interior decorator, and "love" becomes the absolute of her emotional life. She has no awareness that the absolute is after all grounded in history and is ultimately political and thus historically contingent (namely, not absolute). Her uncontesting acceptance of "forever" leads her to a reacceptance of the code of patriarchy: "Just tell me where you want to meet."

The representation of Maerose in the film follows the trajectory of her divided behavior and ideas. To the extent that she, like Irene, transgresses the code of patriarchy, she is punished and treated as "whore," whereas her final act of submission and acceptance is rewarded. Similarly, Maerose's clear sense of her goal makes her, like Irene, come across—in the patriarchal common sense of the film—as a scheming woman who stops at nothing to get what she wants. An exemplary scene is her encounter with Charley and the account she gives of this incident to her father. Charley goes to Maerose to get her advice about Irene ("Do I ice her? Do I marry her?"), but rather than attending to Charley's urgent pleas, Maerose seduces him and in a sense forces him to make love to her "on the oriental" in the livingroom of her Manhattan apartment, thus affirming the code of the "whore." When she reports this event to her father, whom she hopes to enrage so that she can get back at Charley, she reverses the entire situation. She tells her father that Charley raped her, "screwed" her several times, and then proceeds to describe the size of Charley's penis, again violating the code of virginity—she is indeed represented as a scheming "whore." However, the crucial representation not only of her deviousness but also her utter insensitivity and cruelty is her treatment of her father's ulcer. Responding to his pain and plea for water, Maerose runs the tap water, making a convincing noise while she pours liquor in a glass and then hands it to her suffering father. She breaks the filial bond. Yet the film does not make clear that the man involved in this scene, her father, is the same one who had banished her from his home and family and caused her years of anguish for transgressing his sexual code. Maerose tries to undermine her father's restrictive sexual code in this scene by equating Charley, the person her father wanted her to marry, with the man with whom she had a brief affair. In Dominic Prizzi's eyes, Charley is almost asexual; he knows Charley as well as he knows his own daughter since they grew up together. Maerose by calling her love making with Charley a "rape" and by describing the size of his penis is simply drawing her father's attention to the fact that Charley is, like any other man, a sexual being and that under the code of patriarchy all "love making" is in fact a form of rape. Maerose wants her father to see Charley, his asexual "son," the other men of the family, and perhaps himself differently—as constructed by the code of patriarchy at the core of which is the owning of women as sexual beings.

Again like Irene, Maerose is a knowing woman: to document Irene's theft, she retraces the other's routes, finding witnesses that can testify that Irene was indeed involved in the casino affair. She is also capable of planning a scheme through which her grandfather will be forced to act upon her findings and "get" Irene. Her plan, however, is only partially successful. She is unable to persuade her grandfather to do what she wants immediately, but her scheme and evidence prompt Don Corrado to insist that Irene return the stolen money "within five days" with interest. Despite participating in all the signs of female otherness, Maerose, unlike Irene, accepts romance as the test of her identity and the uncontested ground of womanhood. As a result of this acceptance she is reinscribed in patriarchy and allowed to live. A mere dissident is no real threat to the prevailing economic and political order but rather provides a safety valve for protest and by disagreeing, purges the system, allowing it move on structurally intact.

In annihilating Irene while allowing Maerose to survive, *Prizzi's Honor* acts out contemporary American society's repressed fantasies that no longer can be openly articulated in the domain of the public sphere. That which is not possible in the center is transferred and executed in the margin. The patriarchal codes thus maintain their legitimacy: all that has happened is a transference of the site from which ideology interpellates the subject and places her in capitalism. The new site is as powerful a place of "hailing" as the previous one without being as politically and culturally vulnerable. The transference, in other words, is in the end a strategy of containment, and thus its psychic space is traversed by the forces of exploitation and domination.

2

Jean-Jacques Beineix's *Diva* has been viewed by most as a beautiful film that is subtly entertaining in part because of its delightful visual jokes and references to film and media culture.

Some critics have suggested that it should be approached as a metafilm: a self-delighting visual space that goes beyond mimeticity and uses the realistic details required by its plot as a mere "excuse to have fun making a movie." Emphasizing the "enlightened playfulness" of the film, at least one critic has attempted to make it into an apolitical statement depicting a "hedonist trapped in a world politicized to the extreme."

This is not the place to discuss the poetics and politics of metafilm, but because a metafilmic vocabulary and frame have become common in discussing films similar to *Diva,* it might be helpful to point out that there is a radical difference between a film that merely quotes from previous visual texts and thus desediments the quoted images and releases new, often parodic meanings in them, and those films that aim at exploring the filmicity of film and thus their own status as film. However, in either case, such a self-reflexivity by no means would imply that the visual space of the film lies beyond ideology; ideology is the conditon of meaning and communication in all discourses, and metafilms are no exception: there is a politics to self-reflexive discourses as well as to discourses that represent themselves as transparent and mimetic. But judging from various commentaries, *Diva* has indeed succeeded in creating the illusion that it is a film about itself as a floating signifier and without troubling "contents." It is, according to another critic, "the most purely pleasurable movie," full of "visual wit and style."

Interrogation of the film, however, reveals the ideology inscribed in this "witty" visual space to be a profoundly disturbing statement about the politics of gender, the contemporary crisis in the relationship between men and women in the West and the transgressions it causes. The film is committed to the ideal of the sovereign (male) self and its free and unencumbered growth through emotional, intellectual and aesthetic fulfillment—all presented as universal and thus transcultural values. The world, events, and other people are seen as occasions for self-enhancement on the part of the protagonists who seemingly are struggling with the contemporary world in which individualism and private spaces have lost their values. The contradictions repressed in such a liberal humanist view of the self and its connection with others are so overwhelming, however, that the film,

which ostensibly sets out to support such an ideology by drama-
tizing it, becomes in actuality not an affirmation of liberalism but
a deconstruction of the very philosophical grounds upon which it
is founded. For the central male characters, Jules and Gorodish,
to achieve self-governing and fulfilling independence through
emotional encounters and aesthetic knowledge, they have to
negate the very principles of liberalism that authorize their
search and their world view. Liberalism and its underpinning
pluralism are articulated in the unsaid of the film as mere strategies of containment in capitalist patriarchy—as discourses for
interpellating women as the "subjects" of men's desires.

The current crisis in the relationship between men and
women in the West (a mode of relating that is part of a larger
view of an imperial self and its relations to the outside world) is
foregrounded in recent years partly because of the rapid shifting
of patterns of behavior under new social forces. The traditional
codes of connection in male-female relationships have been prohibited in the public discourses of postmodernism, and Western
women are no longer represented in these discourses as a mere
actant of men's erotic and domestic fantasies. As a result the
Western middle-class male has had to search for this lost center
(so necessary for orienting his sense of self and emotional well-
being) in the margins. In *Prizzi's Honor* the margin that reinscribes the prohibited centering codes is the Mafia family, the
underground world that is not in the public sight but circum-
scribes it. In *Diva* the Mafia family is replaced by the world of
white mercenaries, corrupt officials, and Third World merchants,
which although removed from the center of values and subjectivities of the West, nonetheless circumscribe it. This "excess" of
the center, in other words, operates in *Diva* as the margin in
which the codes of patriarchy—suspended in the public postmodern discourses of gender—are given a dark and powerful
force. As *Diva* clearly indicates, the search for a new erotic and
emotive site (following a familiar pattern in Western history) has
led to the emotional and sexual colonization of the dark woman:
an exploitative relations that deprives the nonWestern woman of
the very self-sovereignty for which Gorodish and Jules strive.
Beneath the playful and glittering surfaces of *Diva*, the calm
Zen-like gestures Gorodish and the innocent-looking face of

Jules lie a deep, destructive aggression and emotional cruelty. The film is an allegory of what Cynthia, the film's "black American diva," calls "un viol" (a rape) of the dark woman by the Western man who no longer can unleash his unchecked erotic fantasies upon the postmodern Western woman.

On the surface, *Diva* devolves around a complicated plot consisting of a double chase. In the rather intricate interstices of these chases, however, quietly and perniciously a third chase takes place that, like the first two, aims at restoring the lost state of affairs. The overt chases of the film are about the destiny of two voices: both private voices that should not be made public. If the Taiwanese record pirates get hold of the tape of Cynthia's rendition of Catalani's *La Wally* (made surreptitiously by Jules), her aesthetic purity and performative integrity will be violated, and she will be reduced to a mere commercial property and descend to the rank of popular singer. ("Vous me prenez pour les Beatles?") She is the dark singer who refuses the status of "celebrity," believing in the totality of the performative situation. The "publication " of the second taped voice is also equally ruinous of a career. This is a tape made by a white prostitute, Nadia, recounting the crimes of the chief of police who, along with a private army of thugs, is involved in prostitution rings, drug trafficking, and murder.

Alongside these two actual chases, a third chase takes place in the film. In this one, the searchers also struggle to retrieve something that is of vital importance: the traditional erotic order and patriarchal ideal of womanhood and femininity Jules and Gorodish need for securing their own power of masculinity and perpetuation of their exploitative relation with women. This search, however, is equated in the film with the search for spontaneity, poeticity, and affirmation of the right of the individual to shape his life and world according to his sovereign desires. Unlike the first two chases, this search takes place not on the streets of Paris, but in the dark interiors of quiet lofts; the awesome inside of a lighthouse; the dreamy terrain of a "fairy tale" told over the telephone; and in the textuality of surrealistic jokes. The object of this search is a woman(hood) tantalizingly placed on the moving boundaries of the figure of nuturing mother and seductive mistress. This peculiar combination, in which

woman is projected as a self-negating person, requires traditional gender arrangements for its existence, but these are in crisis in
the West. To a very large extent the postmodern Western
woman, in comparison to the Eastern woman, refuses to respond
to the image of herself projected by male fantasies rooted in the
cultural representations generated by the patriarchal social
order. The white European man is thus forced to go outside contemporary Europe to find a woman who could be interpellated
into the order of his (political) desires. However, in *Diva* the
white man, whose gender hegemony is being challenged,
revenges himself by punishing the white woman throughout the
film—presenting her as self-absorbed, insensitive, inhumanly
efficient, and, on the whole, nonsexual.

The first European woman the film focuses on is Nadia, a
prostitute who is fleeing from being forcibly kept as the chief of
police's mistress. Before being murdered by his henchmen, she
conceals in the mailpouch of Jules's moped an audio tape cassette
recording her miseries and revealing the crimes of the chief of
police. Nadia is the white woman as burden—by dropping the
"burden" of her confession (her history) on Jules, she pits him
against the corrupt forces and sets in motion their nearly fatal pursuit of him. Barefoot and barely clothed, Nadia is a "professional"
woman stripped of all "womanly" qualities. The blonde policewoman, Paula, is also a "professional." Although in her professional capacity she saves Jules in his loft and protects him from his
adversaries, she only partly succeeds as the redeeming woman.
She is the meddling, punishing mother who takes care of Jules
only as part of preserving her own image. She is, significantly,
indifferent to sensuality and uninterested in touching and contact.
While on a stake-out with her partner, who brags about his athletic
prowess as a runner and somewhat facetiously invites her to feel
his leg muscles, she becomes nervous and refuses. The other white
women presented in the film do not fare any better: all are presented as lacking spontaneity and warmth. In one of the chase
scenes a wounded Jules feeling his pursuers takes shelter in a
video-games arcade. Bleeding from a wound and almost losing
consciousness, he leans on the shoulder of a young white woman
for support. Paranoid and unfeeling, the woman mistakes his gesture for a sexual pass and shoves him away. It is also a white prosti-

tute who instigates the betrayal of Jules that results in his being shot; she persuades a dark prostitute who has befriended Jules, letting him hide from his pursuers in her apartment, to reveal his location to the thugs seeking him. The futility and frustration in the relationship between contemporary Western men and women is summed up in a powerful visual gesture: tired, taking refuge in a friend's apartment, Jules lies down fully clothed next to his friend's white companion and burrows his head—still shielded in his motorcycle helmet—into the irritated woman's shoulder; she then punches his helmet away. Completely protected and without a trace of vulnerability, Jules is impervious to her. It is also important to notice that in the film none of the white women, including the policewoman who is on the screen more than any other white female, plays an important role in the unfolding of the story and all of them are low in the hierarchy of characters in the film.

In telling contrast to the white woman, who is cold and distant, the dark woman is depicted as warm, loving, resourceful, and above all in emotional and sexual synchrony with man. She is the epitome of ideal womanhood that Jules and Gorodish find in the process of vanishing from their own culture but are striving to retrieve and reestablish as the norm.

One embodiment of this ideal is Cynthia—the dark goddess whose beauty, quiet but powerful sexuality, and sheltering strength must be preserved and protected at all costs. She is Jules's "private property," "his diva," and must remain his and only his; Jules's arduous efforts to keep the tape of her voice out of the hands of the Taiwanese record pirates is an enactment of his refusal to share with the public. The owning of her (voice) is, of course, very significantly based not on any "right" but on a "theft": Jules's taping of her voice without her consent or even knowledge. Having "stolen" her voice, Jules, the postmodern Mafia man and neocolonialist, acquires the right of ownership, and throughout the film he behaves as if he does indeed have a legitimate claim on her voice. As Cynthia reminds him, the illegal taping is nothing short of a rape. However, Cynthia is presented in the film as the forgiving mother-mistress: unlike the blonde policewoman, Paula, who searches Jules's apartment for evidence of wrongdoing that could lead to his punishment, Cynthia, who has the evidence of Jules's wrongdoing, not only does not punish him but embraces him, and the film ends with Jules in her arms reaffirming his sense of true womanhood.

The spectator makes this relation intelligible in his tale by viewing ideology's hailing as a natural and organic relationship between man and woman, thus universalizing the codes of gender in capitalist patriarchy. This naturalization is emphasized by the elaborate camera shots of Jules's "romantic" walk with Cynthia, resplendent in a flowing gown and carrying a white parasol, through the Tuileries Gardens where the two are shown in silent communion with each other and nature. Such "romantic" acts as Jules bringing Cynthia an enormous bouquet of flowers and his fascination with lyrical music are in stark contrast to Jules's own contemporary urban language and life-style symbolized by his apartment: a virtual storehouse of postmodern electronic technology located on the top floor of a garage, packed with discarded machinery and vehicles, and decorated with large wall murals of 1950s automobiles. Jules's "romantic" gestures thus point to his deep-seated nostalgia for recapturing the lost world in which patriarchy, with its gender codes and exploitative modes of living, is uncontested.

The latent sexual dimension of Jules's relationship with Cynthia is alluded to when the camera cuts from the scene of their walk to a close-up of Jules the following morning lying under blue satin sheets in Cynthia's room. As the camera pans the room, it turns out he is sleeping alone on the couch, but in an earlier scene, he acts out his sexual desires for "his Diva" using a dark prostitute as a stand-in.

Alba is to Gorodish what Cynthia is to Jules: nurturing, loving, and ethereal. Her movements around Gorodish, for the most part, occur on rollerskates that keep her skimming above the floor and beyond the hard resistance of earth (the realities of the crisis of patriarchy). Her manners and speech are also displaced—she is a woman-child symbolizing an everlasting childhood. Her language is charged with fables, jokes, stories, and verbal gestures that pressure the banality of daily talk toward the poetry of the street. If Cynthia is, in Jules's words, the "Queen of the Night," calm, restful, mysterious, then Alba, whose name means "dawn," is the angel of the day bringing with her freshness, movement, and openness. She is in tune with higher realities, and not only her talk and carefree gestures point to a "beyond," but her saluting the sun with her bare breasts while taking care of Jules in the lighthouse is a central visual image reminding the audience of the lyrical space in which Jules and Gorodish's search is taking place. She is uninhibited: she shoplifts an album from a record shop, hiding it in a portfolio of nude photos she has made of herself, as if to signal her disregard for such material codes as private property and such moral ones as propriety. She is the spirit of freedom from the social. Unlike the "serious" contemporary white woman, she is the instance of playfulness; and also unlike the white woman, she not only does not "burden" the man but, as her acts of disregard for the routine demonstrate, she "lifts" him to a higher region of reality with her surreal tales and fantastic fables. The politics of her gestures and the contradictions upon which this notion of freedom is based are revealed when one realizes that she is herself a piece of private property owned by Gorodish and subject to his sense of propriety as when he jealously chides her for coming late, threatening to put her back where he found her—on a road in Vietnam with her VC friends—if she does it again.

The women of the film are thus separated along a color line with white representing lifelessness, lack of love, and a deadly indifference to emotions and art, which symbolize life-giving energies, warmth, and protectiveness. The white women are all unaware of the inner needs of the men around them whereas the dark women center their lives around the desires of men and are thus shaped by men according to their needs. The film carefully points out that the emotional and erotic power of the dark woman is not just a question of relative personal perception but a universally perceived fact. One way in which the film signals this universality is to permeate those environments encompassing the harmony of white men and dark woman with blue lighting (or blue objects). Even when Jules is with the prostitute, the film plays with the color of the lighting: harsh colors shattering the calm dark light symbolize her failure. More important, the film attempts to show how this notion transcends the particular by studying the relationship between dark women and white men from two entirely different perspectives: the view of Gorodish and that of Jules.

Gorodish is the intellectual involved in the discovery of the underlying structures of reality. Through his analytical powers he sees the connections between events (including the two conspiracies behind the two chases) and by manipulating the relationship between the two manages to achieve his goals and arrange the deaths of all the bad guys: not only the chief of police and his henchmen but also the Taiwanese record pirates. He is a frightening new, postmodern combination of intellectual-technocrat-guru whose voracious, imperial "I" does not recognize any boundaries. He is the exemplary man of the new patriarchy— fully involved in the technologies of exploitation and power. He is equipped with the latest high-tech electronic and technological devices and gadgets and at the same time maintains a nostalgic reification of earlier low-tech industrial products such as his fleet of CV Citroens and the lighthouse itself as well as the social arrangements supported by them. He obviously has the resources to indulge his taste for both state-of-the-art and "antique" technologies as well as spend entire days meditating on puzzles and cultivating the Zen art of buttering bread. The source of his income (and thus his freedom to meditate) is not quite clear, although his understanding of the criminal mind and ability to anticipate and control the actions (even arrange the deaths) of various felons, suggests his own involvement in underground activities. The world is a mere projection of his wishes and desires; he molds events almost according to his whims. Jules, on the other hand, is the intuitive man who delights in the sensuous. Although he is unanalytical, he is also a manipulator of events and people and like Gorodish does not stop at any boundaries in satisfying his desires.

Both men are living on the margins of contemporary life, but this does not mean that they are marginal. They are located, in fact, at the heart of the postmodern world. They have a postmodern life style, are conversant with technology, and are at home with the many languages and codes of postmodern living. Similar to other colonialists, they keep abreast of the technological developments of their time and are simultaneously nostalgic for earlier social values. They are romantics with a high degree of self-reflexivity about their own acts and beliefs; their talks and discussions constantly include themselves. For Gorodish this self-reflexivity is analytical—there is hardly a moment in which the subject of his thinking is not thinking itself—whereas for Jules it is primarily intuitive and phenomenological—a way of feeling and acting. However, for both such a high degree of self-consciousness does not preclude a rather twisted naivete, which they seem to welcome as a relief from the oppressiveness of constant self-examination.

Although unknown to each other at the start of the film, once introduced by Alba, Gorodish and Jules recognize their shared affinity and act as if they have long been intimate. They are in fact the two postmodern sides for the European mind. Whereas one represents the analytical and the other the intuitive, they are both the film's heroes—the forces of good resisting the forces of evil—and are united with the dark women who are also representative of art, innocence, and self-knowing. The world of the film is thus divided between the good (Western men and dark women) and the evil or ignorant (the chief of police, his cohorts, the Taiwanese record pirates, and a number of white women who are all too busy surviving to be aware of the higher realities of living). The world around the criminals and white women is one of corruption, prostitution, self-interest, and unthoughtful living, but the world around Jules and Gorodish is one of purposeful living and aesthetic and erotic purity. The moral purity in the film is presented through the use of such visual cliches as the two henchmen. The brutality and vulgarity of one is communicated by drawing on the negative racial and cultural stereotypes of a Spaniard in French culture. The other henchman is represented in terms of the international imagery of punk: not only do his clothes, manner, and weapon (an icepick) signal his criminality, but more important in terms of the film, even his aesthetic anarchism is a sign that he is the emissary of disorder. He hates everything from Beethoven to elevators, preferring only to listen to kitschy accordion music through his earphones. The film is made intelligible in terms of a framing ideology that unequivocally polarizes the world and posits Jules and Gorodish as unquestionably "angels" of goodness. Gorodish's arrival in one of the last scenes of the film (in which the chief of police is about to murder Jules and the policewoman) is to be decoded by the viewer—in the subject position offered by the film—as a climactic rescue scene in which the bad guys are vanquished.

But the film's association of Jules-Gorodish with the forces of good breaks down under its own inner contradictions, which deconstruct the philosophical ground of the film: Jules-Gorodish, far from being uncontaminated goodness, partake in the same crimes for which the chief of police is doomed. For Jules and Gorodish to obtain a fulfilling relationship, which for them is the main purpose of life, they find themselves taking those very same qualities away from others. Gorodish steals Alba from Indochina. Jules steals Cynthia's voice and dress, not only causing her agony but also forcing her into an abhorrent situation that threatens to destroy her integrity, identity, and art. The target of these acts of violence are dark women who are vulnerable in a white world. Gorodish and Jules exploit this vulnerability in the same fashion the chief of police exploits prostitutes and drug addicts and in the same tradition that eighteenth- and nineteenth-century colonialists exploited the Third World. In the film the dark woman replaces the Western woman, who is moving away from this position of total vulnerability to the Western man's oppressive desires, as the site where aggression is unleashed. The film legitimizes this aggression and resecures the code of patriarchal gender relations by presenting Jules and Gorodish on the side of goodness, poise, sensitivity, and aesthetic harmony. However, their patriarchal acts—subjugating women to reinstate the codes of masculinity—are based on the same principles as those of the criminals: the exploitation of others. The polarization of good and bad in the film thus collapses under the weight of its own arbitrariness. The film's seeming coherence is achieved through love, but the coherence is based on an incoherence, a violation of its professed values and founding ideas. This situation is itself an extension of a larger historical change: the current political crisis in the relationship between men and women in the West and its underlying economics, a crisis masked by the seeming order of an imported love.

The subject of the film turns out to be the transgressions committed against those whose victimization is necessary for the heroes to reach the desired level of gender security in the threatened codes of patriarchy. That dark women are the objects of aggression is a telling indication of the changing political economy and geoerotics of the times: the colonization of women may come to an end in one part of the world but the domination of the imperialist male continues in other corners of the globe. The emotional expansionism of the white male, however, is legitimized in the language of flight from the emotionally dead white woman and embrace of the resurrecting dark female: the interpellation of dominant ideology merely changes sites.

CHAPTER 8

THE POLITICAL ECONOMY OF ART: INGMAR BERGMAN'S *FANNY AND ALEXANDER*

ALEXANDER

Alexander is an artist in the making: he is involved in the construction of a more genuine and stable reality than the one that surrounds him. He is thus indifferent to mundane actualities because he is in touch with a higher level of being. From the very opening shots of the film, in which he is shown absorbed in his toy theatre, Alexander is represented in the film as being "different" from the people around him. He is constantly seen hiding under tables, behind objects, and in the recesses of rooms where he is provided with a post of observation. He can see without being seen and without having to participate in what he sees. He is—as a true romantic artist is assumed to be—"not engaged" in the affairs of the world. The film does not inquire into the reasons for his (the artist's) difference from ordinary people but offers this difference as the given and obvious of culture, almost as a "natural," inevitable fact. The unsaid of the film assumes that all artists-visionaries who have access to a higher reality are different from those who are engulfed in the dailiness of living, and Alexander is no exception. The theory of art and creativity behind the film presupposes that art is otherworldly; it is transcendental, and its manifestation through human agency seems almost a matter of accident. This romantic view of art enables the film—by direct appeal to culture's common sense view of art, which is a normalized form of this romantic theory—to state a position for the artist without seeming to have stated one, to offer a philosophy of art without seeming to have done so. It allows the film, in other words, to mystify its master code: life as a dream play.

Throughout the film, Alexander is mostly quiet and does not seem to be able to communicate with ordinary people. The only time he is involved in any sustained talking, it is with extraordinary individuals such as the mad boy, Ishmael, and his equally "imaginative" craftsman-artist brother in Uncle Isak's house. His two constant companions are his stuffed animal, which he carries with him everywhere in wakefulness as well as in sleep, and the ghost of his father. Neither of these can talk back: Alexander seems to be more at home with silence that he fills by inventing alternative versions of reality. His first invention is the story he circulates among his classmates about his mother selling him to a circus and for which he is severely chastised by the bishop and his mother. The second story he invents to "correct" reality is about the bishop's previous wife and their two children. In Alexander's version of that life, the bishop drove them to drown themselves; he is thus a murderer. For this Alexander is again punished; this time he is flogged and confined to the attic. Both stories are expressions of a desire to reshape empirical reality in the light of his higher knowledge of the true nature of things. He is a "player" in the dream world of a circus, and the bishop is "really" a murderer: Alexander knows. As the film progresses Alexander's distance from everyday reality increases to such a degree that when he is in Uncle Isak's house he seems to think he is talking to God himself. It is here also that, when visiting Ishmael, he develops the power to see not only the visible but also the invisible: he is able to see both that which is in Ishmael's room as well as what is taking place in the bishop's house. He envisions the Bishop's aunt knocking over a lamp that actually starts a fire engulfing her, the house and the bishop himself. Through Alexander and his visions, the film represents the artist as knower of the reality that lies behind the real: the eternal verities that are beyond the reach of ideology, language, politics, and the quotidian.

However, in spite of his deep desire to be a fabulist, inventor of tales and stories that erase mundane reality and in their place inscribe a higher reality, Alexander does not seem to be a firm believer in his own invented reality. Under pressure he often withdraws his fables and yields to the ordinary reality of, for instance, the reprimand from his mother or the flogging from the bishop. Both of these punishments for his fabulations are represented in the film as instances of the artist being misunderstood by literal-minded philistines. It is implied that Alexander's reality exceeds the frames of intelligibility employed by his mother or the bishop. However, one cannot but wonder about the politics of this theory of art and creativity and thus the portrait of the artist presented in the film. Isn't the other (and in the film the unexplored) side of the artist as fabulator, as eraser of the quotidian reality, the artist as complicit with this same quotidian reality? The artist succumbs to the dominant power because he has mystified the production of power in culture by mystifying the production of reality itself. Isn't a depoliticized imagination inevitably a collaborationist one—one that in its refusal to inquire into the constitution of politics allows its undeconstructed domination?

In constructing Alexander as a fabulist, Bergman is in fact reiterating the ideological move of many contemporary films that function to produce a unitary subject—a coherent, centered, "organic" self as the ultimate ground of reality. The unitary subject, unbroken by the intervention of the dailiness of cultural practices, is the effect of the mode of negotiation with the real that Jacques Lacan calls the *Imaginary*. The Imaginary is the unmediated contact with the world modeled after the relation of a child to its own specular image or its connection with its own mother, both instances of plenitude and fullness. Bergman produces Alexander in the space of the Imaginary and hints at his refusal to enter what Lacan names the *Symbolic Order* (language and the other symbolic practices of culture that constitute reality as the effect of difference, absence and dailiness). The Symbolic is, of course, the domain of the father; and Oscar's death in the film literally signals the suspension of the symbolic—the public space of the interrogation of cultural values. Alexander's obsessive attachment to his Grandmama (Helena) is, on the other hand, his reaffirmation of the Imaginary, the regressive plenitude, which is another way of stating that Bergman's theory of art is based on the idea of the artist as neurotic, an essentially "sick" person who attempts to bypass the order of the Symbolic and reside in the Imaginary. By refusing the Symbolic, he produces himself as a sovereign imagination in touch with unmediated reality.

CARL

Alexander is a person of imagination whereas his Uncle Carl is a man of reason—he is a professor (a reasoner) in the local university. It is part of the romantic transcendentalism of the film that the man of reason (professor) is constructed as a childlike clown. As a defense against his unrelenting depression, Carl often gets drunk and acts like a buffoon. In one scene he even passes wind, blowing out the candles that the children hold close to him. He, like Alexander, does not belong to the world of adults, but unlike Alexander, he is not an artist. He does not have access to an integrative reality and is therefore buried under the mess of dailiness without ever being able to discern in it a pattern, an overall shape. In Carl, Bergman ridicules reason and portrays the rational man as helpless and without insight. "How is it," Carl asks, "that one becomes second rate?" Carl is one of the few members of the family who does not have much to do with the theatre and acting (except, of course, for his degraded form of clowning for the children). Limited by rationalism, he does not have the imaginative generosity that characterizes most members of the family. His unhappiness, however, acquires a symbolic dimension in the film and goes beyond a mere personal trait: it captures in its bleakness the repressed side of the family that his brother, Gustav, tries so hard to conceal. Although this repression is "read" psychoanalytically in the Freudian interpretive frame of the film, it is, in the final analysis, a social one—the underside of the structure of domination (e.g., Carl's own subjugation of his wife) that is the precondition of the hegemony of his class. The spectator is led to produce a "tale" from the film in which the child artist in touch with extradiscursive reality is a mature negotiator of reality whereas the grown-up professor is imprisoned by "reason," becoming a helpless, infantile clown. The petty bourgeois mistrust of "reason" and intellectuality provides further cues to the spectator, who is thus resecured into the prevailing ideology of sympathy and the ethics of the "heart."

CHILDHOOD

Childhood is the space of plenitude, clarity, imagination, and magical realities. In the light of the enchanting realities perceived by children the world of adults is tested and found wanting. The true wisdom is the wisdom of the child (Alexander, for instance) or at least of the adult who has the ability to understand children. Uncle Gustav and Grandmama Helena are exemplary figures who empathize with the child. Bishop Edvard, on the other hand, is the dark villain of the film partly because he is so alien to the world of children and so insistent on educating children into the logic of responsibility, literal truth, and the disciplined routines of the adult world. It is symbolic that the bishop's own children were drowned, and one of Alexander's inventions is a tale about them being murdered by their own father. Edvard's childlessness is a symbol of his lifelessness. His house, in contrast to the rich profusion and playfulness of the Ekdahl's, is the house of adults—drab, confining, and chillingly cold.

The strong sense of nostalgia expressed for childhood in the film, however, is symptomatic of the unhappiness about adult life in contemporary Western European society, in which the protocols of a consumer culture turn adulthood into a space of frustrated desires. The adoration of children, in other words, is not merely a natural phenomenon but is directly related to the disjuncture that capitalism inserts between childhood and adulthood: the world of play and the domain of work. The Ekdahl's worshiping of children is, in spite of the film's overt values, an acknowledgment of their own repressed unhappiness of which Carl's insomnia is yet another mark.

CHRISTMAS EVE

On the Christmas Eve with which the film opens its first major segment, the world is presented as an ongoing feast. The real is decomposed, de-real-ed and then reconstituted as an aesthetic experience. The world is framed like a work of art and presented to the senses for their aesthetic consumption. The real is emptied of its contents. The labor that is a precondition for such an elaborate party and feast for the senses is concealed under the happy-looking faces of the maids serving the Ekdahl household. However, there are symptoms of tension. The muttering of the "sulking" maid, who after having been chastised by Helena for being moody and thus spoiling the feast calls Helena a "bitch," is a sign of the strained relationship between master and servant. Also during one of the communal Christmas dances Gustav flirts with the maid, Maj, and informs her that he will pay her a visit later that night: the sexual desire of the master for the maid hints at both Gustav's unhappiness in his own life as well as his unhindered power over subordinates.

COMMERCE

Commerce is the absent cause in the film. The world of the film is its effect. The film is silent on the source of income for the Ekdahl family. True Gustav owns a restaurant and the family owns and runs the theatre. However, the theatre has been operating at a loss nearly every year, borrowing money from Helena to keep going rather than contributing any income to the household. The mere cost of maintaining the Ekdahl's palatial residence, not to mention their generous life-style and country residence, far exceeds any ostensible income depicted in the film. *Fanny and Alexander* backgrounds material conditions so that it can be free to highlight the ideal: the everyday world of exchange and labor is silenced while daily life is constructed as an uninterrupted gaiety. When unhappiness intrudes, as in the middle section of the film while Emilie and her children live for a short time in the bishop's house, it is treated as an aberration of the real; its causes are privatized (Emilie made a bad choice).

The only figure through whom the material world of finance enters the film is Isak Jacobi—the moneylender. But as a Jewish merchant, he is a deviation from the high bourgeois norms that determine the world in which the Ekdahls live. Even his moneylending is suppressed in the film. He is constructed first and foremost as "uncle" to the children and a lover of their grandmama, Helena, and his trading to rescue the children from the evil that has befallen them in the bishop's house is mystified as black magic. His shop—the realm of moneylending and trade—is also dematerialized. It is represented as the site of mystery, fantasy, and magic: a house full of beautiful objects, giant talking marionettes, and strange happenings. All traces of money, finance, and labor are thus erased from the world in which the story of the film unfolds.

EDVARD VERGERUS (THE BISHOP)

Edvard, the bishop, is against the consumer culture and prevailing self-indulgence and hedonism that he sees dominating the life of the upper bourgeoisie. His anticonsumptionism generates most of the negative reactions to his character in the film. His stance toward consumer culture, however, is depoliticized in the film and represented simply as a moral position. The viewer is thus situated so that he will view Edvard in the tale of the film as a stern puritan: that antithetical force to the bourgeois ethics of pleasure. The desire to moralize the bishop's position is so intense because the implications of his views are politically intolerable for the Ekdahl family and their class. In fact, the frame of dominant cultural intelligibility governing the film requires that the spectator regard Edvard's position to be so threatening it is equated with an opposition to and denial of life itself. By identifying with the frame of knowing that the film offers, the spectator acquires his own subjectivity in opposition to the one represented by Edvard. The bishop's anticonsumptionism (evident in his demand that Emilie and her children enter the new cycle of their lives in his house without the luxury of extra clothes, toys, and other objects that they do not urgently need) has lead some of viewers to see him as an "ogre" and to interpret his practices as instances of "sensory deprivation," equating them with "depletion" of the "soul" itself.

Although Edvard's anticonsumptionism is moralized in the film and rejected as a mode of puritanism, it is, in the last instance, a political position: an expression of his opposition to the wealthy and the culture that perpetuates their values and dominance. His challenge of the dominance of consumerism dooms him. Traditionally the function of the clergy has been to ideologically justify the hegemony of the ruling classes and explain their mastery as "natural." As bishop, Edvard occupies a high position in the clergy, but historically that class as a social group has been at the service of the dominant power. In contesting that power, he also defies the subserviance of his own class. His desire to marry Emilie is an attempt to occupy the space of power that she and her children symbolize. The film punishes his desire to transgress class lines by demonizing him and consuming him in flames.

EMILIE

It is never made clear in the film why Emilie is attracted to Oscar. Oscar is a decidedly ordinary person—a mediocre actor lacking energy and vitality. Emilie, on the other hand, is a strikingly beautiful woman and a talented actress. Emilie's attraction to Oscar seems to be related more to the position of power and wealth that he occupies than his physical or intellectual attributes. Oscar is the manager of the theatre and both in terms of his family wealth and age represents for Emilie the authority figure who might enable her to have a successful career. Emilie's need for a figure of authority is confirmed by her subsequent marriage to the bishop. Her remark toward the end of the film that she and Helena will go back to the theatre and take over its management ("From now on we will make the decisions") is more an organizational effort than a political understanding of gender relations—it does not show Emilie's awareness of her position as a woman in the hierarchy of power. As the new manager, the play she selects to perform, "A Dream Play," by Strindberg ("that woman hater," Helena calls him) is an elaborate poetic statement on the fleeting unreality of existence. It affirms the commonsensical and dominant view of art as dream and fantasy, something that might provide solace or distraction for people, rather than assert the function of art as an interrogation of cultural practices: including the questions why beforehand she, as a woman, had not been given the opportunity "to make all the decisions" in running the theatre or why she was denied all her rights as an individual and mother while married to the bishop and prevented by the patriarchal order from leaving him and taking her children with her.

ENDING

Nowhere in the film does its ideological stance and politics surface more clearly than in its ending. The ending of *Fanny and*

Alexander is a recuperation of all the class values that were displaced in the middle of the narrative by Edvard. In the end Edvard is burned to death, and the Ekdahls are seen celebrating the births of two new babies (new life). But the celebration is as much one of death (Edvard's) as of life.

The fete in a sense announces the end of the threat of the petty bourgeoisie (Edvard) and the reinstatement of the hegemony of the upper class. Part of the ideology of this hegemony is for the upper bourgeoisie to represent itself as a tolerant, democratic, and pluralistic order. The symbol of this pluralism and secular tolerance is the Ekdahl's double commemoration of Emilie's legitimate child along with Maj's illegitimate child. No distinctions are made between legitimate and illegitimate, and the implications are that the upper class love of human life transcends the narrow moralistic concerns of the half-civilized petty bourgeois Edvard. Tolerance and pluralism here are, of course, merely a means of legitimating the sexual transgressions of the upper bourgeoisie and its manipulation of those who serve it.

FAMILY

Family is mystified in the film as are its main historical functions: preserving the patriarchal order of heterosexual coupling and the transferring of private property from one generation to the next. The class structures reproduced by the family are concealed by representing them as the nuturing site of unquestioned love and the ultimate space of happiness. By chronicling the lives of three generations of the Ekdahls, the film constructs the family as an instance of continuity, cohesion, and community: an entity, in other words, that provides a stablizing force against the displacements of history. The film, therefore, substitutes a sequentiality for an interrogation of history. The family saga represents history as "chronology"—an unbroken chain of events—instead of inquiring into history as a set of relationships. Such a maneuver represents events as "the way things are" and the present (the obvious) as the "natural" outcome of history, thus producing the illusion of permanence and transhistoricality. In dehistoricizing the Ekdahl family, the film universalizes its mode of living, associating it with warmth, affection, opulence, abundance of food, and a diverse plenitude of objects and possessions, and offers the Ekdahls as a "natural" paradigm of family life.

The film projects this naturalized universality of the Ekdahl family by mystifying the very real social, material, and historical differences between it and the other families in the film—the Jacobis and Vergeruses—arising out of their different class positions by treating these other families as aberrations. The bishop's family is represented as half-civilized moralists who have chosen a life of dark austerity, whereas the Jacobis are Jewish and as such, by definition in the realm of the film, "different," even bizarre. Both instances are treated as individualized and privatized deviations from the norm of the Ekdahls' joyous abundance. But the Ekdahls' happiness, despite the manifest desire of the film, becomes problematized in symptoms that hint at the darker side of family life such as Carl's depressions and his sadistic relation to his wife; Emilie's hasty escape from the Ekdahl family into the arms of the bishop; Fanny's constant gaze; the neglect of the eldest grandchild (Gustav's daughter), and the despair of the seduced, now pregnant maid, Maj.

FANNY

In a family most of whose members are child-adults, Fanny is an adult-child. She is also one of the few who are not actor-artists. These traits situate her in a cognitive space opposite Alexander. Alexander is a dreamy, intuitive, imaginative artist; Fanny is the cerebral and interrogative knower. Alexander is self-absorbed and thus withdrawn. Fanny is inquiring, and the precondition of this inquiring cast of mind is distance from events. Bergman plays Fanny's intellectualism against Alexander's intuitionism, and although Fanny's name is in the title of the film, he excludes her from any significant participation in the narrative. He also associates her intellectualism with coldness and insensitivity: while Alexander is being flogged in the bishop's house, Fanny looks on without any visible emotion on her face. If she is affected at all, she seems to be offended more by the violation of Alexander's human rights as a philosophical matter than by his pain. During the funeral procession for her father, she has a contemplative smile on her face while Alexander tries to get rid of his emotional pain by muttering all the swear words he knows.

FREUD

The overall interpretive arc of the film is the Freudian family romance. The exemplary analytical case in the film is the relationship among Alexander, his mother, and her lover-husband, Edvard. In a charged scene, the bishop first reprimands Alexander for having fabulated a story about his mother selling him to a circus and then intrudes between Alexander and Emilie who is comforting her son. Placing his head between Alexander and Emilie's, Edvard flirts with her by whispering in her ear. The situation echoes the arch-Freudian triangular relationship in *Hamlet* (Claudius, Gertrude, and Hamlet). But this rather overt allegorical statement is by no means the only Freudian interpretation of relationships in the film. Freudian concepts provide the matrix of intelligibility at all levels of the narrative. Carl, the neurotic failed professor, is seen as a man who has not completed the process of oedipalization and suffers from a weak superego; his brother Gustav, on the other hand, is an oral person with a well-developed sense of reality and pleasure.

In using the family as the frame of intelligibility through which all human relationships are accounted for, Freudian psychoanalysis reduces the social dimension of relationships to a quasi-private one and thus denies the constitutive function of politics, class, gender, and race. Bergman employs this privatizing device in analyzing, understanding, and naturalizing the relationship between the Ekdahls and the theatre as well as their relationship with their servants. The result of such a heavy emphasis on Freudian psychoanalysis is that the film contains and backgrounds political and social reality while foregrounding the inner world of the individual as the origin of all human and social realities.

GUSTAV ADOLF

Gustav is the youngest of Helena's three sons and the happiest, most optimistic, and confident one. He is sexually fecund and quite successful as a businessman. His open, hopeful, and tolerant personality seems to reflect the world of business he inhabits; he is neither an artist (like his eldest brother Oscar) nor an intellectual (like his brother Carl). He is a pragmatic person whose philosophy of life consists of the common sense of his class and profession. Although he is affiliated with the theatre and makes a big production out of the annual party that he and his family give for the actors, his interest in the theatre is not artistic. He is concerned mostly about the financial benefits he derives from the theatre as the manager of its restaurant.

His vision of reality, to a considerable extent, coincides with the underlying philosophy of the film, so much so in fact, that his concluding speech can be taken as the manifesto of the entire film about how to live. The occasion for the speech is the grand party he is giving to celebrate the birth of his own illegitimate child (by Maj, the nursery maid) and the child born to Emilie from her marriage to Edvard. The party, in its abundance and inclusivity, is itself a sign of his deeply pluralistic, tolerant, and liberal approach to life affirmed by the speech (as a businessman he cannot afford to be otherwise). "It is necessary and not in the least bit shameful," he tells his family and guests, "to take pleasure in the little world—good food, gentle smiles, fruit trees in bloom, waltzes." He concludes by urging everybody, "Let us be happy while we are happy. Let us be kind and generous and affecionate and good." Gustav's speech is the ultimate reconfirmation of the values and spaces of power that were threatened by the austere puritanism of Bishop Edvard. The film completely recuperates Edvard as his child (and Emilie's) is absorbed by the Ekdahls to be raised in the ethics of the upper bourgeoisie. Gustav's "manifesto" is the apotheoisis of consumptionism and the final rejection and negation of Edvard's antihedonistic views ("sensory deprivation") as befits a businessman and a family whose fortune is dispensed according to a business ideology of consumption and used to promote a consumer society.

HELENA

Helena is the grandmama who keeps everything together and makes sure that the present is patterned after the past. Her notion of the past, however, is not a historical one. For her the past is more a state of being; a set of values, attitudes, and conduct. Her past is the space of the uncontested hegemony of her class and its economic domination that has enabled her family to live the opulent life it does. Also by the authority of this past her class as represented in herself is the arbiter of right and wrong and in fact the guardian of civilization itself. She is the one who has the authority to decide that Gustav's behavior toward Maj is not acceptable (he should be more kind to her); she is also the person who, through Isak, arranges the rescue of Fanny and Alexander (who embodies her class values) from the petty bourgeois moralism of Bishop Edvard. Whereas the many women around her live a repressed life of subjugation (the maids, Carl's wife, Emilie, Gustav's wife and daughter), she has lived in almost all the subject positions that a woman can culturally occupy: actress, lover, wife, mother, matriarch, and manager of a large estate. But she conceals the politics of her position and her experience, naturalizing it as the authority of age (as in her talks with Isak).

IMAGINATION

Imagination is the "magic" of life: it can bring about whatever it desires without the constraints of the forces of history, society, and economics. The film places a great deal of emphasis on the constitutive role of imagination to depoliticize reality itself. The imagination of the private individual, it is understood, has supreme power in changing reality. If harsh social realities resist taking the desired form, all one has to do is to imagine them differently. The film moves effortlessly between the imagined and the real, and this intermixing of the two further adds to the mystification of the real, concealing the influence of history in the production of communal reality. The privileging of imagination in the film, and such other devices as employing a psychoanalytic frame of interpretation for the real, are part of the ideology of the film that establishes the unitary subject—the sovereign individual free from the forces of history—as the originator of the real and the source of meaning.

ISAK JACOBI

His power and place in the narrative is naturalized as that of a lover—he and Helena were lovers in the past: a past, by the way, that both treat as the master plan for the present and the future. His position of prominence, however, is actually acquired by his money. He is a moneylender who loans money to the impoverished Carl and pays Edvard in order to rescue Alexander and Fanny from bondage. Bergman in these scenes either marginalizes the power of money and economics or backgrounds it by resorting to the device of magic and imagination. In the scene where the children are rescued from Edvard, Isak conjures up replicas of the children through some obscure magical act that, we are to understand, is the real cause of the successful liberation of the children. Given the marginalization of money in the film, it is significant that the moneylender is Jewish. It is also revealing the way Bergman depicts Isak in terms of a strange, mysterious, even eerie household: he is the embodiment of the "weird" and "different" in the film. There is a strong political undertone in these representations of Isak: he is constructed very much in keeping with anti-Semitic assumptions. Isak is a cunning, bizarre moneylender who is shrouded in secrecy and lives in a mysterious shop with his two nephews, who are represented as equally "strange" as well as degenerate and demented. Located on the margins of society, he is isolated from the mainstream life of the Ekdahls.

ISHMAEL

Ishmael is Isak's mad, visionary nephew. A woman plays the role of Ishmael in the film, evidently as a statement on the unisexuality of the visionary—the ultimate transcendence of political and social situations by defying (rather than interrogating) the code of gender. In the domain of higher realities, the film presupposes, such trivial social codes as gender do not matter. Ishmael is the mad prophet through whom Alexander is initiated into the intricacies of imagination as a maker of the real. It is in Ishmael's cell that Alexander acquires the ability to see not only the visible (what is taking place in front of him in Ishmael's room) but also the seemingly remote and invisible (the fire that is starting in Bishop Edvard's house and that will eventually destroy both the house and the bishop).

MAJ

Maj is the projection of the patriarchal fantasy of a maid-mistress-daughter figure. In the relationship between Gustav and Maj, the class antagonism is covered up and the dominant class is represented as lover, protector, and generous father. For the film to make sense, the spectator must see the ruling class as benevolent protector and source of values. Maj's inclusion in the Ekdahl family (the celebration of the birth of her illegitimate child side by side with the celebration of Emilie's child and her partnership in the dress shop with Gustav's daughter) is a further act of mystification through which the exploitation of Maj by Gustav is concealed in the suspension of class and social differences and in the incorporation of everyone into what Roland Barthes, adapting an exhibition's title, called the *Great Family of Man*. The great family of man is the mythical invention of contemporary capitalism designed to mask the effects of its exploitation of individuals. To mystify the sharp and cruel differences that separate the people of the world because of its political and economic domination, capitalism trivializes these differences by projecting a transcendental "unity." The great family of man is based on the assumption that beneath all the "superficial" differences is a "natural" unity tying all people together. Through such a fantasy of togetherness, the dominant power absorbs and thus neutralizes dissent and the opposition of various subordinate classes and peoples. The inclusion of Maj in the Ekdahl family is, in other words, an ideological move to suspend class and social divisions in the name of an illusory higher reality: it is an instance of the production of "false consciousness."

OSCAR

An ordinary man with ordinary, if not banal, ideas about the theatre, paternity, and life in general, Oscar derives the authority of his views and the attention they command from his position as the manager of the theatre. Although presented as artistic, his authority is ultimately related to the wealth of his family, a wealth that has made it possible for the family to own and run the theatre. It is his power and money rather than his mediocre aesthetic sensibility that might finally account for Emilie's marrying him.

Oscar's views on art and theatre not only have an economic base but also an ideological importance in that they articulate the underlying philosophy of art shaping the film.

> My only talent, if you call it talent in my case, is that I love this little world inside the thick walls of this playhouse. And I'm fond of the people who work in this little world. Outside is the big world, and sometimes the little world succeeds for a moment in reflecting the big world, so that we understand it better. Or is it perhaps that we give the people who come here the chance of forgetting for a while the harsh world outside. Our theatre is a small room of orderliness, routine, conscientiousness, and love.

Oscar's philosophy is also echoed in his brother Gustav's final speech. Both regard art, in the last instance, as an escape from the harsh realities of the world—a haven and a refuge. Neither understands the theatre as a site of interrogation of culture, rather both present it as mere diversion. The film's view of the theatre (art) as mere distraction from the complexity of communal life is one aspect of its overall nonhistorical and depoliticizing tendencies and is in harmony with its other ideological moves that privatize and naturalize class differences.

REALITY

The specificity of time and space and the constraints of history, culture and the political, economic, and ideological forces that produce reality are all erased in the film. External reality is subsumed by the imaginary of unitary individuals. The film manages to trivialize the real by closing the gap between the real and the dream (through the character of Alexander), diminish the distance between here and there (in the figure of Alexander), and transgress the spaces between the living and the dead (by means of the ghosts of Oscar and Edvard). As a result of the strategic use of these characters and devices, the real is demate-rialized in the film and represented as an eternal extension of dreams, fantasies, and acts of imagining.

SELF-REFLEXIVITY

The film is a tissue of self-referring images and sequences. The artist Bergman throughout the film refers to the role and function of the artist, the position of art, and the healing power of the theatre. In a sense the film is about making art and its moral function—how alienation from art leads to horrible cruel-ty and sadism (Edvard).

Self-reflexive art comes into existence not by the verisimi-lar depiction of some external reality but by enacting its own condition of being, exploring its very ground of existence. In representing itself as highly self-aware of its condition of possib-lity, self-reflexive art lays claim to the possibility of direct access to knowledge and thus undermines the assumption that all forms of knowing are mediated, representational, and produced through the agency of communal and cultural discursive prac-tices. The film, from its very opening shot in which Alexander is seen gazing at his puppet theatre, to the final speech by Gustav, attempts to ground itself in its own state of existence and as a self-founding act hint at its independence from all social and historical conditions.

THEATRE

The "theatre" is so represented in the film that the spectator, if she is to make sense of the "tale" of the film, is required to regard it as the "little world" that provides the "big world" with a principle of cohesion, order, and, above all, a sense of totality. The cohesion of the world is not, however, achieved by an interrogation of its pieces; that is to say, it is not a Brechtian inquiry into the relationships among various econom-ic, political, and ideological practices but the cohesion of the (regressive) Imaginary. In the regressive space of the Imaginary, away from the pressures of the differences of the Symbolic order of culture, the spectator overcomes the fragmentary reality that is the product of the real contradictions of contemporary life and thus reaches a state of reassuring tranquility. The resolutions that social practices cannot attain are achieved by aesthetic acts. Historical contradictions remain while an Imaginary cohesion is obtained in the enclosed space of the "theatre."

BIBLIOGRAPHY

Adorno, Theodore. 1973. *Negative Dialectics.* New York: Seabury Press.

Aspinall, Sue. 1983. "Women, Realism and Reality in British Films, 1943–53." In *British Cinema History,* ed. J. Curran and V. Porter. Totowa, N.J.: Barnes and Noble.

Althusser, Louis. 1971. *Lenin and Philosophy,* trans. Ben Brewster. New York: Monthly Review Press.

———. 1977. *Reading Capital,* trans. Ben Brewster. London:New Left Books.

Andrew, J. Dudley. 1984. *Concepts in Film Theory.* New York: Oxford University Press.

Aronowitz, Stanley. 1990. *The Crisis in Historical Materialism.* Minneapolis: University of Minnesota Press.

Bakhtin, Mikhail. 1986. "Extracts from 'Notes' 1970–71." In *Bakhtin: Essays and Dialogues on His Work,* ed. Gary S. Morson. Chicago: University of Chicago Press.

Barthes, Roland. 1968. *Elements of Semiology,* trans. A. Lavers and C. Smith. New York: Hill and Wang.

———. 1975. *The Pleasure of the Text,* trans. R. Howard. New York: Hill and Wang.

———. 1977. *Image, Music, Text,* trans. S. Heath. New York: Hill and Wang.

Belsey, Catherine. 1985. "Constructing the Subject; Deconstructing the Text." In *Feminist Criticism and Social Change,* ed. J. Newton and D. Rosenfelt. New York: Methuen.

Benjamin, Walter. 1973. *Understanding Brecht,* trans. A. Bostock. London: New Left Books.

Bersani, Leo. 1986. *The Freudian Body.* New York: Columbia University Press.

Blonsky, Marshal, ed. 1985. *On Signs.* Baltimore: Johns Hopkins University Press.

Bordwell, David. 1985. *Narration in the Fiction Film.* Madison: University of Wisconsin Press.

————. 1989. *Making Meaning.* Cambridge, Mass.: Harvard University Press.

————, Kristin Thompson, and Janet Staiger. 1985. *The Classical Hollywood Cinema.* New York: Columbia University Press.

Brecht, Bertolt. 1979. *Brecht on Theatre,* trans. John Willett. New York: Hill and Wang.

Browne, Nick. 1970. "The Politics of Narrative Form: Capra's *Mr. Smith Goes to Washington.*" *Wide Angle* 3, no. 3: 4–11.

Brunette, Peter, and David Wills. 1989. *Screen/Play: Derrida and Film Theory.* Princeton, N.J.: Princeton University Press.

Cixous, Helene. 1980. "The Laugh of the Medusa." In *New French Feminisms,* ed. E. Marks and I. de Courtivron. Amherst: University of Massachusetts Press.

Clifton, N. Ray. 1983. *The Figure in the Carpet.* London and Toronto: Associated University Press.

Conklin, H. C. 1955. "Hanunoo Color Terms." *Southern Journal of Anthropology* 11: 339–344.

Culler, Jonathan. 1981. *The Pursuit of Signs.* Ithaca, N.Y.: Cornell University Press.

Dayan, Daniel. 1974. "The Tutor Code of Classical Cinema." *Film Quarterly* 28, no. 1.

DeLauretis, Teresa. 1984. *Alice Doesn't.* Bloomington: Indiana University Press.

―――. 1987. *Technologies of Gender.* Bloomington: Indiana University Press.

――― and Stephen Heath, ed. 1980. *The Cinematic Apparatus.* New York: St. Martin's Press.

Deleuze, Gilles. 1971. *Masochism: An Interpretation of Coldness and Cruelty,* trans. J. MacNeil. New York: George Braziller.

―――. 1986. *Cinema 1: The Movement-Image,* trans. H. Tomlinson and B. Habberjam. Minneapolis: University of Minnesota Press.

―――. 1988. *Bergsonism,* trans. H. Tomlinson and B. Habberjam. New York: Zone Books.

――― and Felix Guattari. 1983. *Anti-Oedipus,* trans. R. Hurley. Minneapolis: University of Minnesota Press.

――― and Felix Guattari. 1987. *A Thousand Plateaus: Capitalism and Schizophrenia.* Minneapolis: University of Minnesota Press.

DeMan, Paul. 1986. *Resistance to Theory.* Minneapolis: University of Minnesota Press.

Derrida, Jacques. 1976. *Of Grammatology,* trans. G. Spivak. Baltimore: Johns Hopkins University Press.

―――. 1978. *Writing and Difference,* trans. A. Bass. Chicago: University of Chicago Press.

————. 1981. *Positions,* trans. A. Bass. Chicago: University of Chicago Press.

————. 1982. *Margins of Philosophy,* trans. A. Bass. Chicago: University of Chicago Press.

————. 1988. "Telepathy." *Oxford Literary Review* 10, nos. 1–2: 3–41.

————. 1989. "Like The Sound of the Sea Deep within a Shell: Paul deMan's War." In *On Paul deMan's Wartime Journalism,* ed. W. Hammacher, N. Hertz, and T. Keenan. Lincoln: University of Nebraska Press.

———— and Mustapha Tlili, eds. 1987. *For Nelson Mandela.* New York: Henry Holt-Seaver Books.

Dieckmann, Katherine. 1984–85. "Interview with Wim Wenders." *Film Quarterly* 38, no. 2: 2–8.

Ebert, Teresa L. 1990. "Writing in the Political: Resistance Post-modernism." Paper delivered at Conference on "Rewriting the (Post)modern: (Post)colonialism/Feminism/Late Capitalism." March 30–31, 1990, University of Utah.

Eco, Umberto. 1985. "How Culture Conditions the Colours We See." In *On Signs,* ed. M. Blonsky. Baltimore: Johns Hopkins University Press.

Fargier, Jean-Paul. 1977. "Parenthesis or Indirect Route." In *Screen Reader 1.* London: Society for Education in Film and Television.

Feuer, Jane. 1982. *The Hollywood Musical.* London: British Film Institute.

Fiske, John. 1989. *Understanding the Popular.* Boston: Unwin Hyman.

Formations of Pleasure. 1983. London: Routledge and Kegan Paul.

Foucault, Michel. 1980. *Power/Knowledge.*, ed. Colin Gordon. New York: Pantheon.

————. 1987. "The Ethic of Care for the Self as a Practice of Freedom." *Philosophy and Social Criticism,* nos. 2–3.

————. 1988. *Politics, Philosophy, Culture,* ed. L. D. Kritzman. New York and London: Routledge.

Freud, Sigmund. 1961. *Beyond the Pleasure Principle,* trans. J. Strachey. New York: W. W. Norton.

Fuss, Diana. 1989. *Essentially Speaking: Feminism, Nature and Difference.* New York: Routledge.

Gallop, Jane. 1988. *Thinking through the Body.* New York: Columbia University Press.

Gidal, Peter. 1976. *Structural Film Anthology.* London: British Film Institute.

Gill, Brendan. 1989. "The Faces of Joseph Campbell." *New York Review of Books* (September 28): 16–19.

Giroux, Henry. 1983. *Theory and Resistance in Education.* South Hadley, Mass.: Bergin and Garvey.

Gomery, D. 1986. *The Hollywood Studio System.* New York: St. Martin's Press.

Hak Kyung Cha, Teresa, ed. 1980. *Apparatus.* New York: Tanam Press.

Heath, Stephen. 1975. "Film and System: Terms of Analysis I & II." *Screen* 16, nos. 1–2.

————. 1976. "On Screen, in Frame: Film and Ideology." *Quarterly Review of Film Studies* 1, no. 3.

————. 1981. *Questions of Cinema.* Bloomington: Indiana University Press.

———— and Patricia Mellencamp, ed. 1983. *Cinema and Language*. Frederick, Md.: University Publications of America.

Hebdige, Dick. 1979. *Subculture: The Meaning of Style*. London: Methuen.

Higson, Andrew. 1983. "Critical Theory and 'British Cinema'." *Screen* 24, nos. 4–5.

Hill, John. 1983. "Working Class Realism and Sexual Reaction: Some Theses on the British 'New Wave'." In *British Cinema History*, ed. J. Curran and V. Porter. Totowa, N.J.: Barnes and Noble.

Hirst, Paul. 1979. *On Law and Ideology*. Atlantic Highlands, N.J.: Humanities Press.

Hjelmslev, Louis. 1961. *Prolegomena to a Theory of Language*, trans. F. J. Whitefield. Madison: University of Wisconsin Press.

Hoveyda, Fereydoun. 1986. "Nicholas Ray's Reply: *Party Girl*." In *Cahiers du Cinema 1960–1968: New Wave, New Cinema, Reevaluating Hollywood*, ed. J. Miller. Cambridge, Mass.: Harvard University Press.

Iser, Wolfgang. 1978. *The Act of Reading*. Baltimore: Johns Hopkins University Press.

Izod, John. 1988. *Hollywood and the Box Office, 1895–1986*. New York: Columbia University Press.

James, David E. 1989. *Allegories of Cinema: American Film in the Sixties*. Princeton, N.J.: Princeton University Press.

Jameson, Fredric. 1980. *The Political Unconscious: Narrative as a Socially Symbolic Act*. Ithaca, N.Y.: Cornell University Press.

Johnson, Barbara. 1987. *A World of Difference*. Baltimore: Johns Hopkins University Press.

Johnston, Claire. 1974. "Women's Cinema as Counter-Cinema." In *Notes on Women's Cinema.* London: Society for Education in Film and Television.

Kirhy, Lynne. 1987. "Temporality, Sexuality and Narration in *The General." Wide Angle* 9, no. 1.

Kuhn, Thomas S. 1970 *The Structure of Scientific Revolutions.* Chicago: University of Chicago Press.

Kuntzel, Thierry. 1980. "Film Work 2." *Camera Obscura* 5.

Lacan, Jacques. 1977. *Ecrits: A Selection,* trans. A. Sheridan. New York: W. W. Norton.

Laclau, Ernesto. 1988. "Building a New Left." *Strategies* 1, no. 1.

——— and Chantal Mouffe. 1985. *Hegemony and Socialist Strategy.* London: Verso.

Le Grice, Malcolm. 1977. *Abstract Film and Beyond.* London: Studio Vista.

Lemon, L. T., and M. Reis, ed. 1965. *Russian Formalist Criticism: Four Essays.* Lincoln: Nebraska University Press.

Levin, Michael. 1989. "Ethics Courses Useless." *New York Times* (November 25).

Levi-Strauss, Claude. 1963. *Structural Anthropology,* trans. C. Jacobson and G. Schopf. New York: Harper and Row.

Lyons, John. 1968. *Introduction to Theoretical Linguistics.* London and New York: Cambridge University Press.

Lyotard, Jean-Francois. 1984. *The Postmodern Condition,* trans. G. Bennington. Minneapolis: University of Minnesota Press.

———. 1987. *The Differend: Phrases in Dispute,* trans. G. Van Den Abbeele. Minneapolis: University of Minnesota Press.

———— and Jean-Loup Thebaud. 1985. *Just Gaming,* trans. W. Godzich. Minneapolis: University of Minnesota Press.

Mannheim, Karl. 1972. *Ideology and Utopia,* trans. L. Wirth and E. Shills. London: Routledge and Kegan Paul.

Martin, Luther H., H. Gutman, and P. H. Hutton, eds. 1987. *Technologies of the Self: A Seminar with Michel Foucault.* Amherst: University of Massachusetts Press.

Marx, Karl. 1974. *Economic and Philosophical Manuscripts of 1844,* trans. M. Mulligan. Moscow: Progress Press.

———— and Frederick Engels. 1975. *Collected Works,* vol. 3. New York: International Publishers.

————. 1976. *Collected Works,* vol. 5. New York: International Publishers.

————. 1978. *Collected Works,* vol. 11. New York: International Publishers.

MacBean, James Roy. 1975. *Film and Revolution.* Bloomington: Indiana University Press.

Metz, Christian. 1982. *Imaginary Signifier: Psychoanalysis and the Cinema.* Bloomington: Indiana University Press.

Miller, J. Hillis. 1987. *The Ethics of Reading.* New York: Columbia University Press.

————. 1989. "An Open Letter to Professor Jon Wiener." In *On Paul deMan's Wartime Journalism,* ed. W. Hamacher, N. Herts, and T. Keenan. Lincoln: University of Nebraska Press.

Modleski, Tania. 1986. "The Terror of Pleasure: The Contemporary Horror Film and Postmodern Theory." In *Studies in Entertainment: Critical Approaches to Mass Culture,* ed. Tania Modleski. Bloomington: Indiana University Press.

———. 1988. *The Women Who Knew Too Much.* New York: Methuen.

Mulvey, Laura. 1975. "Visual Pleasure and Narrative Cinema." *Screen.* 18, no. 2.

———. 1981. "Afterthoughts on 'Visual Pleasure and Narrative Cinema' Inspired by *Duel in the Sun.*" *Framework:* 15–17.

Nichols, Bill. 1981. *Ideology and the Image.* Bloomington: Indiana University Press.

O'Connor, James, and A. Cockburn. 1989. "Their Mullas and Ours." *Zeta Magazine* (April).

Oudart, Jean-Pierre. 1977–78. "Cinema and Suture. *Screen* 18, no. 4.

Penley, Constance. 1989. *The Future of an Illusion: Film, Feminism and Psychoanalysis.* Minneapolis: University of Minnesota Press.

Pleynet, Marcelin. 1978. "Economical-Ideological-Formal." In Sylvia Harvey, *May '68 and Film Culture.* London: British Film Institute.

Prieto, Luis. 1975. *Pertinence et Pratique.* Paris: Minuit.

Saussure, Ferdinand de. 1966. *Course in General Linguistics,* trans. W. Baskin. New York: McGraw-Hill.

Schiller, Herbert J. 1985. "Breaking the West's Media Monopoly." *The Nation* (September 21).

Screen Reader 1. 1977. London: The Society for Education in Film and Television.

Silverman, Kaja. 1980. "Masochism and Subjectivity." *Framework* 12.

———. 1988. *The Acoustic Mirror.* Bloomington: Indiana University Press.

Sontag, Susan. 1967. *Against Interpretation.* New York: Delta Books.

Stam, Robert. 1989. *Subversive Pleasures: Bakhtin, Cultural Criticism, and Film.* Baltimore: Johns Hopkins University Press.

Studlar, Gaylyn. 1988. *In The Realm of Pleasure.* Urbana: University of Illinois Press.

Thompson, E. P. 1978. *The Poverty of Theory.* London: Merlin Press.

Thompson, Kristin. 1981. *Eisenstein's* Ivan The Terrible: *A Neoformalist Analysis.* Princeton, N.J.: Princeton University Press.

Volosinov, V. N. 1973. *Marxism and the Philosophy of Language.* New York: Seminar Press.

Weed, Elizabeth, ed. 1989. *Coming to Terms: Feminism/Theory/Politics.* New York: Routledge.

West, Cornell. 1985. "Afterword: The Politics of American Neo-Pragmatism." In *Post-Analytical Philosophy,* ed. J. Rajchman and C. West. New York: Columbia University Press.

Willemen, Paul. 1971. "Distanciation and Douglas Sirk." *Screen* 12, no. 2.

Zavarzadeh, Mas'ud. 1985. "Semiotics of the Foreseen: Modes of Intelligibility in (Contemporary) Fiction." *Poetics Today* 6, no. 4.

———. 1989. "Theory as Resistance." *Rethinking Marxism* 2, no. 1.

———. Forthcoming. "Argument and The Politics of Laughter." *Rethinking Marxism.*

INDEX